# INDIANA

# Historical

## By D. Ray Wilson

## ON THE COVER

A typical scene on the highways and roads in Indiana Amish Country. This photograph was taken on Indiana 5 south of Shipshewana on a winter day.

Dedicated to my wife, Bea

Author D. Ray Wilson
INDIANA HISTORICAL TOUR GUIDE

First Edition, 1994

Published by Crossroads Communications
Carpentersville, IL 60110-0007
Manufactured in the United States of America

Library of Congress Catalog Number: 93-74003
International Standard Book Number: 0-916445-36-4

## OTHER TOUR GUIDES BY D. RAY WILSON

"Colorado Historical Tour Guide"
"Greater Chicago Historical Tour Guide"
"Illinois Historical Tour Guide"
"Iowa Historical Tour Guide," 1st, 2nd editions
"Kansas Historical Tour Guide," 1st, 2nd, 3rd editions
"Missouri Historical Tour Guide." 1st, 2nd editions
"Nebraska Historical Tour Guide," 1st, 2nd editions
"Wyoming Historical Tour Guide," 1st, 2nd editions

Editor: "Oklahoma Historical Tour Guide"

## ABOUT THE AUTHOR

D. Ray Wilson, a native Californian, has been a journalist for more than 40 years and has served on newspapers in Nebraska, Kansas, California, Arizona, and Illinois. He is author of "The Folks," "Fort Kearny on the Platte," "Episode Hill 616," and "Organizing the Organization" in addition to his series of historical tour guides. Wilson received his journalism degree from Northern Illinois University and is the recipient of an honorary Doctor of Letters degree from Judson College, Elgin, IL. He is listed in several editions of "Who's Who" and is founder and chairman of the board of the DuPage Heritage Gallery, Wheaton, IL.

# Table of Contents

# Introduction

This book is written for those persons who appreciate the uniqueness of American history and are interested specifically in the State of Indiana's colorful past.

Indiana, the Hoosier State, has a unique history. Largely Indian lands from about 1200 A.D. until the European "invasion" or possibly a better description would be "infiltration" dating back as far as the latter part of the 18th century. The English claimed the land first, then the French only to be claimed again by the English. After the American Revolution, it took years for the Americans to resolve the Indian "problem."

There were many famous Indian leaders but probably none more well-known than Tecumseh, chief of the Shawnees. Tecumseh had great ability as an organizer and a leader and is considered one of the outstanding Indians in American history. The Battle of Tippecanoe in November, 1811 was, properly speaking, a drawn battle, though it marked the collapse of the Indian military movement.

George Rogers Clark created his place in history for his daring in 1778 and 1779 in the taking and retaking of Vincennes against the British for the new United States of America.

Robert Owens attempted to establish a new social order at New Harmony in 1825; an experiment short lived.

Abraham Lincoln spent his formative boyhood days in southern Indiana. His mother died in their Indiana home.

Elwood Haynes invented the first successful automobile in Kokomo in 1893-94. He was a noted inventor of metals as well. After his successful test in the summer of 1894, over 200 different automobiles have been brought on the market by Indiana inventors/manufacturers. Probably none were more productive than the Studebaker brothers, who began their business as wagonmakers.

Indiana was the birthplace of Wilbur Wright and Larry Bell, two famous aviation pioneers.

Several Indianans have served as the Vice President of the United States, the latest being Dan Quayle of Huntington.

Indiana raised 28,509 volunteers over quota in President Lincoln's first call for troops by states at the outset of the Civil War. The state legislature refused to fund the first two years of the rebellion and Governor Oliver P. Morton operated the war effort on borrowed money from a friend, J.F.D. Lanier.

Lambkin P. Milligan with others in the *Knights of the Golden Circle*, an outspoken organization against the Union during the Civil War and engaged in subversive activities, were charged with fomenting rebellion. Out of this case came the famous Milligan, ex parte case decided by the Supreme Court in 1866.

7

Several famous authors, poets, songwriters, entertainers and artists were Hoosiers. Just a few of the names that to come to mind are Lew Wallace, James Whitcomb Riley, Booth Tarkington, Gene Stratton Porter, Thomas Dreiser, Mary Jane Ward, Ernie Pyle, Hoagy Carmichael, Cole Porter, Jimmy Dean, Jim Davis, and a host of others.

Seven astronauts have come from Indiana. Two of the best known, perhaps, are Frank Borman and Virgil "Gus" Grissom

Along with the famous there were also the infamous. John Dillinger became Public Enemy No. 1 during the 1930s. The Reno brothers are credited with the first train robbery in the world.

We could go on and on. There are many stories about people, places, and things.

There is so much to see and enjoy in the Hoosier State. This book is written as much for the natives as for the visitors to the state. We have crisscrossed it many times during our research and have to come to appreciate the state more on each visit.

We could have continued the research but all of these projects must come to an end if they are ever to be published. During some of our research we found conflicting or differing stories from time to time. After careful research we selected those stories we felt most comfortable with.

The people here have been friendly and helpful. We received assistance from literally hundreds of persons connected with historical societies and chambers of commerce. Several other interested individuals were also helpful.

We recommend every one have an up-to-date map of the state on any tour.

Please slow down a bit and don't be afraid to take a side road now and then for possible special adventures. Indiana has so many great offerings for every interested traveler. We hope you enjoy this book and find it helpful.

*D. Ray Wilson*
*Sleepy Hollow, IL*

# Chapter 1
# An Overview

Jonathan Jennings, a Pennsylvanian, arrived in Jeffersonville and was admitted to the bar in Vincennes in 1807. Jennings, an abolitionist, was elected to Congress as the representative from Indiana Territory in 1809. On January 5, 1816, Jennings introduced a bill in Congress for an act enabling Indiana Territory to write a constitution and apply for statehood. The petition was approved by President Madison April 19, 1816 and on May 13, 43 representatives were elected to the Constitutional Convention. The convention convened in Corydon June 10 and Jennings was elected president. The constitution was adopted June 29. August 5, Jonathan Jennings was elected Indiana's first governor and assumed office November 7. He was reelected in 1819. (Photograph by Indiana Historical Society Library, Negative No. C5828.)

# Chapter 1
# An Overview

The first permanent white settlement in present day Indiana was Vincennes, fortified in 1732, during the period of the French and Indian War. Vincennes became the capital of the Indiana Territory, created May 7, 1800; and **William Henry Harrison** of Ohio, later to become the ninth president of the United States, was appointed the first territorial governor. The territorial capital was moved to Corydon on March 11, 1813; and it was here, in the summer of 1816, that a constitutional convention was called. Indiana was admitted to the Union on December 11, 1816 as the 19th state. Corydon remained the capital until 1825 when it was moved to Indianapolis.

**Jonathan Jennings** was elected the first governor of the new state. **James Noble** and **Waller Taylor** were selected as the two U.S. Senators and **William Hendricks** to the U.S. House of Representatives. All three legislators were seated in December of 1816.

The earliest known residents were approximately 3,000 Mississippian people who lived at Angel Mounds between 1200 and 1400 A.D. When the first white explorers arrived in 1679, they found only a few hundred Indians, most belonging to the Miami tribe. During the 18th and 19th centuries the Delaware, Mohican, Munsee, and Shawnee had moved to Indiana from the East where they were driven out by white settlers. The Huron, Kickapoo, Piankashaw, Potawatomi, and Wea came from the Great Lakes area about the same time. The Potawatomi, who built villages in the northern section in the late 18th century, were the last indigenous peoples to leave Indiana. By 1836, many Indians had sold their lands to the federal government and the rest were driven out within the next two years by military force.

Virginia was granted a charter from James I for the Northwest country, part of which became Indiana, on May 23, 1609. Explorer Sieur de LaSalle and a party of 28 men are believed to be the first white men in Indiana when they camped near the present day site of South Bend in 1679. LaSalle returned near this site in 1681 where he held council with the Indians at Council Oak.

The French, who had begun trading with the Indians as well as trapping for furs, built a fort at Ouiatenon near the site of present day Lafayette in 1720 and Fort Miami, on the site of present day Fort Wayne, in 1722. Francois Morgane de Vincennes built a fort at the present day site of Vincennes in 1732. Both

11

France and England claimed this part of the country. The French claim lasted from 1671 to 1763 when England took over until 1783.

In 1763, the British took Montreal and France relinquished all claims to the western country, including Indiana. Fort Miami and Ouiatenon became British army posts. In the early part of 1763, the Indians, led by Ottawa Chief Pontiac, captured both forts and destroyed Ouiatenon.

Earlier in the year King George had set aside the lands west of the Alleghenies as an Indian reserve.

The British rebuilt their stockades on the Wabash River in 1777 and began to incite the Indians against the Virginians who had begun to settle in the Indiana area. **Father Pierre Gibault**, representing **Lieutenant Colonel George Rogers Clark**, induced the people of Vincennes to swear allegiance to the United States as Clark and his men occupied Fort Sackville in July, 1778. The British took to the offensive and recaptured Vincennes in December as Virginia organized the lands northwest of the Ohio River as Illinois Country. On February 24, 1779, Clark retook Vincennes. The next day Fort Sackville was surrendered by the British and was renamed Fort Patrick Henry by the Americans. In 1779-80, the Virginia legislature gave 150,000 acres of land in Indiana to George Rogers Clark and the men who had fought with him.

Virginia conveyed the territory northwest of the Ohio River to the United States in 1784.

In 1787 Congress created the Northwest Territory and **Arthur St. Clair** became the first territorial governor. The fort at Vincennes was rebuilt and renamed Fort Knox.

In 1790, **Winthrop Sargent**, territorial secretary, created Knox county, embracing all of Indiana and parts of Ohio, Michigan, Illinois and Wisconsin. During most of the next decade, the American army went about destroying Indian villages; and, as a consequence, there were several skirmishes and battles between the army and the Indians during this period.

Shortly after his appointment as governor of Indiana Territory, Governor Harrison negotiated with the Indians to give up their titles to lands in most of Indiana. In a 1805 treaty the United States gained title to the Indian lands in eastern Indiana.

The others who served as governors of the Indiana Territory include **John Gibson**, who also served as the Territory's secretary under Harrison, and **Thomas Posey**, who held the military rank of brigadier general.

In 1803 grape culture was introduced into Indiana by Swiss colonists who had settled in Switzerland County in the southern part of the state.

Aaron Burr's so-called western conspiracy, beginning in 1806 after his duel with Alexander Hamilton, remains unclear

William Henry Harrison was perhaps more important than any other man in opening Ohio and Indiana to white settlement, negotiating several treaties with the Indians, particularly the Treaty of Fort Wayne in 1809. He studied medicine before joining the army in 1791. In 1798 he resigned to become secretary of the Northwest Territory. He was named the first governor of the Territory of Indiana (1800-1812), became the hero of Tippecanoe and was elected ninth President of the United States in 1841. He died a month after his election. (Photograph by Indiana Historical Society Library).

in history. **Major Davis Floyd**, who joined Burr's forces, recruited men to build boats near present day New Albany near Louisville for the "conspiracy" in 1806. Major Floyd deserted the scheme and was later arrested for treason. He was tried in Indiana Territory in a federal court and convicted. Sentiment was so divided over the trial that the dishonored major was fined $20 and spent only a few hours in jail. Burr was later arrested and tried for treason in Richmond, Virginia. He was found not guilty by the court. Major Floyd, by the way, was elected a delegate to the constitutional convention held in Corydon in 1816.

In 1810, Governor Harrison met with **Tecumseh** at Vincennes as the Americans were anxious to end their fighting with the Indians. The following year, Harrison defeated **Prophet**, Tecumseh's brother, at the famous Battle of Tippecanoe.

The war with England began in June, 1812. William Henry Harrison ended his tenure as governor of Indiana Territory and joined in the fight against the British who had again incited the Indians to strike out against the Americans. Twenty-four white settlers were massacred by Indians at Pigeon Roost in Scott County on September 3 and during the two days that followed an Indian force attacked Fort Harrison but were repelled by the garrison commanded by **Captain Zachary Taylor**, who would later become president of the United States. British and Indian forces laid siege to Fort Wayne, September 5-12, but the garrison was relieved September 12 upon the arrival of reinforcements commanded by General Harrison. The last Indian battle fought in Indiana occurred December 17-18, 1812 when the Miami Indians were defeated on the banks of the Mississinewa River in Grant County.

In September, 1814, the Farmers and Mechanics Bank at Madison and the Bank of Vincennes were chartered. The State Bank of Indiana was established by the state legislature in 1834.

The **Thomas** and **Nancy Lincoln** family, including seven year old Abraham, arrived in Spencer County, Indiana, from Kentucky in 1816. Nancy died in 1818 and Tom Lincoln married Sarah Bush Johnston, a widow, a short time later. The family remained in the state until 1830 when they moved to Illinois.

The Rappites, an ascetic religious group that had come from Germany to Pennsylvania, founded New Harmonie on the Wabash River in 1815. These colonists were led by **George Rapp**, who had dreamed of a perfect co-operative community. The Rappites sold the village in 1825 to **Robert Owen**, a Scottish social reformer, who attempted to establish a new social order. His group included scholars, teachers, and scientists. They adopted a number of progressive ideas for their community, especially in education. The colony prospered briefly and leaders from countries from afar came to study Owen's methods.

14

Civil War Governor Oliver P. Morton (1823-1877) was one of the ablest of the war governors and a strong supporter of President Abraham Lincoln's administration. In 1867 he resigned to enter the Senate where he served until his death. (Photograph by Indiana Historical Society Library).

This experiment failed in 1827 because of the lack of cooperation of all of the colonists.

The first stage coach line in Indiana was established in 1820 and operated between Vincennes and Louisville. On April 10, 1824, U.S. mail was transported by stage between the two cities. The National Road began at the state line just east of Richmond in 1827 and reached Terre Haute in 1838. In 1828 a stage route was established between Madison and Indianapolis. The first railroad track in Indiana, one mile long, was laid at Shelbyville in 1834. The first steam train arrived in Indianapolis from Madison October 1, 1847. The first Union Station in the United States was built in Indianapolis in 1853.

**Hanover College**, the first denominational college in Indiana, was established in 1827 by the Presbyterians.

The first public subscription library in Indiana opened in Vincennes in 1807. State law provided for county libraries in 1818, and for the Indiana State Library in Indianapolis in 1825.

U.S. Congress granted land to the state to build the **Wabash and Erie Canal** in 1827. Construction of the canal did not begin for another five years, in 1832, and it was not formally opened until July 4, 1843. Construction began in Fort Wayne on February 22, 1832. It was not completed until 1853, running 452 miles from Toledo, Ohio, to Evanston, Indiana; the longest canal in the United States. From Fort Wayne, the canal ran southwest through Huntington, Lagro, Wabash, Peru, Logansport, Lockport, Pittsburg, Americus, Lafayette, Attica, Covington, Lodi, Montezuma, Terre Haute, Riley, Worthington, Bloomfield,

Newberry, Washington, Rogers, Petersburg, Francisco, Port Gibson and Evansville.

The **Underground Railroad** began operations at Cabin Creek, in Randolph County, in 1831. This operation assisted runaway slaves seeking freedom in Canada.

Coal was first mined near Cannelton in 1837 to service river steamers. The first major coal mining operation began 17 years later in Sullivan County. Coal continues to be the state's most valuable mineral resource.

The Panic of 1837 forced Indiana into bankruptcy in 1838.

**William Henry Harrison**, Indiana's first territorial governor and hero of the Battle of Tippecanoe, was elected President of the United States in March, 1841, but died in office 30 days later.

Indiana was called upon to raise three regiments during the Mexican War of 1846-1847. Approximately 5,000 Indianans served in that war with 542 Hoosiers either killed in action or died of diseases. Lew Wallace, later to become a general, served as lieutenant stationed on the Rio Grande, well away from any action during the Mexican War.

The **Studebaker brothers** opened their blacksmith shop in South Bend in 1852. They became famous for their wagons and carriages and in 1904 introduced their motorcar, popular for several decades.

**James Oliver** received a patent for his famed chilled-steel plow in 1868.

Indiana's economy improved in the 1850s as railroads pushed into the state providing expanded markets for farmers. This resulted in the creation of new cities.

While Indiana provided for a statewide system of free public schools in 1816 the legislature did not establish taxes to pay for them until 1849. Up until that time children were schooled locally with parents providing the resources or taking turns to educate them.

The office of State Superintendent of Public Instruction and the State Board of Agriculture were created in 1851. The State Board of Education was created the following year. The state legislature also passed a law in 1852 allowing vigilantes to enforce the law against horse thieves and other lawbreakers.

The first official U.S. air mail flight occurred in the summer of 1859 when a balloon was released from Lafayette destined for New York. The brief flight went only six miles.

The Civil War brought many changes to the Hoosiers. Indiana voted for **Abraham Lincoln** in the 1860 election, and the Civil War governor, **Oliver P. Morton**, held the state unswervingly to the Union cause. On April 6, 1861, two days after the fall of Fort Sumter, Governor Morton issued a call for six Indiana regiments. **Lew Wallace** was appointed adjutant general of the state. In 1861, 61,341 Indianans enlisted in the

16

Union Army while the state's quota was only 32,832. During the war Indiana raised 196,363 men for service, 7,243 were killed in battle and 17,785 died of diseases. During the first two years of the war, Governor Morton ran the state government without the approval for the funding by the state legislature.

Millionaire **J. F. D. Lanier,** a New York banker formerly of Madison, Indiana, outfitted several regiments of Indiana troops during the Civil War and kept the state from bankruptcy a second time by advancing $400,000 to the State and Governor Morton.

Indiana troops saw their first action June 3, 1861 at Philippi, Virginia. They saw their last action at Palmentto Ranch, Texas, May 13, 1865.

There was some opposition to the war and as it dragged on, opposition became open. Resistance to the draft was state-wide and violence occurred in some 30 counties with attacks on newspapers, political demonstrations and activities of secret organizations. Some enrolling officers were killed during this period.

Indiana was given a quota of 9,000 Confederate prisoners of war. Among the POW camps was one in Lafayette. Some 3,700 captured Confederate soldiers were actually imprisoned in Indiana during the war.

Confederate sympathizers created the *Knights of the Golden Circle* in 1862 in an attempt to thwart Governor Morton's efforts on behalf of the Union. The secret organization's goal was to conquer Mexico and establish a Gulf empire based on cotton and slavery. Several influential men, among them **Lambdin P. Milligan, Dr. William A. Bowles** and **Horace Heffren,** were arrested and convicted as leaders of the *Order of American Knights,* whose membership had grown to an estimated 50,000, the Indiana branch of the *Knights of the Golden Circle.* The conspirators planned to kidnap Governor Morton, hold him hostage and launch an insurrection on August 16, 1864. The movement was dissolved when a military tribunal convicted the offenders of treason, sentencing the leaders to be hanged. The U.S. Supreme Court later overturned the sentences.

**Brigadier General John Hunt Morgan** and 2,500 Confederate troops raided through southern Indiana, July 8-13, 1863. During this brief raid, involving the towns of Corydon, Palmyra, Salem, Vienna, and Lexington, Morgan's men destroyed property and looted stores and homes. Earlier, July 18, 1862, **Adam R. "Stovepipe" Johnson** and a band of Confederates raided and pillaged Newburgh.

Indianan **Richard Gatling** invented the first practical machine gun in 1862 to add to the Army's arsenal.

**Frank Reno** and his outlaw gang robbed a Jefferson, Madison & Indianapolis train in Jefferson County in 1868 in one

Indiana's first natural gas well was discovered about two miles southwest of Francesville, off US 421, in 1867.

of the richest robberies up to that time netting the bandits nearly $100,000. It is claimed that in this robbery, Frank Reno "invented" train robbery. Actually the gang had held up two trains earlier, the first in 1866.

The first Indiana Grange was formed in Vigo County in 1869 and was organized statewide by **John Wier** in 1872. The Grange advocated railroad regulation that favored farmers.

Petroleum was discovered at Terre Haute in 1865 and the first oil well was drilled on the farm of **D. A. Beyson**, near Keystone in Wells county in 1889. That same year, Standard Oil Company built the world's largest refinery at Whiting. Natural gas was discovered at Eaton in 1876. The first natural gas well came in at Portland in 1886.

Indiana's first newspaper was the *Indiana Gazette* published in 1804 by **Elihu Stout**. *WBBA*, owned and operated by Purdue University, the oldest radio station in the state, was granted its license in April, 1922.

The first Protestant church in Indiana, serving a Baptist congregation, was organized at Owen's Creek in Knox county in 1798. The earliest church was the Vincennes Roman Catholic Church established before 1750.

The Panic of 1873 brought labor unrest to the country. The Whitecaps, a hooded secret organization, operated in 18 southern counties to enforce morality of rural society during the 1870s. At first victims were warned but as time went on violence

18

and corruption within the organization led to whippings and in some cases, executions. The Whitecaps were dissolved in 1893 when they falsely accused two boys in Harrison County of murdering their father. While protecting themselves against the Whitecaps, the boys killed five vigilantes and were later exonerated of any unlawful acts.

The State Board of Health was established in 1881.

In 1889, **Benjamin Harrison**, a grandson of William Henry Harrison, became President of the United States.

The first successful gasoline-powered autocar was introduced by **Elwood Haynes** of Kokomo in 1894. He is also credited with inventing stainless steel.

The invention set off a wave of car manufacturers and Indiana was home to over 100 of these companies.

Here is a list of automobiles once manufactured in the Hoosier state: Albany, American, American Simplex, Amplex, American Underslung, Amsted, Apperson, Auburn, Avanti, Bendix, Brooke-Spache, Bryan, Champion, Clark, Cole, Colonial, Comet, Continental, Cord, Crosley, Crow-Elkhart, Crown, DeSoto, Diamond, Dixie Flyer, Duesenberg, Dumore, Economy, E.I.M., Elcar, Elkhart, Empire, Erskine, Evansville, Frontenac, Gary, Great Western, Harper, Hassler, Haynes, Haynes-Apperson, H.C.S., Henderson, Hercules, Herff-Brooks, Hoosier Scout, Howard, Huffman, IMP, Inter-State, Izzer, James, Kelsey, Kenworthy, Kiblinger, Lambert, Laurel, Lawter, Leader, and Lexington.

Also Lindsay, Lyons, Madison, Marion, Marmon, McFarlan, McIntyre, Mercer, Merz, Meteor, Mier, Model, Mohawk, Moore, Moorriss-London, Munson, National, Parry, New Parry, Pathfinder, Perfection, Pilot, Postal, Pratt, Pratt-Elkhart, Princeton, Real, Reeves, ReVere, Richmond, Ricketts, Rider-Lewis, Roosevelt, Sellers, Senator, Shad-Wyck, Sheridan, Shoemaker, Simplicity, Single-Center, South Bend, Sperling, Stanley, Star, Sterling, Stratton, Studebaker, Stutz, Sun, Tincher, Traveler, Tricolet, Union, Waverly, Pope-Waverly, Wayne, Westcott, Williams, Overland, Windsor, and Zimmerman.

A call for Indiana troops for the Spanish-American War came in April, 1898. Indiana was the first state to fill its quota. Only a few Indiana soldiers were called to fight in this brief war.

The newly organized Socialist Democrat Party held its national convention in Indianapolis in 1900 and nominated **Eugene Debs** as its candidate for the U.S. presidency. Debs received less than one percent of the vote in Indiana. Debs was also a candidate for the presidency in 1904, 1908, 1912, 1920.

In 1906, the United States Steel Corporation began building the city of Gary where the company built its largest steel plant.

In 1911, the first 500-mile Memorial Day automobile race was held on the Indianapolis Motor Speedway.

Among some of the most noted writers from the state are **Edward Eggleston** (*"The Hoosier Schoolmaster,"* 1871), **Lew Wallace** (*"Ben Hur,"* 1880), **James Whitcomb Riley** (*"The Bear Story"*) **Thomas Dreiser** (*"An American Tragedy,"* 1925), **Booth Tarkington** (Pulitzer Prizes for *The "Magnificent Ambersons,"* 1919; *"Alice Adams,"* 1922), **Gene Stratton Porter** (*"Freckles,"* 1904; *"The Girl of the Limberlost,"* 1909), **Albert J. Beveridge** (Pulitzer Prize for *"Life of John Marshall,"* 1920), and **Mary Jane Ward** (*"Snake Pit"*).

Another Pulitzer Prize winning writer was World War II newspaper correspondent **Ernie Pyle**.

In the field of music, such names as **Hoagy Carmichael** and **Cole Porter** stand out. The famed actor **James Dean** was a native of Indiana. The nationally syndicated cartoonist and creator of "Garfield," **Jim Davis** is also a native as are **Phil Jones**, Emmy Award winning journalist, and **Robert C. Sheets**, Director of the National Hurricane Center.

Indiana has produced five United States vice presidents including **Thomas R. Marshall, Charles W. Fairbanks, Thomas H. Hendricks, Schulyer Colfax** and **J. Dan Quayle**. Several others have been appointed to cabinet posts. President Lincoln appointed **Caleb Smith** as Secretary of Interior in 1861 and replaced with another Indianan, **John P. Usher**, in 1863. In 1865, Lincoln appointed **Hugh McCulloch** as Secretary of the Treasury, a post he held until 1869 under President Johnson. Indianan **William H. H. Miller** served as U. S. Attorney General from 1889 to 1893. **John W. Foster** was appointed Secretary of State by President Harrison in 1892 and served until the next year when he was replaced by another Indianan, **Walter Q. Gresham**. In 1895, **John Hay** was appointed Secretary of State by President McKinley and served in this post until 1905. **Claude R. Wickard** served as Secretary of Agriculture, 1940-45, appointed by President Roosevelt. President Nixon appointed **Clifford M. Hardin** as Secretary of Agriculture in 1969 and replaced with another Indianan, **Earl L. Butts**, in 1971. **Dr. Otis P Brown** was apppointed as head of Health and Human Services Department in 1985 by President Reagan.

**John Dillinger** became the most notorious bank robber of the 1930s, committing many of these robberies in Indiana as he spread terror across the midwest. The FBI named him "Public Enemy No. 1," when he committed his first federal offense, interstate auto theft. Another notorious outlaw band, the Barrow (**Clyde Barrow** and **Bonnie Parker**) gang ventured into Indiana on May 8, 1933 and robbed the Lucerne Bank in Cass County of $300.

Indiana has had its share of natural disasters and a few are listed.

Tornadoes and floods that struck Indiana in March, 1913,

resulted in 732 deaths and some $180 million in damages. Railroad and highway bridges were washed out and the National Guard was called out. Tornadoes killed 60 and injured several hundred when they touched down in Princeton in Gibson County and Griffin in Posey County in March, 1925. Both communities suffered heavy damage. In January, 1937, the Ohio River flooded much of the southern part of the state causing some $500 million in damages. Martial law was declared with a call out of the National Guard.

In April, 1965, tornadoes destroyed the communities of Russiaville, Alto, Greentown and Dunlap. National Guardsmen helped to recover 137 bodies and hundreds of injured. In April, 1974, tornadoes killed 41 and injured 769 while creating damages exceeding $70 million. In January, 1978, 19 Indianans died in the worst blizzard of record for the state.

Thirty one persons were killed in a mine explosion January 28, 1931.

Indiana contributed 130,670 men to the armed forces during World War I but only the 115th Field Artillery was distinctly a Hoosier outfit. **James B. Gresham** of Evansville was one of the first three Americans to be killed in action. Indiana lost 3,354 men and 15 women nurses in the conflict.

The Ku Klux Klan emerged in the 1920s and became powerful in the political structure of the state. **K. C. Stephenson**, the Grand Dragon, was convicted of murder in 1925 and sentenced to a life term in the Indiana State Prison.

The last lynching in Indiana occurred in Marion in 1930 when two black youths accused of rape and murder were hanged. Martial law was declared to keep the peace in the black community.

Prohibition, the stock market crash of 1929 and the depression that followed contributed to a crime wave across the entire country and Indiana was not immune to this problem. Law enforcement officers had their hands full investigating and chasing down bank robbers, murderers, bootleggers and racketeers.

Some 338,000 Indianans answered the call during World War II with 10,000 losing their lives during military service.

The battleship *U.S.S. Indiana* was launched November 20, 1941.

About 1,000 Indiana service personnel lost their lives during military service in the Korean War. Nine Indiana National Guard pilots flew combat missions during that conflict.

Company D, 151st Infantry of Indiana arrived in Vietnam in 1968 and became one of the most decorated units during that war.

Indiana is credited with seven astronauts, **Joseph P. Allen, Frank Borman, Mark N. Brown, Anthony W. England,**

21

**Virgil I. Grissom, Jerry L. Ross**, and **Donald E. Williams**.
Joseph Allen, of Crawfordsville, entered the space program as a civilian in 1967 and flew on flights STS-5, November 11-16, 1982, and STS-51A, November 8-16, 1984.

Frank Borman, of Gary, entered the space program as an Air Force officer in 1962. He flew on Gemini 7, December 4-18, 1965, and Apollo 8, December 21-27, 1968. Borman received the Congressional Space Medal of Honor.

Mark Brown, of Valparaiso, entered the space program as an Air Force officer in 1984.

Anthony England, of Indianapolis, entered the space program as a civilian in 1967. He flew on STS 51-F, July 29-August 6, 1985.

Virgil "Gus" Grissom, of Mitchell, entered the space program as an Air Force officer in 1951. In the first group of astronauts selected Grissom flew on Mercury 4, July 21, 1961, and Gemini 3, March 23, 1965. He was the second American in space. He died January 27, 1967 at NASA John F. Kennedy Space Center during preparations for the first Apollo flight. Grissom was awarded the Congressional Space Medal of Honor posthumously.

Jerry Ross, of Crown Point, entered the space program as an Air Force officer in 1980. He flew on STS 61-B November 26-December 3, 1985.

Donald E. Williams, of Lafayette, entered the space program as a Naval officer in 1978. He flew on STS-51-D April 12-19, 1985.

Seventy service men who were born in Indiana or joined the military in Indiana have been recipients of the Congressional Medal of Honor (1862-1973). The first Indianan to receive the award was 2nd Lt. Frederick W. Fout of the 15th Battery, Indiana Light Artillery, near Harpers Ferry, West Virginia, September 15, 1862. He voluntarily gathered the men of his battery, remanned the guns, which had been ordered abandoned by an officer, opened fire, and kept up the same on the enemy until after the surrender. Eight privates serving in the 83rd Indiana Infantry were awarded the CMH at Vicksburg, Mississippi, May 22, 1863. Another Indianan, Pvt. Lewis T. Hunt, serving with the 6th Missouri Infantry, also received the CMH at Vicksburg on May 22nd. Thirty of the 70 Indiana service men held the rank of private when they were awarded the medal.

Indiana's Constitution was adopted in 1851 to replace the original one adopted in 1816. The governor of Indiana is elected to a four year term and can serve any number of terms, but may not serve more than two terms consecutively. The other state officers, who also serve four year terms, include the lieutenant governor, attorney general, secretary of state, auditor, and treasurer.

The Indiana legislature, called the General Assembly, consists of a 50-member Senate and a 100-member House of Representatives. Senators serve four-year terms; Representative serve two-year terms. The legislature meets annually.

The courts in Indiana are headed by the state Supreme Court and the Court of Appeals. The Supreme Court consists of a chief justice and four associate justices. The chief justice is selected by a nonpartisan judicial commission and serves for five years.The Court of Appeals has nine judges. The judges of the Supreme Court and the Court of Appeals are appointed by the governor to serve for two years and then they are placed on a ballot for the voters to retain or reject them for a new 10-year term. Circuit courts cover one or more of all the counties and some counties maintain superior and special courts.

The state is composed of 92 counties.

The state gained its name from the earliest inhabitants, the Indians. Called the "Hoosier State," it is not clear where the name came from. It could be from "Who's here?" – a reply to a knock at the door, or from "hoozer", an early English dialect for something large, or from "husher," a slang word for a fighter or a man who could "hush" others with his fists. It also may refer to a person, Samuel Hoosier, a contractor who preferred Indiana workers for the building of a canal along in the Ohio River in 1825.

*The Crossroads of America* is the state's motto. The state song is *On the Banks of the Wabash, Far Away*; the state flower, the Peony; the state bird, the Cardinal; and the state tree, the Tulip Poplar.

Indiana is a leading agricultural state. Corn is the major crop and the state is a leader in growing soybeans and tomatoes. Other crops include wheat, hay, oats and grain sorghum. Important vegetables crops grown are cabbage, onions, and potatoes. The main fruit crops include apples, melons, peaches and strawberries. Hogs are the state's most valuable livestock product with beef production second.

About 60 percent of the building limestone mined in the United States comes from the state.

There are 16 state museums and historical sites operated by the Division of State Parks, Department of Natural Resources. These include the Indiana State Museum, Indianapolis; Angel Mounds, Evansville; Corydon Capitol, Corydon; Culbertson Mansion, New Albany; Ernie Pyle Birthplace, Dana; Gene Stratton Porter's "The Cabin in the Wildflower Woods, Rome City; Indiana Territorial Capital, Vincennes; the Jones House, Gentryville; Lanier Mansion, Madison; Levi Coffin House, Fountain City; Old State Bank, Vincennes; Limberlost, Geneva; the town of New Harmony; Pigeon Roost, south of Scottsburg; T. C. Steele Home, Nashville; and Whitewater Canal, Metamora. All of these are described more fully in the following chapters.

23

There are 18 State Parks in Indiana. They are listed here with telephone numbers for additional information:

Bass Lake State Beach, Rt. 5 (IN 10), Knox, (219) 772-3382 (Memorial Day weekend to Labor Day weekend).

Brown County, off IN 46, Nashville (812) 988-6406.

Chain O'Lakes, 2355 East 75 South, Albion (219) 636-2654.

Clifty Falls, 1501 Green Road, Madison (812) 265-1331.

Falls of the Ohio, on the banks of the Ohio River, Clarksville (812) 945-6284.

Harmonie, Route 1 Box 5A (on the banks of the Wabash), New Harmony (812) 682-4821.

Indiana Dunes,1600 North 25E, Chesterton (219) 926-1952.

Lincoln, adjacent to the Lincoln Boyhood Home Memorial, Lincoln City (812) 937-4710.

McCormick's Creek, Route 5 Box 82 (along the White River), Spencer (812) 829-2235. This was Indiana's first state park.

Mounds, 4306 Mounds Road (off I-69), Anderson (317) 642-6627.

Quabache, 6720 E. 100 South, Bluffton (219) 824-0926.

Pokagon, 450 Lane 100 Lake James (off I-69), Angola (219) 833-2012.

Potato Creek, 25601 IN 4, North Liberty (219) 656-8186.

Shades, Route 1 Box 72 (off I-74), Waveland (317) 435-2810.

Shakamak, Route 2 Box 120 (off IN 48), Jasonville (812) 665-2158.

Spring Mill, off IN 60, Mitchell (812) 849-4129.

Summit Lake, 5993 North Messick Road, New Castle (317) 766-5873.

Tippecanoe, Route 4 Box 95A (off US 35), Winamac (219) 946-3213.

Turkey Run, Route 1 Box 164 (IN 47), Marshall (317) 597-2635.

Versailles, US 50, Versailles (812) 689-6424.

Whitewater Memorial , Route 2 Box 194 (off IN 101), Liberty (317) 458-5565.

# Chapter 2
# Indianapolis, State Capital

*This chapter presents the historical sites in and around the state capital. Some of the personalities involved in its history are also introduced.*

Samuel Bigger, a Whig from Rushville, was elected governor of Indiana in 1840 but was defeated in 1843 by Democrat James Whitcomb of Bloomington. (Photograph by Bass Photo Co. Collection, Indiana Historical Society Library, Negative No. 29717.)

# The Procession of Governors

Jonathan Jennings, the first governor, ran for the U.S. Congress and was elected during his second term in office. Lieutenant Governor Ratcliff Boon served as acting governor from September 12 to December 5, when Democrat-Republican William Hendricks assumed the office of governor.

In August 1825, James B. Ray was elected governor and was reelected for a second term in August 1828. He was an Independent. In August 1831, Noah Noble, a National Republican, was elected to the governor's seat. In 1834, Noble, now a Whig, was reelected. In 1837, David Wallace, a Whig from Covington, was elected governor. He had served previously as the lieutenant governor. Wallace was replaced in 1840 by Bigger.

# Chapter 2
# The Capital, Indianapolis

INDIANAPOLIS (pop. 1,236,600) was settled in 1820 with the first non-Indian settler arriving on February 26. It was selected as the site of the state capital June 7, 1820 and the state legislature accepted the site in January, 1821. The sale of town lots in Indianapolis began October 9, 1821.

State government moved to the new capital in 1825, although work on the capitol building was not completed until 1835. In 1825, the state government created new jobs that brought many people to Indianapolis. Growth continued when the National Road (US 40) was routed through the town in 1834 and reached its peak in 1836 with the building of the Central Canal on White River.

The city was incorporated in 1847 and serves as the county seat of Marion county, named for **Francis "The Swamp Fox" Marion** of Revolutionary War fame. Marion County was established April 1, 1822.

It also serves as an educational center and is home of **Butler University**, founded by the Disciples of Christ in 1850; **Marian College**, established by the Roman Catholics in 1853; **Indiana Central College**, created by the Evangelical United Brethren in 1902; and **John Herron Art Institute** and units of Indiana University, including the **Indiana University Medical Center**.

The Youth for Christ movement began in Indianapolis in 1943 and has become a world-wide organization.

January 1, 1977, **Reverend Jaqueline Means**, ordained in Indianapolis, became the first woman priest in the Episcopal Church of America.

The National Headquarters of the American Legion is located at 700 North Pennsylvania Street. It was dedicated in August, 1950.

The first theatrical performance was held in Indianapolis in 1823. The first Indiana Democratic Convention was held here in 1828. In 1829, the Indiana Colonization Society was founded for the purpose of sending black Americans to Liberia.

The Navy cruiser *U.S.S. Indianapolis* was launched in 1931 and served as a flagship for President Franklin Roosevelt on some of his ocean trips. During World War II, the ship and its crew served admirably in combat. On March 31, 1945, the ship was damaged and nine crew members killed in a kamikaze attack between Guam and Leyte. The Indianapolis was sunk by Japanese submarine I-58 on July 30, 1945 with a loss of 880 crew

27

members. The ship had carried parts of the atomic bomb dropped on Japan from the West Coast to Tinian Island earlier.

**Henry Ward Beecher**, later to become a noted leader in the anti-slavery movement, accepted the pastorate of the Second Presbyterian Church, then on Monument Circle, in 1836 and served until 1847. In addition, he served as editor of the *Indiana Farmer and Gardener*. He was the brother of Harriet Beecher Stowe, author of *"Uncle Tom's Cabin."* His sister, a frequent visitor, castigated Indianapolis in her novel, *"From Dawn to Daylight,"* a best seller everywhere but Indianapolis where it was banned. During the 1850s Reverend Beecher provided Sharps carbines to colonists in Kansas in their fight against slavery and these colonists established The Beecher Bible and Rifle Church in Waubansee.

The first steam train arrived in Indianapolis from Madison on October 1, 1847. The first street cars were introduced in 1864. The first belt railroad in the United States was built in Indianapolis in 1873. In September, 1904, the largest interurban terminal station in the country was opened in the city.

Indiana's first state fair was held in Indianapolis October 20, 1852. The State Board of Agriculture was established February 14, 1851.

President-elect **Abraham Lincoln** visited Indianapolis April 16, 1861 enroute to Washington, D. C. and his body lay in state in the capitol building April 30, 1865 when the funeral train stopped enroute to Springfield, Illinois. Almost 100,000 persons came out in the rain to pay their respects to the fallen president.

Indianapolis hummed during the Civil War. It became the state recruiting headquarters. Camp Morton, named for Governor **Oliver P. Morton**, was established as an Army training center and was occupied by six regiments of Union troops. Altogether 24 army camps, a soldiers' convalescence home, and an arsenal/supply depot operated here during the war. Camp Morton also served as a prisoner-of-war camp for 3,700 Confederate soldiers. A large ammunition factory was established in the city.

**Dr. Richard Gatling** of Indianapolis invented a hand-cranked rapid-fire gun in 1862, named for him, that fired 250 rounds per minute.

The Grand Army of the Republic held its national convention in the city in 1866.

The post war period, from 1865-73, saw rapid growth and the expansion of the city. This boom, resulting in inflation, collapsed in 1873. The economy recovered slowly and it was not until 1890 that the city experienced another period of expansion. During this depressed period, the population had grown to 170,000.

President Andrew Johnson's visit to the city to recruit

Eli Lilly was the founder during the Civil War era of the pharmaceutical company bearing his name. The company, through its Lilly Foundation established in 1937 has contributed millions of dollars to numerous philanthropic endeavors, especially in the area of education. (Photo by Bass Photo Collection; Indiana Historical Society Library).

support for his soft policy toward the South created riots and state and local public officials snubbed him.

**Dr. John S. Bobbs** performed the first successful gall bladder operation on a local seamstress. His Dispensary for the Poor became part of the newly-opened Indiana Medical College.

**Catherine Merrill** became a professor of literature at Butler University, the second woman in the country to win a professorship.

**Colonel Eli Lilly** opened a pharmaceutical company at 15 West Pearl Street with $1,400 in assets and a staff of three. Out of this grew the giant pharmaceutical firm of Eli Lilly whose company and Canadian researchers developed insulin. The Eli Lilly company is one of the city's best known benefactors.

**Mrs. Fanny Osbourne** of the city married Author Robert Louis Stevenson.

Indiana's Woman's Prison was established in Indianapolis in 1873.

Two tragic fires in Indianapolis, at the Bowen-Merrill booksellers and at the Surgical Institute, killed 34 persons and led to improved fire safety laws.

**Harry** and **Albert Von Tilzer** (also known as Gumbinsky), who grew up on the city's Southside, wrote the hit song, *"Take Me Out to the Ballgame."*

The stage and screen actor **Clifton Webb** (1891-1966) was born in Indianapolis as Webb Parmalee Hollenbeck. Principally a Broadway dancer and singer, he appeared in several films. He may be best known for playing the part of crusty but lovable

Lynn Belvidere. He appeared in three Mr. Belivdere films, 1948, 1949, and 1951. He was nominated for the Oscar's best actor award in the role of Mr. Belivdere in the 1948 film *"Sitting Pretty."* He was also nominated for best supporting actor as Waldo Lydecker in the 1944 release of *"Laura"* and for his 1951role as Elliott Templeton in *"The Razor's Edge."*

**Charles H. Black** built an automobile with an internal combustion engine here in 1891. Black could have been recognized as the inventor and builder of the first successful automobile except that he used a kerosene torch for the ignition that blew out on windy days. The auto business flourished in Indianapolis before World War I and many innovations in motorcar manufacturing originated here. Among these innovations were four-wheel brakes and the six-cylinder engine.

By the turn of the century Indianapolis was recognized as the leader in the new automobile industry. Sixty-five different kinds of automobiles were in production before World War I, including Stutz, Coasts, Duesenberg, and Cole. Among the early automobiles built in Indianapolis were the American Underslung, 1906-1914, manufactured by the American Motor Car Company; the Brooke-Spacke, 1919-1921, by Spacke Machine & Tool Company; the Cole, 1909-1925, by Cole Motor Car Company; the Colonial, 1917-1921, by Colonial Automobile Company; the Comet, 1914-1915, by Comet Cyclecar Company; the De Tamble, 1908-1913, by Speed Changing Pulley Company when production moved to Anderson in 1909; the Duesenberg, 1920-1937, by Duesenberg Motor Company; the Economy, 1914, by Economy Car Company; the Empire, 1909-1919, by Empire Motor Company until 1912 when the company moved to Pennsylvania; the Frontenac, 1922, by Frontenac Motor Corporation; the Hassler, 1917, by Hassler Motor Company; H.C.S., 1920-1925, by H.C.S. Motor Company; the Henderson, 1912-1915, by the Henderson Motor Car Company; the Herff-Brooks, 1914-1916, by Herff-Brooks Corporation; the Hoosier Scout, 1914, by Hoosier Cyclecar Company; the Lindsey, 1907-1908, by J. V. Lindsey; the Lyons-Atlas and Lyons Knight, 1912-1915, by Lyons-Atlas Company; the Marion, 1904-1915, by Marion Motor Car Company; the Marmon, 1903-1933, by Nordyke and Marmon Company (1902-1925) and Marmon Motor Car Company (1926-1933); the Merz, 1914-1915, by Merz Cyclecar Company; the Mohawk, 1903-1904, by the Mohawk Auto & Cycle Company; the National, 1900-1924, by National Automobile & Electric Vehicle Company, whose name changed two other times during production; the Parry, 1910-1911, by Parry Auto Company; the New Parry, 1912, by Motor Car Manufacturing Company; the Pathfinder, 1911-1918, which succeeded the New Parry by Motor Car Manufacturing Company and then was reorganized in 1916 to become The Pathfinder Company; the Roosevelt, 1929-1931, by Marmon

Motor Company; the Stratton, 1924, by Stratton Motor Corporation; the Tricolet, 1904-1906, by H. Pokorney Automobile & Gas Engine Company; the Waverly, 1898-1903; 1908-1914, and the Pope-Waverly, 1903-1907, by a series of companies beginning with the Indiana Bicycle Company in 1898 and ending with the Waverly Company in 1908; and the Overland, 1903-1929, by Overland Company (1905-1907). The Moore, 1917, was built in Indianapolis but the manufacturer is unknown.

Indianapolis was home to four U.S. vice presidents including **Thomas R. Marshall** (1912 under Woodrow Wilson), **Charles W. Fairbanks** (1904 under Theodore Roosevelt), **Thomas H. Hendricks** (1884 under Grover Cleveland) and **Schulyer Colfax** (1868 under Ulysses S. Grant).

Author **Booth Tarkington** was born in Indianapolis in 1869. He won two Pulitzer Prizes for his writing: *"The Magnificent Ambersons"* in 1919 and *"Alice Adams"* in 1922. Among his many other books are *"Penrod "* (1914) and *"Penrod and Sam "* (1916).

The Raggedy Ann doll originated in Indianapolis in 1914 when Cartoonist **John Gruelle** took his daughter Marcella's old

Booth Tarkington with his dog, Figaro. (Photograph by Indiana Historical Society Library, Negative No. C5827.)

31

rag doll found in the attic and drew in a face and pinned on the doll's breast the famous heart with "I Love You." The daughter died in childhood. Gruelle, born in Arcola, Illinois, wrote 26 Raggedy Ann and Andy books, loved by children and adults around the world.

**Kurt Vonnegut, Jr.**, a native of Indianapolis, gained famed as a novelist in 1922 with the publication of his book, *"Slaughterhouse-Five."*

**Madame C. J. Walker,** born Sarah Breedlove in Louisiana, arrived in Indianapolis in 1910 where she built a successful business in cosmetics for black women. When she died nine years later, she had already become the first black female millionaire.

More Hoosiers enlisted in the military services during World War I than from any other state. One of the first American units in France was the famed 150th Field Artillery of the Rainbow Division, commanded by **Colonel Robert H. Tyndall**. A 500-bed Eli Lilly Base Hospital was established in France by Indianapolis physicians.

Indianapolis was one of seven stops on the first transcontinental commercial airflight in 1929. Transcontinental Air Transport (TAT) began their two-day, two night trip across the U.S. from New York's Penn Station July 7. The flight terminated in Glendale, California. The one-way airfare was $351.94.

The Ku Klux Klan, with more than 250,000 members in Indiana in the 1920s, was led by Grand Dragon **K. C. "I-am-the-Law" Stephenson**. The Indiana Klan was the largest in the nation at the time. At the height of his power, Stephenson was the leader of the Klan in 23 northern states. He was convicted of the murder of 28-year old **Madge Oberholtzer**, a statehouse worker, in 1925 and sentenced to life imprisonment in the Indiana State Prison. Once in prison, Stephenson revealed that he and the Klan were involved in state politics going all the way to the governor's mansion. His revelations of political corruption brought indictments against **Governor Ed Jackson**, Indianapolis **Mayor John Duvall**, six Republican Klan members on the Indianapolis city council, and several county officials. Earlier, Jackson had replaced **Governor Warren T. McCray** who had been sentenced to a prison term for mail fraud. Stephenson claimed that mayors of three major cities and 40 smaller towns around Indiana were indebted to him. The Klan had its tentacles throughout the state's political structure during its heyday. *The Indianapolis Times* received a Pulitzer Prize in 1928 for its campaign against the KKK.

Miss Oberholtzer was the victim of a bizarre kidnapping-and-rape involving Stephenson. He abducted the young woman and on the night train ride to Hammond savagely raped her. In Hammond, he took her to a hotel where they spent the night. The next morning, under guard, Miss Oberholtzer was permitted to go to a drug store and there she secretly purchased poison which she took on her return to the hotel. She became violently ill so Stephenson returned her to her home. A month later, she died a painful death, but not before giving lawyers a deathbed statement about the kidnap-rape by Stephenson. His trial was held in November, 1925, in Noblesville, just north of Indianapolis where he was found guilty and given a life sentence. He spent 31 years in prison, the longest term ever served in Indiana on a charge of second-degree murder. He was released from prison in 1956 and died in Tennessee ten years later.

In late October 1963, 62 persons were killed and 385 injured in a gas explosion at the Indiana State Fairgrounds Coliseum during the finale of a performance of "Holiday on Ice."

**Harry C. Stutz** had designed cars for 14 years or more before the first vehicle to bear his name appeared. The Stutz car was initially produced in the Indianapolis factory of the Ideal Motor Car Company. In 1913, the company name was changed to the Stutz Motor Car Company of America. The Stutz Bearcat, one of motoring history's most legendary models, was introduced the next year and became an immediate success.

**Howard Marmon** was another pioneer automaker. Ray Harroun won the first Indianapolis 500 in 1911 driving a specially-built 6-cyclinder Marmon, the Wasp. Marmons did well in contemporary competition, with 54 first places logged between 1909 and 1912.

**Fred Duesenberg** began by making bicycles and designed his first car, the Mason, in 1904. He and his brother, August, founded Duesenberg Motors in 1913. They concentrated on building racing cars until 1920 when their first production car made its debut.

**John Dillinger**, the most notorious bank robber of the 1930s, was born in Indianapolis June 22, 1903. He and two others robbed the Massachusetts Avenue State Bank of $24,000 on September 6, 1933. He was named "Public Enemy No. 1" by the FBI in March, 1934.

**Benjamin Harrison**, the 23rd president of the United States, had deep roots in Indiana. Born in North Bend, Ohio, he moved to Indianapolis with his wife, Caroline, to establish a law practice after receiving his education in Cincinnati. In 1862, Governor Morton asked Harrison to form a volunteer regiment. He recruited and organized the 70th Indiana Infantry which he also commanded as a colonel. The regiment saw action in the Atlanta campaign and at Nashville. At the end of the war he was promoted to the rank of brevet brigadier general.

After the war, Harrison returned to duty as Indiana Supreme Court reporter, a post which allowed him to continue his law practice. In 1880 he was elected to the U.S. Senate but was defeated in a re-election bid at the end of his first term. In 1888

33

Benjamin Harrison (1833-1901) was the 23rd President of the United States. He became a resident of Indianapolis in 1854. After military service with an Indiana regiment during the Civil War he became a well-established corporation lawyer. He served in the U.S. Senate (1881-1887). He was elected president in 1888, defeating Grover Cleveland. (Photograph by Indiana Historical Society Library, Negative No. C5826). Below is a photo of his Indianapolis home on North Delaware Street, open to the public.

he was nominated for the Presidency and defeated **Grover Cleveland** in a close race. During his four year term as the President, Harrison is credited with establishing a modern Navy and was a pioneer in the conservation movement. Following his stint in the White House, Harrison returned to Indianapolis to resume a successful law practice. He died on March 13, 1901.

PRESIDENT BENJAMIN HARRISON HOME, 1230 North Delaware Street, was completed in 1875 for Harrison and his wife, Caroline, at a cost of $24,818.67. Unfortunately Caroline died while they were still in Washington, D.C. and Harrison returned to his Indianapolis home alone. In the 1890s, about the time of his second marriage, he added central heating, plumbing, electricity, and a front porch. After his death in 1901, his wife, Mary, and their daughter moved to New York until 1937, when Mrs. Harrison sold the home to the Arthur Jordan Foundation, who rented out the home as a boarding house. The foundation has, with the help of family members, completely renovated the home. It is operated today by the President Benjamin Harrison Foundation as a memorial to President Harrison. The home has been designated a National Historic Landmark and is listed on the NRHP. It is open to the public from 10:00 a.m. to 3:30 p.m. weekdays and from 12:30 to 3:30 p.m. Sundays. It is closed Saturdays, the month of January, and the holidays Easter, Thanksgiving, and Christmas. An admission is charged.

The famous INDIANAPOLIS MOTOR SPEEDWAY, a National Historic Landmark and listed on the NRHP, stands unchallenged as the world's greatest sports spectacle. It was built in 1909 by four Indianapolis businessmen, **James A. Allison, Carl G. Fisher, Arthur C. Newby** and **Frank H. Wheeler**. It has been the scene of the International 500-mile automobile races since 1911.

The first auto races were during a three-day program beginning August 19, 1909. Several drivers averaged a little over 70 miles per hour. **Barney Oldfield** claimed a new world record for one mile averaging 83.2 miles per hour. The first 500-mile race, held May 30, 1911, was won by **Ray Harroun** and his backup driver, **Cyrus Patschke**, driving a six-cylinder Marmon Wasp in six hours, 42 minutes and eight seconds. **Arie Luyendyk** averaged 185.981 miles per hour to win the 1990 race, earning $1,090,940. Races were not held in 1917-18 and 1942-45 because of the world wars. During World War I, the Speedway was used as an aviation repair depot and landing field for military aircraft. The Speedway was closed during World War II because of rationing of rubber and petroleum products.

The Speedway was purchased by **Eddie Rickenbacker**, a one-time Indianapolis race driver and World War I aviation ace, in 1927. Rickenbacker sold it to **Anton "Tony" Hulman** in 1945 and ownership has been held by the Hulman family ever since.

35

An Indy 500 exhibit displayed at the Indiana State Museum.

INDIANAPOLIS MOTOR SPEEDWAY HALL OF FAME MUSEUM, 4790 West 16th Street, Speedway, is home to over 33 Indianapolis 500 winning cars including the Marmon Wasp driven by Ray Harroun in 1911. The museum also includes a section for a variety of special interest race cars and a collection of antique and classic passenger cars, many of which were built in Indiana in the early part of this century. The museum is located within the 2 1/2 mile race track. It is open from 9:00 a.m. to 5:00 p.m. daily except Christmas Day. An admission is charged.

James Whitcomb Riley (1847-1916) lived in Indianapolis for several years and died here in 1916. Born in nearby Greenfield, he enjoyed expressing himself through verse from an early age. His success as a poet led him to a full time career composing and reciting, the latter before packed houses around the country, including a performance in New York's Carnegie Hall. Creator of such classics as *"Little Orphant Annie," "The Raggedy Man," "When the Frost is on the Punkin,"* and *"The Bear Story,"* Riley wrote and had published 1,044 poems and was Indiana's Poet Laureate.

JAMES WHITCOMB RILEY HOME, 528 Lockerbie Street, was actually the home of Major and Mrs. Charles L. Holstein and the poet was a paying guest for the last 23 years of his life. Riley moved here in 1893 and died in his bedroom July 22, 1916. The home was built in 1872 by Mrs. Holstein's father, John R. Nickum. The home is considered one of the two most perfectly preserved Victorian houses in America. Many of the poet's personal collections are on exhibit. The home is a National Historic Landmark and is listed on the NRHP. The home is open daily from 10:00 a.m. to 4:00 p.m., except Monday and from 12:00 noon to 4:00 p.m. Sundays. An admission is charged.

INDIANA STATE MUSEUM, 202 North Alabama Street, is located in the former Indianapolis City Hall. Among the exhibits are a 450-million-year-old fossil, the state's first television camera used to telecast the 1949 Indianapolis 500, and the landscape works of Indiana artist T. C. Steele. The museum is listed on the NRHP. The ISM includes 16 historic sites throughout the state. The museum is open from 9:00 a.m. to 4:45 p.m. Monday through Saturday and from 12:00 noon to 4:45 p.m. Sunday. Admission is free.

INDIANA HISTORICAL SOCIETY, 315 West Ohio Street, collects, preserves, and promotes Indiana history through outreach programs, exhibits, publications, and an extensive research library. The collection includes manuscripts, photographs and other visual material, maps, and books. The library is open from 8:00 a.m. to 4:30 p.m. weekdays and from 8:30 a.m. to 4:00 p.m. Saturdays. It is closed on Saturdays from June through August, state holidays, and during the Society's fall and spring conferences. Admission is free.

INDIANA HISTORICAL BUREAU, 140 North Senate Avenue. Created in 1915, the Indiana Historical Bureau's duty is to edit and publish documentary and other material relating to the history of the state and to promote the study of Indiana history through traditional and alternative learning methods in the arts, humanities, and sciences. The Indiana Governors'

Poet James Whitcomb Riley lived in this house on Lockerbie Street in Indianapolis for 23 years and died here in 1916.

Portraits Collection and special exhibits are on display from 8:00 a.m. to 4:30 p.m. weekdays, except state holidays. Admission is free.

MORRIS-BUTLER HOUSE, 1204 Park Avenue, was built as a lavish 1865 mansion and today serves as a museum of the mid-Victorian (1850-1890) period. The house features high-ceilinged, vivid colored interiors with exuberant stencilling, gleaming silver and glassware, and rare Victorian furniture and artwork. It is listed on the NRHP. The museum is open from 10:00 a.m. to 4:00 p.m. Tuesday through Saturday and from 1:00 to 4:00 p.m. Sundays. Tours occur every half hour with the last tour of the day scheduled at 3:30 p.m. It is closed on Mondays and holidays. An admission is charged.

THE HERITAGE PRESERVATION CENTER, 340 West Michigan Street, serves as the state headquarters of Historic Landmarks Foundation. It includes the restored 1879 Kuhn House linked by a glass atrium to a complementary modern addition. The center is open for tours by appointment, 8:30 a.m. to 5:00 p.m. weekdays. During the months of June through August, the Foundation's sightseeing service offers tours of the center combined with walking tours of the historic canal area (other times by appointment). An admission is charged for the tours. The center is closed on holidays. For additional information, call (317) 639-4534.

EITELJORG MUSEUM OF AMERICAN INDIAN AND WESTERN ART, 500 West Washington, boasts one of the finest collections of American Western and Native American artifacts in the country. It is open from 10:00 a.m. to 5:00 p.m. Tuesday through Saturday and from 12:00 noon to 5:00 p.m. Sundays. Tours are conducted daily at 2:00 p.m. It is closed on Mondays, except during June through August, and is also closed Thanksgiving, Christmas and New Year's Day. An admission is charged.

INDIANAPOLIS MUSEUM OF ART, 1200 West 38th Street, is comprised of four art pavilions, the Eli Lilly Botanical Garden, a theater, restaurants and shops on a 152-acre campus. The permanent and changing exhibitions, ranging from ancient artifacts to works by contemporary artists, are housed in the pavilions. The permanent collections include the J. M. W. Turner Collection of watercolors and drawings, the Holliday Collection of Neo-Impressionist Art, the Clowes Fund Collection of Old Masters, the Eli Lilly Collection of Chinese Art, and the Eiteljorg Collection of African Art. The museum offers a full schedule of public programs as well as a variety of lectures, films, classes, concerts, and other special events. It is open from 10:00 a.m. to 5:00 p.m. Tuesday, Wednesday, Friday and Saturday; 10:00 a.m. to 8:30 p.m. Thursday, and from 12:00 noon to 5:00 p.m. Sunday. It is closed on Monday and most major holidays. Admission is free.

38

THE CHILDREN'S MUSEUM OF INDIANAPOLIS, 3000 North Meridian Street, is the largest children's museum in the world. Here the entire family can explore the past and the future of the world, discover the arts, the sciences, and world cultures. The museum claims the largest water clock in the world. More than 4,000 programs are offered annually. It is open 10:00 a.m. to 5:00 p.m. Tuesday through Saturday and from 12:00 noon to 5:00 p.m. Sunday from Labor Day through Memorial Day and the same hours with Monday added during the summer months. An admission is charged. From 5:00 to 8:00 p.m. each Thursday the museum is open and admission is free during these hours.

INDIANA MEDICAL HISTORY MUSEUM, 3000 West Washington, is housed in the Old Pathology Building on the grounds of Central State Hospital. As the nation's oldest surviving pathology laboratory, the building originally provided physicians in the late 1800s and the early 1900s with state-of-the-art facilities in which to study mental and nervous disorders. Today, the museum uses its more than 15,000 artifacts to educate visitors about developments which made possible today's advanced medical treatment and health care. The museum has 12 historic rooms and a changing exhibits gallery. It is open from 10:00 a.m. to 4:00 p.m. Wednesday through Saturday and other days by appointment. An admission is charged.

The INDIANA SOLDIERS AND SAILORS MONUMENT is in the center of Monument Circle and is considered one of the world's most outstanding works of monumental architecture. Standing 284 feet, six inches high, the monument is only 15 feet shorter than the Statue of Liberty. Work on the monument was begun in 1887 and completed in 1902. Four epochs of Indiana history are commemorated by bronze statues of representative men: George Rogers Clark, the period of the Revolution; William Henry Harrison, the War of 1812 and the Battle of Tippecanoe; Governor James Whitcomb, the Mexican War; and Governor Oliver P. Morton, the Civil War. The monument is open from 10:00 a.m. to 7:00 p.m. daily. An elevator carries visitors to the glass-enclosed observation deck.

The INDIANA WAR MEMORIAL, 431 North Meridian Street, was conceived and built in honor of Indiana's World War I veterans. Construction begin in 1924, the cornerstone was laid July 4, 1927 by **General John J. "Black Jack" Pershing**. The building was completed in November, 1933. The name of every serviceman from Indiana who served during World War I is displayed on the walls. Also displayed are the names of Indiana veterans who were casualties of World War II, Korea, and Vietnam. The Shrine Room has a magnificent setting of the American flag, above which shines the crystal Star of Destiny. Beneath the flag is the Altar of Consecration. In each corner of the Shrine Room stand the flags of the Allied Nations and along

39

The 1865 Morris-Butler House serves as a museum in Indianapolis.

two walls are portraits of the World War I Allied commanders. Outside of the south steps stands the largest sculptured bronze casting made in the United States which represents the spiritual concept of the soldier. While military artifacts are displayed throughout the building, the main museum is housed in the lower concourse and occupies 29,000 square feet. On November 11, 1987, the Memorial was rededicated to honor all Indiana war veterans from World War I to the present. It is open from 8:30 a.m. to 4:30 p.m. daily.

NATIONAL TRACK AND FIELD HALL OF FAME, One Hoosier Dome, features the greatest names in track and field with the sports greatest achievements. Among the more than 130 athletes honored here are Jim Thorpe, Jackson Scholz (known from the film *"Chariots of Fire"*), Babe Didrickson, Jesse Owens, Wilma Rudolph, and Bruce Jenner. It is open daily during Hoosier Dome tour days. For information on hours and schedules call (317) 262-3410. An admission is charged.

INDIANA STATE FAIRGROUNDS HISTORIC MINI MUSEUM/VISITOR'S CENTER, 1202 East 38th Street, chronicles the state fair's history through photographs, documents, and artifacts. The Fairgrounds works with the Indiana State Archives Commission on Public Records in presenting an updated display at the Fairs. Information about other Indianapolis attractions also is available. The Museum/Center is open from

9:00 a.m. to 10:00 p.m. daily through the Fair dates and at other times by special arrangement, (317) 927-7500. Admission is free.

HOOK'S HISTORICAL DRUG STORE AND PHARMACY MUSEUM, on the Indiana State Fairgrounds, 1202 East 38th Street, is an authentic example of a 19th century drug store with ice cream sodas still on tap. This historic drug store is located adjacent to the Indiana State Fairgrounds Historic Museum/

The Indiana War Memorial in Indianapolis was completed in 1933.

Visitors' Center. It is open from 11:00 a.m. to 5:00 p.m. daily. Admission is free.

CONNER PRAIRIE, 13400 Allisonville Road, Fishers (northeast of Indianapolis) is a 55-acre restoration of an 1836 Indiana village, complete with costumed residents and farm on the 1823 estate of William Conner. There is also a hands-on Pioneer Adventure Center. It is open from 10:00 a.m. to 5:00 p.m. Tuesday through Saturday and from 12:00 noon to 5:00 p.m. Sundays, May through October, and the same hours Wednesday through Saturday, and same hours on Sundays, in April and November. Admission to the museum center is free. There is an admission charge for the other offerings on the site.

INDIANA TRANSPORTATION MUSEUM, at Forest Park on IN 19, Noblesville, features historic transportation vehicles. Rides are available on restored interurban cars on the museum's operating railroad. It is open weekends and holidays from 12:00 noon to 5:00 p.m. Special guided tours for groups can be arranged by calling (317) 773-6000. An admission is charged.

U.S. ARMY FINANCE CORPS MUSEUM, off the front lobby of the Major General Emmett J. Bean Center, Fort Benjamin Harrison, traces the history of pay in the Army from 1775 to the present using documents, uniforms, and an extensive military currency collection. It is open from 8:00 a.m. to 4:30 p.m. weekdays except on federal holidays, and the first Saturday of the month, 10:00 a.m. to 3:00 p.m. Tours on request. Admission is free.

HERRON SCHOOL OF ART AND GALLERY of Indiana University, 1701 North Pennsylvania Street, is the professional art school for the Indiana University-Purdue University of Indianapolis campus and Indianapolis' Center for Contemporary Art. The Gallery focuses on visual art of the last 10 years with emphasis on works by internationally known contemporary artists as well as faculty and students. There are about eight exhibitions presented every year. The Gallery is open from 10:00 a.m. to 7:00 p.m. Monday through Thursday, and from 10:00 a.m. to 5:00 p.m. Friday. Admission is free. Free parking is available on Pennsylvania and Talbot Streets.

GARFIELD PARK CONSERVATORY, 2450 South Shelby Street, features a year-round display of tropical plants producing unusual fruits and exotic blooms. The Conservatory was established in 1913 and the world-renown Sunken Gardens were designed by Vonnegut & Bohn in 1916. Tours are available from 10:00 a.m. to 5:00 p.m. Tuesday through Saturday, and from 12:00 noon to 5:00 p.m. Sunday. It is closed on Monday. Admission is free, however, there is a charge for special shows.

NATIONAL ART MUSEUM OF SPORTS, Bank One Center, Tower, second floor, is recognized as America's largest and most diversified holder of sports art. Founded in 1959, with its original location at Madison Square Garden in New York City, the museum maintains a collection of more than 250 paintings and sculptures and over 1,400 photographs. The museum was moved to Indianapolis in 1991. Exhibition galleries change quarterly, bringing new artists, subject matter and mediums to the Indianapolis community, the state of Indiana, and the rest of the country. The museum is open from 9:00 a.m. to 5:00 p.m. week days and from 10:00 a.m. to 4:00 p.m. Saturday. Admission is free.

PHI KAPPA PSI FATERNITY HEADQUARTERS, located in historic Lockerbie Square, 510 Lockerbie Street, houses a collection of Victorian furnishings and serves as the central office and museum for the men's national fraternity. It is open from 8:00 a.m. to 4:30 p.m. weekdays. Admission is free.

J. I. HOLCOMB OBSERVATORY & PLANETARIUM at Butler University, 4600 Sunset Avenue, features a one-meter (38-inch) Cassegrain reflecting telescope, the largest telescope in the state. It is open for tours, including a planetarium show, a visit to the clockroom with its Geochron world time indicator and telescope viewing. An admission is charged.

Indianapolis is home to the professional National Football League Colts and the National Basketball Association Pacers. Originally the Boston Yanks, 1944-1948; then the New York Bulldogs, 1949; the New York Yanks, 1950-1951; Dallas Texans, 1952; they became the Baltimore Colts in 1953 gaining the name via a fan contest and remained in Baltimore through 1983—a period of 30 years. The franchise was moved to Indianapolis March 28, 1984 and now play in the Hoosier Dome. The Indianapolis Pacers were established here in 1967.

The National Headquarters of the **American Legion**, the largest veterans organization in the world, is located at 700 N. Pennsylvania Street. The American Legion was founded in 1919 and today has more than three million members.

There are numerous buildings, not previously identified, in Indianapolis listed on the NRHP.

Among these are the **Administration Building** (1904), Indiana Central University; **Allison Mansion** (1914) 3200 Cold Spring Road; **Anderson-Thompson House** (1860), 6551 Shelbyville Road; **Arsenal Technical High School** (1866-1929), 1500 East Michigan Street; **Aston Inn** (1852), 6620 North Michigan Road; **The Athenaeum** (1894), 401 East Michigan Street; **Bals-Wocher House** (1870), 951 North Delaware Street; **Bates-Hendricks House** (1860, 1865) 1526 South New Jersey Street; **Benton House** (1873), 312 South Downey Avenue; **Broad Ripple Park (Children's Museum), Dentzel Carousel** (c. 1900), 3000 North Meridian Street; **William Buschman Block** (c. 1879), 968-972 Fort Wayne Avenue; **Butler Fieldhouse (Hinkle Fieldhouse)** (1928), Butler Uni-

Demonstrations of how the early pioneers may have fared on the Indiana frontier are features of Conner Prairie on the 1820s estate of William Conner.

versity Campus; **Byram-Middleton House** (1870), 1828 North Illinois Street; **Central Library of Indianapolis-Marion County Public Library** (1916), 40 East St. Clair Street; Christ **Church Cathedral** (1858), 125 Monument Circle; **Christamore House** (1926), 502 North Tremont Street; **Circle Theatre** (1916), 45 Monument Circle; **City Market** (1886), 222 East Market Street; **Henry P. Coburn Public School No. 66** (1915, 1929), 604 East 38th Street; **Cole Motor Car Company** (1914), 730 East Washington Street; **Columbia Club** (1924), 121 Monument Circle; **Cotton-Ropkey House** (c. 1850), 6360 West 79th Street; **Coulter Flats** (1907), 2161 North Meridian Street; **Crispus Attucks High School** (1927), 1140 North Martin Luther King Jr. Street; **Esplanade Apartments** (1913), 3015 North Pennsylvania Street; **Fidelity Trust Building** (1915), 148 East Market Street; **Calvin I. Fletcher House** (1895) 1031 North Pennsylvania Street; and **Fort Harrison Terminal Station** (1908), Building 616.

Also **General German Protestant Orphans Home** (1872), 1404 South State Street; **Alfred M. Glossbrenner Mansion** (1910), 3202 North Meridian Street; **Hammond Block** (1874), 301 Massachusetts Avenue; **Hannah-Oehler-Elder House** (1859-1872), 3801 South Madison Avenue; **Hiram A. Haverstick Farm** (1879), 7845 Westfield Boulevard; **Heier's Hotel** (1916), 10-18 South New Jersey Street; **Hollingsworth House** (1850), 6054 Hollingsworth Road; **Hotel Washington** (1912), 32 East Washington Street; **Independent Turnverein** (1914), 902 North Meridian Street; **Indiana Oxygen Company** (1930), 435 South Delaware Street; **Indiana Theatre** (1927), 134 West Washington Street; **Indianapolis News Building** (1910), 30 West Washington Street; **Jackson Buildings** (1882, 1923), 419 and 425 East Washington Street; **Johnson-Denny House** (1862), 4456 North Park Avenue; **Arthur Jordan Memorial Hall** (1928), Butler University; **Julian-Clark House** (1873), 115 South Audubon Road; **Charles Kuhn House** (1879), 340 West Michigan Street; **Louis Levey Mansion** (1905), 2902 North Meridian Street; **Lockefield Garden Apartments** (1937), 900 Indiana Avenue; **Lombard Building** (1893), 22-28 East Washington Street; **Majestic Building** (1896), 47 South Pennsylvania Street; **Horace Mann Public School No. 13** (1893, 1918), 714 Buchanan Street; **Marott Hotel** (1926), 2625 North Meridian Street; **Marott's Shoes Building** (1900), 18-20 East Washington Street; **McCormick Cabin Site** (1820), off US 40; **George Philip Meier House "Tuckaway"** (1907), 3128 North Pennsylvania Street; **Michigan Road Toll House** (1850, 1882), 4702 Michigan Road NW; **Minor House (Indiana State Federation of Colored Women's Clubs)** (1897), 2034 North Capitol Avenue; and **Thomas Moore House** (c. 1860), 4300 Brookville Road.

Also **Morrison Block** (Morrison Opera Place) (1870), 47 South Meridian Street; **Mount Pisgah Lutheran Church** (1875), 701 North Pennsylvania Street; **Pearson Terrace** (1902), 928-940 North Alabama Street; **Pierson-Giffiths (Kemper House)** (1873), 1028 North Delaware Street; **The Propyleaum** (1891), 1410 North Delaware Street; **Prosser House** (c. 1880), 1454 East Tenth Street; **Reserve Loan Life Insurance Company** (1925), 429 North Pennsylvania Street; **Rink's Women's Apparel Store** (1910), 29 North Illinois Street; **Roberts Park Methodist Episcopal Church** (1876), 401 North Delaware Street; **St. James Court** (1919), 2102-2108 North Meridian Street; **Saint John's Church and Rectory** (1871), 121 South Capitol Avenue and 124 and 126 West Georgia Street; **Saint Mary's Catholic Church** (1912), 317 North New Jersey Street; **Schnull-Rauch House** (1904), 3050 North Meridian Street; **Scottish Rite Cathedral** (1929), 650 North Meridian Street; **Selig's Dry Goods Company Building** (1924, 1933), 20 West Washington Street; **The Seville** (1921), 1701 North Illinois Street; **Shortridge High School** (1928), 3401 North Meridian Street; **August Sommer House** (1880), 29 East McCarty Street; **State Capitol Building** (1888), Washington Street and Capitol Avenue; **State Soldiers and Sailors Monument** (1902), Monument Circle; **Stewart Manor (Charles B. Sommers House)** (1924), 3650 Cold Springs Road; **George Stumpf House** (1872), 3225 South Meridian Street; **Taylor Carpet Company Building** (1897, 1906), 26 West Washington Street; **Test Building** (1925), 54 Monument Circle; **William N. Thompson House** (1920), 4343 North Meridian Street; **U.S. Courthouse and Post Office** (1905), 46 East Ohio Street; **Union Railroad Station** (1888), 39 Jackson Place; **The Vera and The Olga** (1901), 1440 and 1446 North Illinois Street; **Madame J. Walker Building** (1927), 617 Indiana Avenue; **West Washington Street Pumping Station** (1871), 801 West Washington Street; **John Greenleaf Whittier School No. 33** (1890), 1119 North Sterling Street; and **YWCA Blue Triangle Residence Hall** (1927), 725 North Pennsylvania Street.

There are a number of listings under Apartments and Flats of Downtown Indianapolis Thematic Resources (1886-1929). Under this listing is **Alameda** (1925), 37 West St. Clair Street; **Alexandra** (1901), 402-16 North New Jersey Street and 332-36 East Vermont Street; **Ambassador** (1924), 39 East 9th Street; **Baker** (1903), 310 North Alabama Street, and 341 Massachusetts Avenue; **Blacherne** (1895), 402 North Meridian Street; **Burton** (1919), 821-23 North Pennsylvania Street; **Cathcart** (1909), 103 East 9th Street; **Chadwick** (1925), 1005 North Pennsylvania Street; **Colonial** (1900), 126 East Vermont Street and 402-408 North Delaware Street; **Dartmouth** (1929), 221 East Michigan Street; **Delaware Court** (1917), 1001-15 North

Delaware Street; **Delaware Flats** (1887), 120-28 North Delaware Street; **Devonshire** (1929), 412 North Alabama Street; **Emelie** (1902), 326-30 North Senate Avenue and 301-03 West Virginia Street; **Glencoe** (1901), 627 North Pennsylvania Street; **Grover** (c. 1913), 615 North Pennsylvania Street; **Harriett** (c. 1905), 124-28 North East Street; **Lodge** (1905), 829 North Pennsylvania Street; **Martens** (c. 1899), 348-56 Indiana Avenue; **Massachusetts** (1906), 421-27 Massachusetts Avenue; **Mayleeno** (1913), 416-18 East Vermont Street; **McKay** (1923), 611 North Pennsylvania Street; **Myrtle Fern** (1923), 221 East 9th Street; **Oxford** (1902), 316 East Vermont Street; **Pennsylvania** (1906), 919 North Pennsylvania Street; **Plaza** (1907), 902 North Pennsylvania Street and 36 East 9th Street; **Rink** (1901), 401 North Illinois Street; **Savoy** (1899), 36 West Vermont Street; **Shelton** (c. 1925), 825 North Delaware Street; **Sid-Mar** (1887), 401-403 Massachusetts Avenue; **Spink** (c. 1922), 230 East 9th Street; **St. Clair** (1899), 109 West St. Clair Street; **Sylvania** (c. 1906), 801 North Pennsylvania and 108 East St. Clair Street; **Vienna** (1908), 306 East New York Street; **Wil-Fra-Mar** (c. 1886), 318 East Vermont Street; **Wilson** (c. 1890), 643 Ft. Wayne Avenue; and **Wyndam** (1929), 1040 North Delaware Street.

There are 20 historic districts (in 1992) and include **Chatham-Arch Historic District** (1836-1900), roughly bounded by I-65, 11th, North and East Streets; **Cottage Home Historic District** (1870-1939), Dorman and St. Clair Streets; **Fletcher Place Historic District** (1855-1924), bounded by I-65/70, Penn Central railroad tracks, East Street, and Virginia Avenue; **Forest Hills Historic District** (1911-1935), bounded by Monon Railroad tracks, Kesseler Boulevard, College and Northview Avenues; **Fountain Square Commercial Areas Thematic Resources** (1871-1932); **Laurel and Prospect District** (1871-1932), 1335 to 1419 East Prospect Street; **State and Prospect District** (1871-1932), State Avenue and Prospect Street; **Virginia Avenue District** (1871-1932), roughly bounded by Virginia Avenue from Grove Avenue to Prospect and Morris Streets; **Herron-Morton Place Historic District** (c. 1855-1930), roughly bounded by Central Avenue, 16th, Pennsylvania and 22nd Streets; **Holy Rosary-Danish Church Historic District** (1857-1930), roughly bounded by Virginia Avenue, I-65/70 and South East Street; **Indiana Avenue Historic District** (1869-1935), 500 block of Indiana Avenue between North Street, Central Canal, Michigan and West Streets; **Indiana World War Memorial Plaza** (1921-1950), bounded by St. Clair, Pennsylvania, Vermont, and Meridian Streets; **Indianapolis Union Station-Wholesale District** (c. 1863-1930), roughly bounded by Capitol Avenue, Maryland, Delaware, and South Streets; **Irvington Historic District** (1870-1936), roughly

47

bounded by Ellenburger Park, Pleasant Run Creek, Arlington Avenue, the B&O Railroad, and Emerson Avenue; **Lockerbie Square Historic District** (1855-1930), bounded by Michigan, Davidson, New York, and New Jersey Streets; **Massachusetts Avenue Commercial District** (1865-1930), roughly bounded by one block on either side of Massachusetts Avenue from Delaware Street to I-65; **Meridian Park Historic District** (c. 1892-1933), bounded by 34th Street, Washington Boulevard, 30th Street, and Pennsylvania Street; **New Augusta Historic District** (1852-1939), roughly bounded by E. 71st Street, Coffman Road, and New Augusta Road; **North Meridian Street Historic District** (1900-1936), 4000-5694 and 4001-5747 North Meridan Street; and **Woodruff Place Historic District** (1872-1930), roughly bounded by 1700-2000 East Michigan and East 10th Streets.

Also listed on the NRHP is **University Park** (1887-1938), bounded by Vermont, Pennsylvania, New York, and Meridian Streets, and **Crown Hill Cemetery** (1877), roughly bounded by Northwestern Avenue, Boulevard Place, 32nd, and 38th Streets. Many of Indiana's famous are buried in Crown Hill Cemetery from President Benjamin Harrison to James Whitcomb Riley. Also buried here is the bank robber John Dillinger.

Screen star Carole Lombard is congratulated by Indianapolis civic and veteran leaders for her part in a war bond drive at the outset of World War II. She was killed in a plane crash in January 1942. (Photograph by Bass Photo Co. Collection; Indiana Historical Society Library).

# Indianapolis man invents
# deadly rapid-fire gun in 1862

The sight of wounded men from the battlefield inspired Richard J. Gatling, a 44 year old Indianpolis man, to invent the Gatling gun.

He was best-known at the time for his invention of an automatic wheat-planting machine.

He was issued a patent on November 4, 1862 for his gun that used a cluster of rotating barrels to fire 500 rounds per minute. By cranking a handle each barrel fired once per rotation.

After seeing wounded men from the early Civil War battles, Gatling was prompted to invent a gun that would make war so terrible that nations would want to turn against it.

His first models were destroyed in a fire which meant that for the next several months production was limited. The Gatling gun was not expected to be used widely during the Civil War but as the war wore on it did see use in several engagements.

Units of the frontier Army were equipped with the Gatling gun in their campaigns against the Plains Indians. While it could produce a withering fire, it also had a tendency to lock up because of the heat produced during intensive use. The gun was also mounted on a two-wheeled caisson which sometime slowed fast-moving troops in the field.

# USS Indianapolis Memorial

A memorial to the 881 sailors and Marines who died when the *USS Indianapolis (CA-35)* went down in the Pacific is located in the Neslar Naval Armory, 1802 West 30th Street, Indianapolis (dedicated summer of 1995).

The ship, with a record of 10 battle stars, was sunk by a Japanese submarine Sunday, July 30, 1945. The *Indianapolis* took only 12 minutes to sink after being hit amidships by the second torpedo. The first had blown off the *Indianapolis'* bow and tons of seawater poured through the interior walls.

It is believed that about 880 of the 1,197 sailors and Marines survived long enough to abandon ship. Many of the initial survivors were badly wounded and burned. On Monday the shark attacks began. In the days to follow some went mad and others died from swallowing seawater and fuel. Some were drowned when their lifejackets absorbed too much seawater.

It was four days (Thursday) later before the survivors were spotted by the pilot of a Navy Ventura PV1 bomber. Lt. j.g. Charles Qwinn first spotted the oil slick from the sunken ship and then some of the survivors. A call for help brought a plane load of life rafts and supplies to the survivors. The pilot of the Catalina PBY seaplane, Lt. j.g. Adrian Marks defied orders and landed his seaplane on the ocean and rescued 56 survivors when he learned they were being attacked by sharks. The PBY was not flyable but the men had been saved.

Eventually five other Navy ships reached the stricken survivors and those still alive were rescued.

Already over 500 of the survivors of the sinking had drowned or been attacked by sharks. In all, 316 men survived the disaster.

The U.S. Congress has declared the *USS Indianapolis* as a national memorial. As with all lost ships, the Navy lists its status as "still at sea."

# Chapter 3
# South on I-65

*This tour begins in Merrillville and visits such communities as Crown Point, Cedar Lake, Lowell, Rensselaer, Monticello, Woolcott, Idaville, Kentland, Brook, Lafayette, West Lafayette, Delphi, Willliamsport, Frankfort, Lebanon, Thorntown, Franklin, Columbus, Hope, Vernon, Hayden, Seymour, Brownstown, Scottsburg, Henryville, Madison, Salem, Jeffersonville, Clarksville, and New Albany.*

# 4 Year Term for Governor in 1852

The first Indiana governor to be elected to a four year term was Joseph A. Wright from Rushville. Elected to a three year term in 1849, in 1852 he was reelected, this time to a four year term.

Governor James Whitcomb was reelected in 1846. In 1848, he ran successfully for a seat in the U.S. Senate. The office of governor was filled by Lieutenant Governor Paris C. Dunning from December 1848 to December 1849 when Democrat Joseph White was elected.

Elected in 1856, Ashbel P. Willard, a Democrat from New Albany, assumed the governorship in January, 1857.

Henry S. Lane was elected governor in 1860 but was appointed to the U.S. Senate before taking office. His running mate, Oliver P. Morton, served out the four year term and was elected to another term in 1865. Morton faced many difficulties during the Civil War years with a recalcitrant legislature and those who opposed the war.

# Chapter 3
# South on I-65

The trip south from Gary on I-65 to Indianapolis is 162 miles and another 120 miles from Indianapolis to the Kentucky state line at Louisville.

Hammond, Gary, East Chicago, Munster, and Hobart are included in Chapter 5, by traveling on I-80-90, the Indiana Toll Road.

This chapter starts at Merrillville at the junction of US 30 and I-65 in Lake County.

MERRILLVILLE (pop. 27,257) boasts a long history even though the town did not officially exist until incorporation in 1971. It was named in honor of the Merrill brothers, William and Dudley. It emerged as a stop-off point for wagon trains heading west. Sixteen trails radiated in all directions from Merrillville.

**St. Constantine** and **Helen Greek Orthodox Cathedral** in Merrillville is the only Greek Orthodox Cathedral in Indiana. It can be reached from US 30 West exit off I-65, three stop lights west then a half block north.

A historical marker at the Homer Iddings School, 7749 Van Buren, commemorates the **Great Sauk Trail** route through Merrillville.

The **John Wood Old Mill** (1838) east of Merrillville on IN 330, is listed on the National Register of Historical Places (NRHP).

About three miles south of Merrillville on I-65 and a mile or so west on US 231 is CROWN POINT (pop. 17,800), county seat of Lake County, established February 15, 1837. The county was named for **Lake Michigan**. The town was founded in 1834 and incorporated in 1868.

The **Lake County Courthouse**, completed in 1878, is a county landmark. It has been the scene of several historical events such as the visit here on October 7, 1896 of **William Jennings Bryan**, the "Great Commoner," during his campaign for the U.S. presidency. One of the early auto road races was held south of the courthouse over a 25-mile track on June 19, 1909. The winner, who received the winner's cup on the east steps of the courthouse, was **Louis Chevrolet**, a Swiss-born master mechanic who later developed the Chevrolet automobile. The courthouse is listed on the NRHP.

The old **Lake County Jail**, 232 South Main Street, was completed in the fall of 1882. Originally the jail featured six steel cells for men and four for females. In 1926, an addition to the back of the jail increased the space to accommodate up to 150

The notorious John Dillinger, a native Indianan, robbed banks throughout the midwest in the early 1930s. The fake pistol he is holding is said to be the one he used in his escape from the Lake County Jail. (Photograph by Bass Photo Co. Collection, Indiana Historical Society Library).

prisoners and was claimed to be escape proof. Bank robber **John Dillinger** proved jail officials wrong when he escaped from the jail March 3, 1934 by fashioning a fake gun carved from a piece of wood from the top of a washboard, darkening it with shoe polish and forcing a jailer to release him and another prisoner, Herbert Youngblood, being held for murder. Dillinger was being held on charges he had killed a policeman during a bank robbery in East Chicago on January 15, 1934. He had been arrested in Tucson, Arizona, on January 25th on the murder charge and brought to Crown Point to await trial. Dillinger and Youngblood drove away in Sheriff Lillian Holley's car and by crossing the Illinois state line he committed his first federal offense, interstate car theft. The FBI immediately named him "Public Enemy No. 1." Dillinger was killed by G-Men in Chicago in July, 1934, betrayed by **Anna Sage**, the "Lady in Red." The **Lake County Sheriff's House and Jail** are listed on the NRHP

HOMESTEAD MUSEUM, a half block from the old Lake County Courthouse and across the street from the Crown Point Library, is located in the first homestead in Crown Point, built in 1843. It is only open by appointment.

The mural in the Crown Point Post Office, one block east of the Courthouse, was the work of WPA muralist **George Mellville Smith** and depicts the **Solon Robinson** family in the 1830s. Robinson was the first settler in Crown Point, arriving in 1834.

East of I-65 on US 231 eight miles is HEBRON (pop. 2,696). The **Clinton D. Gilson Barn** (1892), 522 West 650S, is listed on the NRHP.

Southwest of Crown Point, just off US 41, is CEDAR LAKE (pop. 8,754).

LAKE OF THE RED CEDARS MUSEUM, 7807 West 138th Place behind the police department (on Constitution Avenue) on the lake, features a wide range of historical artifacts and exhibits featuring lifestyles of the past. Special seasonal exhibits are another special feature of this museum. The building is listed on the NRHP. It is open Thursday through Sunday, May 1 through October 31. An admission is charged.

West six miles on IN 2 exit off I-65 is LOWELL (pop. 5,827). Lowell is three miles east on IN 2 off US 41. **Melvin Halstead** was the founder of Lowell.

The **Melvin A. Halstead House** (1850), 201 East Main Street, and the **Buckley Homestead** (1849), 3606 Belshaw Road, are listed on the NRHP.

The BUCKLEY HOMESTEAD, a living history farm, depicts three time periods of Lake County rural history: a 1910s farm, a one-room schoolhouse, and an 1850s pioneer farm. It is open from 10:00 a.m. to 5:00 p.m. on weekends beginning May 1 through October 31. The grounds are open daily the year-round from 7:00 a.m. to dusk. An admission is charged.

55

Lake of the Red Cedars Museum is housed in this historic building on Cedar Lake.

Married hired men on the Buckley Homestead just outside of Lowell lived in small cottages like this.

Continuing south on I-65 it is 25 miles to the exit to RENSSELAER (pop. 4,944), county seat of Jasper County. Rensselaer was laid out and platted as Newton on June 12, 1839. The name was changed to Rensselaer, for **James C. Van Rensselaer**, on February 18, 1840, and was incorporated in 1849. Jasper County was established March 15, 1838 and named in honor of a young sergeant stationed at Fort Moultrie in 1776 when the British attacked the fort. When the flag was shot down, **Sergeant Jasper** rescued it and nailed it to the broken staff, a signal to people watching from the mainland that the fort had not been captured.

**Major General Robert H. Milroy** (1816-1890), who practiced law in Rensselaer before and after the Civil War, spent most of the war years in West Virginia engaging Lee's Confederate troops. A statue was erected in the city's Milroy Park after his death in 1890. He was born in Washington County.

**Earle "Skater" Reynolds** (1868-1954), who won 16 national and international roller skating championships, called Rensselaer home for 74 years. He was born in Battle Ground, Indiana, in 1868 but his family moved here when he was six. Reynolds, who spent 1938-39 with the Ringling Brothers Circus, performed for King George and Queen Mary of England in 1908.

Songwriter **James F. Hanley** (1892-1942) was a native son and is best known for his World War I hit, *"Back Home Again in Indiana."* He collaborated on more than 100 movies and wrote music scores for a number of Broadway productions.

Another native son was **Edison Marshall** (1894-1967), a best-selling author, who wrote such novels as *"Benjamin Blake," "Yankee Pasha,"* and *"Caravan to Xanadu."* Four of his novels developed into motion pictures, among them *"The Viking."*

**Charles Halleck** (1900-1986), a Jasper County native, served 18 consecutive Congressional terms. He served as Minority Leader for over two decades and was Majority Leader while the Republicans were in power in the 1947-48 and 1953-54 sessions. He was born in DeMotte.

Football great **Tom Harmon** (1919-1990), two-time All-American halfback, 1940 recipient of the Heisman Trophy, and a star for the Los Angles Rams, was also a native son.

**Frederick "Rick" Kupke**, the last American to be captured in the Iranian hostage crisis, was born in Rensselaer in 1947. On November 4, 1979, 52 Americans were taken hostage at the American embassy in Teheran and were held for 444 days.

**St. Joseph's College** was founded by the Roman Catholics in 1889. The **Indian Normal School** (1888), on the college campus, is listed on the NRHP.

The two other structures listed on the NRHP include the **Jasper County Courthouse** (1898), on W. Washington Street, and the **Independence Methodist Church** (1872), southeast

The Parr Postoffice, shown here on the fairgrounds in Rensselaer, was one of the smallest in the U.S. It was only 9 by 11 feet and is dwarfed by the country school in the complex.

of Wheatfield in the northern part of the county.

PIONEER VILLAGE AT THE JASPER COUNTY FAIRGROUNDS, operated by the Jasper County Historical Society, includes a log cabin built c. 1870; the Parr postoffice, one of the smallest in the nation and once the scene of a robbery with the robbers captured later in Oklahoma by the FBI; and Rosebud School, dating back to 1874. The 9 foot x 11 foot Parr postoffice building was owned by **Mrs. Vera Randolph**.

Continuing south on I-65 it is 14 miles to the Wolcott/ Remington Exit on US 24. It is 20 miles east on US 24 to MONTICELLO (pop. 5,162), county seat of White County. The county was established April 1, 1834, and named in honor of **Colonel Isaac White**, killed in the Battle of Tippecanoe in 1811.

WHITE COUNTY HISTORICAL MUSEUM, 101 South Bluff Street, features a collection of artifacts pertinent to the county's history. Among the memorabilia displayed are the epaulets worn by Colonel White on his uniform and his ivory-handled engraved sword, originally owned by his father. The museum is open from 8:00 a.m. to 2:00 p.m. Monday, Wednesday, and Friday. It is closed on all holidays. Admission is free.

A devastating tornado struck Monticello the afternoon of April 3, 1974, killing eight persons and destroying several buildings including the 80-year old courthouse.

Two structures in Monticello are listed on the NRHP–the

The Wolcott House dates back to 1859 and was built by Anson Wolcott, influential in state politics and founder of the town of Wolcott, five miles off I-65 on US 24.

The White County Historical Museum has preserved the county history in this building in Monticello.

The Parrish Pioneer Farm is set in a pioneer Amish settlement just east of Idaville off US 24.

**James Culbertson Reynolds House** (1873), 417 North Main Street, and **South Grade School Building** (1892), 565 South Main Street. The **Wolcott House** (1859), 500 North Range Street, Wolcott, is also listed on the NRHP. The Wolcott House, constructed in 1859 by **Anson Wolcott,** founder of the town, is open by appointment. For an appointment call (317) 563-6662 or 279-2123.

Six miles east of Monticello on US 24 is IDAVILLE (pop. 700) and another mile east is the PARRISH PIONEER FARM, a pioneer Amish settlement. There are several historical buildings on the site, among them the **Abner Shafer** house built in 1850, a loom house, a smoke house, log barn, and blacksmith shop. The display building houses a 50-year collection of antiques, memorabilia, horse drawn carriages, and spinning and weaving items used by early settlers. This outdoor Living Historical Museum is open from 11:00 a.m. to 5:00 p.m. daily, May 1 through November 1. An admission is charged.

Sixteen miles west on US 24 at the I-65 exit is KENTLAND (pop. 1,936), county seat of Newton County. The county, named in honor of **Sergeant John Newton** who served with General Francis Marion during the Revolutionary War, was established on December 9, 1859. Kentland was settled in 1860.

**George Ade** (1866-1944), noted humorist, playwright, author, newspaper columnist, and philantropist, was born in

Kentland, February 9, 1866. After graduating from Purdue University he worked on midwestern newspapers and published several books. From 1900-1910, Ade wrote seven books, 12 full length plays, assorted articles, and ephemeral publications. His most successful play, *"The College Widow,"* written in 1904, earned Ade $5,000 per week while it ran on Broadway, and in the course of his lifetime netted $2 million in royalties for the author. His best-known work, *"Fables in Slang,"* was published in 1900. His first play, written in 1902, was a musical, *"The Sultan of Sula."* It had a short run in Chicago, then went to Broadway where it was such a success the producers had to open a second theatre and hire a second cast to accommodate the overflow crowds. George Ade, after suffering a stroke and several heart attacks in 1943, died May 23, 1944.

North of Kentland, east on IN 16, and east of BROOK (pop. 926) is the **George Ade House (Hazelden House)** (1904), listed on the NRHP. It was here that George Ade hosted four U.S. presidents, Theodore Roosevelt, William Howard Taft, Warren G. Harding, and Calvin Coolidge. Many famous personalities were also guests of Ade at Hazelden.

The Hazelden Compound today includes an 18-hole Country Club, the George Ade Memorial Hospital and Extended Care Facility, the George Ade Clinic, and the restored home.

From Kentland it is nine miles south on US 41 and four miles on US 52 to FOWLER (pop. 2,319), county seat of Benton County. It can also be reached from I-65, 13 miles south of the Wolcott/Remington Exit, then 18 miles west on IN 18, then a mile north on US 52. Benton County was established February 18, 1840. Fowler was laid out in 1871.

The **Presbyterian Church Building** (1902), northwest of Benton and Justus Streets, Oxford, south of Fowler is listed on the NRHP.

It is about 15 miles south on I-65 from the IN 18 Exit to Lafayette.

LAFAYETTE (pop. 43,900) is the county seat of Tippecanoe County, established on March 1, 1826. The county was named for the **Tippecanoe River** and the **Battle of Tippecanoe**. Lafayette, named in honor of the French general who participated in the American Revolutionary War, was platted on May 25, 1825 by **William Digby**, a river boat captain. WEST LAFAYETTE (pop. 21,247) emerged from the town of Kingston platted in 1855. In 1866 the town's name was changed to Chauncey and then became West Lafayette in 1888.

The **Battle of Tippecanoe** in 1811 was a major event in early American history for it was here that white settlers established supremacy over the Indians relative to the ownership of the land. As early as 1805, **Shawnee Chief Tecumseh** and his brother, the **Prophet**, spoke out against witchcraft, use of alcohol, mixed marriages with whites, the adoption of the white man's dress, and the practice of selling Indian lands to the members of their tribe. They worked to unite other tribes to fight off the intrusion of white settlers on Indian hunting lands.

By 1809, the United States had acquired nearly 30 million acres of land from the Indians. Tecumseh and his brother denounced these land acquisitions maintaining the treaties were signed by only a few of the tribes. In 1810-11, Tecumseh, with the support of his followers, demanded the U.S. cede back to the Indians the land acquired in the 1809 Treaty of Fort Wayne involving 2,900,000 acres. **Territorial Governor William Henry Harrison**, representing the federal government, refused.

By September, 1811, Harrison realized that all of this may lead to open hostilities and prepared an expedition to **Prophet's Town**, about seven miles north of today's Lafayette. This force of about a thousand men, including the 4th Infantry Regiment, led by **Colonel John P. Boyd**, and militiamen from the Territory and Kentucky, left Vincennes September 26th. They arrived at what is now Terre Haute October 3, and spent the next 25 days building a fort named **Fort Harrison** in honor of the leader of the expedition. The army arrived at the Indian village the afternoon of November 6th. They camped for the night in sight of the Indian village but Harrison, uncertain of the actions the Indians might take, placed his men in battle positions and established a large detail for sentry duty. Tecumseh, in the south at the time, warned his brother against provoking an attack

This sketch portrays action during the 1811 Battle of Tippecanoe. (Photograph by Indiana Historical Society Library).

Tecumseh, chief of the Shawnee Indians, is considered one of the outstanding Indians in American history. (Photograph by Indiana Historical Society Museum Library).

until after the Indians were organized.

The Prophet ignored his brother's warning and ordered an early morning surprise attack on Harrison's men. It is estimated between 600 and 700 Indians were involved in the attack. The Indians attacked about 4 a.m. on November 7th but met stiff resistance that soon had the Indians in retreat. The official report of the battle shows 37 soldiers killed, 25 died later of wounds, and 126 were wounded. The Indian losses were never quantified but they had been soundly defeated.

Harrison fortified his camp immediately after the battle, expecting Tecumseh to return with reinforcements. Every man in Harrison's forces was kept on full alert throughout the night.

Prophet's Town was destroyed by fire the day after the battle on order of Harrison. Tecumseh returned three months later, gathered up the remaining Indians and went north to join the British. Many Indians returned the following year and planted corn and partially rebuilt the town only to have it destroyed by an expedition led by **General Samuel Hopkins** in November, 1812. This skirmish occurred a few miles east of Prophet's Town and was called **"Spurs' Defeat,"** referred to at times as **The Second Battle of Tippecanoe.** A mounted contingent of Hopkin's forces was ambushed by Indians, sending the cavalry in wild retreat, referred to as the troops' spurring their horses to escape.

Prophet's Town came into existence in May, 1808, when Tecumseh and the Prophet, whose Indian name was **Tenskwatawa**, moved here from their native Ohio. They were granted permission by the Potawatomis and Kickapoos to settle on their tribal lands to promote a plan to unite the Indian tribes to resist white settlement. It became the capitol of the Indian Confederacy led by Tecumseh.

Tecumseh was killed October 5, 1813, in the **Battle of the Thames.** The Prophet was scorned by the Indians for their loss at the Battle of Tippecanoe and his brother spurned and renounced him. He received a pension from the British for his service and lived near Cape Girardeau, Missouri, from 1815 until 1828 when he and his small band moved to Wynadotte County, Kansas. He died there in November, 1834.

William Henry Harrison remained as governor of Indiana Territory until September, 1812, when he was assigned command of the Northwestern frontier in the War of 1812. He was in command at the capture of Detroit and the Battle of the Thames. After the war he returned to public life in North Bend, Ohio, and served in the Ohio state senate, the U.S. House of Representatives, and the U.S. Senate. He was the unsuccessful Whig candidate for President in 1836. He won the Whig nomination four years later and it is reported that more than 30,000 supporters held a massive rally at the Tippecanoe Battlefield on May 29, 1840. One of the campaign slogans during the election was "Tippecanoe and Tyler, Too!" Harrison won the election but died only after serving a month as President.

The **Tippecanoe Battlefield** has been designated as a National Historic Landmark and is listed on the NRHP.

Long before the establishment of Prophet's Town and the Battle of Tippecanoe, **Fort Ouiatenon** was established by the

This monument marks the Tippecanoe battlefield of November 7, 1811. William Harrison led the troops in this battle that ended major Indian hostilities in Indiana Territory.

French in 1717, five miles southwest of Lafayette. It was the first fortified European settlement in what is now Indiana and was established primarily as a trading post and provided some security to the region.

Between 1720 and 1760, the settlement prospered and grew. French traders traveled from Quebec annually to trade their goods for furs trapped by Indians. Some remained to establish homes and at its height some 2,500 persons may have inhabited the area.

**Anthony Foucher,** born in Ouiatenon in 1741, became the first Catholic priest born in Indiana. The French lived in harmony with the Indians of this region until the French and Indian War (1754-63).

The British defeated the French and forced them to give up all their North American lands, including Fort Ouiatenon. **Lieutenant Edward Jenkins** took command of the fort for the British in 1761. In 1764, **Ottawa Chief Pontiac** moved to drive the whites back to the other side of the Appalachian Mountains. In this move, his Indians attacked 12 frontier posts and captured eight of them, including Ouiatenon which fell without a shot on June 1, 1763. Lieutenant Jenkins and his men were taken prisoners and later exchanged for Indians held captive in Detroit.

**"Pontiac's Uprising"** ended as a result of the chief's meeting at Fort Ouiatenon with **Colonel George Croghan,** deputy supervisor of Indian affairs for the English colonies of America, who had been captured by the Indians and brought to the fort. He met with Pontiac in the summer of 1765 and suggested the Indians and whites sign a peace treaty to end the stalemated uprising. Pontiac responded by throwing his tomahawk so the blade was buried in the ground. This gesture, meaning to end hostilities, gave rise to the phrase "bury the hatchet."

After this treaty, Fort Ouiatenon was not regarrisoned but remained a small French trading and trapping post as well as a large Indian settlement. By 1778, only a handful of whites remained while the nearby Wea village had an estimated 1,000 warriors capable of bearing arms. At this same time a British agent stayed at the post to spy on the Americans. He left the fort to George Roger Clark's men, under command of **Captain Leonard Helm.** Helm rejoined Clark at Vincennes as soon as he received pledges of loyalty to the American cause from the residents.

Later, that same year, British **Lieutenant Governor Henry Hamilton** arrived with plans to recapture **Vincennes** from **George Rogers Clark** and the Americans. Clark turned the tables and captured Hamilton in one of the more surprising British defeats of the Revolutionary War.

For a period after the Revolutionary War, Fort Ouiatenon remained as a small French settlement and a popular gathering spot for the area's Indian tribes. The Indians used Ouiatenon as a staging area for raids on white settlers in Kentucky and by 1786 the white settlers evacuated the post for fear of their lives. In 1791, President George Washington ordered the destruction of the Wabash Indian villages and a command led by **General Charles Scott** burned all crops and houses bringing an end to Ouiatenon. By the early 1820s the existence of this fort was all but forgotten.

Fort Ouiatenon was established by the French as a fortified trading post in 1717.

In the late 19th century, local historians took a renewed interest in Ouiatenon, and in 1930, the present blockhouse was constructed by a local physician. In 1968, archaeological excavations and document research began under the auspices of the Tippecanoe County Historical Association. The excavation uncovered the actual site of the original stockade approximately a mile down river from the blockhouse. The actual site was placed on the NRHP in 1970.

Members of the Society of Friends (Quakers) settled in the area in the late 1820s. They soon established a monthly meeting and erected an Academy in 1851, called Farmers Institute. The Quakers still hold their meetings here today.

The **Wabash & Erie Canal** reached Lafayette in 1840 and was a major transportation line until the arrival of the Wabash and Western Railroad in 1856.

The second **Indiana State Fair** was held in Lafayette in October, 1853. Site of this event was on the southeast corner of Washington and Kossuth, now occupied by the Miller School. The practice of rotating the fair to different cities ended in 1855 in favor of permanent facilities in Indianapolis.

**Buddell Sleeper**, a Quaker, operated a "station" in the basement of his home on the **Underground Railroad** before the Civil War.

The first U.S. Air Mail flight occurred August 17, 1859, when the balloon *Jupiter* took off from Lafayette for New York. Southerly winds diverted the flight south to Crawfordsville.

During the Civil War **Camp Tippecanoe** was established as a military training camp near present day 4th Street and Hickory in 1861. Among the regiments mustered here were the 72nd and 86th Indiana Volunteer Infantry. The 86th Indiana Infantry saw action at Murfreesboro, Chattanooga, and served with General Sherman in Georgia. The camp was deactivated in 1865. A prisoner-of-war camp was established in February, 1862, in the Old Red Warehouse and Sample Porkhouse near Canal and Green Streets. A total of 712 Confederate prisoners, largely from the 32nd and 41st Tennessee Regiments, were held here. Illness among the prisoners created the need for a make-

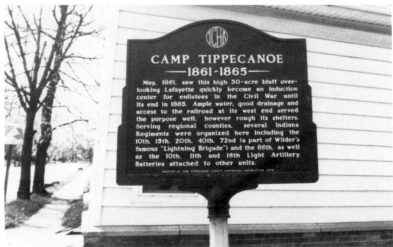

Camp Tippecanoe, a Civil War Army induction center, was located on a 30-acre site at US 231 and South 4th Street in Lafayette.

shift hospital nearby.

**Deadman's Curve** is the designation given to a spot on the **Lafayette & Indianapolis Railroad** line where 30 were killed and 35 injured in a train accident that occurred October 31, 1864. A cattle train left a siding early and crashed into an express passenger train on the main line. Most of those killed and injured were soldiers on furlough.

In early June 1947, two diesel powered freight trains collided one and a half miles north of Battleground killing two trainmen.

The Wabash River flood of March 11, 1913, caused $500,000 in property damage and claimed three lives.

Tornadoes have often struck Tippecanoe County. One on April 9, 1953, along IN 28 in the Lafayette area injured six and caused millions of dollars in damage. The 1965 Palm Sunday tornadoes hit 15 Indiana north and central counties, including Tippecanoe, causing over 100 deaths and hundreds of injuries.

The first Caesarian operation in Indiana was performed by **Dr. Moses Baker** on November 6, 1880, in a farmhouse east of Lafayette. The mother and baby both survived.

**Purdue University** was founded in what is West Lafayette in 1869 and named in honor of its chief benefactor, **John Purdue**. **Amelia Earhart**, the famed aviatrix, served as a consultant in careers for women at the university. She and her co-pilot, **Fred Noonan**, were lost in the Pacific on their around-the-world flight in 1937. John Purdue is buried on the campus.

**John T. McCutcheon** (1870-1949), an alumnus of Purdue University and noted cartoonist, was born in the county. He achieved national fame as the greatest cartoonist of his time and a collection of his work may be found in the Tippecanoe County Historical Museum. (See photo on page 96.)

Two students were killed and hundreds injured when the east bleachers of Purdue's Fieldhouse collapsed during half time of a Purdue-Wisconsin basketball game in late February 1947

**Malcolm D. Ross**, West Lafayette native, gained fame as a Navy balloonist. In 1956 Lieutenant Commander Ross took his "space laboratory" balloon to an altitude of 76,000 feet and received the Harmon International Trophy in 1957 for "outstanding contributions to the science of aeronautics." In 1961, Commander Ross and his co-pilot reached an altitude of 113,500 feet in a balloon. The pair ran into problems on descent and plunged into the Gulf of Mexico in their balloon. In the rescue attempt by a helicopter crew that followed, the co-pilot drowned.

**Harold L. Gray**, creator of the *"Little Orphan Annie"* comic strip was raised on a farm west of west Lafayette. Gray introduced his comic strip in 1924.

Lafayette's **George Souders** won the 1927 Indianapolis 500.

The 1851 Moses Fowler House houses the Tippecanoe County Historical Museum in Lafayette.

Two automobiles, the American (1916-1920) and the Dumore (1918) were built in Lafayette by the American Motor Vehicle Company.

In 1979, Purdue's **Dr. Herbert C. Brown**, Wetherill Research Professor Emeritus of Chemistry, was awarded the Nobel Prize in Chemistry.

TIPPECANOE BATTLEFIELD AND INTERPRETIVE CENTER, seven miles north of Lafayette, just off IN 43 exit from I-65, is a must on a visit to the area. An 85-foot marble obelisk stands on the battlefield. The Interpretive Center houses the museum and gift shop, and serves as a central meeting place for the thousands who tour the battlefield. The Center is open from 10:00 a.m. to 5:00 p.m. daily March through November, and from 10:00 a.m. to 4:00 p.m. December through February. It is closed on Thanksgiving, Christmas, and New Year's Day. An admission is charged.

A historical marker is located at the site of PROPHET'S ROCK. It is reportedly on this stone bluff where the Prophet, Tecumseh's brother, stood during the Battle of Tippecanoe. After laying out the battle plan to the Indians, he retired to this bluff to pray to the Great Spirit.

FORT OUIATENON BLOCKHOUSE is on South River Road. The museum and trading post in the blockhouse are open in the afternoons daily, except Monday, from mid-April through October.

TIPPECANOE COUNTY HISTORICAL MUSEUM, is located in the **Moses Fowler House**, corner of 10th and South Streets. The home is listed on the NRHP. Fowler, one of the area's leading merchants and cattlemen, built his English Gothic

70

home in 1851. The museum contains several rooms of exhibits and memorabilia depicting the history and heritage of Tippecanoe County. It is open from 1:00 to 5:00 p.m. daily, except Monday and during the month of January. Admission is free.

THE WETHERILL HISTORICAL RESOURCE CENTER, across the street at 1001 South Street and operated by the Tippecanoe County Historical Association, houses the library providing easy access to books and microfilms, family files, photos, and card catalogs listing thousands of individuals who have lived and worked in the area. It is a resource center for genealogists, historians and writers.

The **Ninth Street Hill Historic Neighborhood Association**, formed in 1986, has encouraged the preservation and enhancement of the architecture on six-blocks of this historic street, from South to Kossuth Streets. All the buildings on both sides of the street have been mapped and identified for visitors. The homes of Ninth Street Hill date from the 1840s to the 1950s and provides a vignette of the history of life in Lafayette. Information about this tour is available at the museum.

Included in the structures listed on the NRHP in Lafayette are the **Judge Cyrus Ball House** (1869), 402 South Ninth Street; **Enterprise Hotel** (c. 1890), 1015 Main Street; **Farmers Institute** (1851-1874), 4626 West 660 South; **Falley Home** (1863), 601 New York Street; **Marian Apartments** (1907), 615 North Street; **Mars Theatre** (1921), 111 North Sixth Street; **William Potter House** (c. 1880), 915 Columbia Street; **St. John's Episcopal Church** (1853), 315 North Sixth Street; **Scott Street Pavilion** (c. 1900), Columbian Park; **Temple Israel** (1867), 17 South Seventh Street; **Tippecanoe County Courthouse** (1884), Public Square; **Waldron-Beck House and Carriage House** (1878), 1829 North 21st Street; and **James H. Ward House** (c. 1860), 1875, 1116 Columbia Street.

The historic districts in Lafayette listed on the NRHP include the **Centennial Neighborhood District** (1830-1940), bounded by Union, Third, Fourth, Ferry and Ninth Streets; **Downtown Lafayette Historic District** (1825-1930), bounded by Union, Third, Fourth, Ferry and Ninth Streets; **Ellsworth Historic District** (1844-1936), bounded by Columbia, Norfolk & Western Railroad tracks, Alabama, Seventh, South and Sixth Streets; **Perrin Historic District** (1873-1923), bounded by Murdock Park, Sheridan Road, Columbia, Main, and Union Streets; and **Upper Main Street Historic District** (c. 1845-1939), bounded by Ferry, Sixth and Columbia Streets, and the Norfolk & Western Railroad tracks.

There are two houses in West Lafayette listed on the NRHP. These are the **Jesse Andrew House** (1859), 123 Andrew Place, and the **James Pierce, Jr., House** (1884), 4623 North 140 West.

Other structures in the Lafayette area listed on the NRHP include **Ely Homestead** (1847), 4106 East 200 North, northeast of town; **Hershey House** (1856), 1904 North 725 East, east of town; and **Indiana State Soldiers Home Historic District**, off IN 43, north of town.

Thirteen miles northeast of Lafayette is DELPHI (pop. 2,781), county seat of Carroll County. The county was established May 1, 1828 and named in honor of **Charles Carroll**, the last surviving signer of the Declaration of Independence. Delphi was platted the same year by **Samuel Milroy** on 100 acres donated by **William Wilson** for the seat of Carroll County. The town was incorporated in 1866.

The community was served by the **Wabash & Erie Canal** in 1840. The **Wabash Railroad** arrived in 1856.

**James Whitcomb Riley**, the Hoosier poet, spent a great deal of time in Delphi with his friend, **Dr. Wycliffe Smith**. They often explored the county together.

**Pfc William Whistler** (1858-1884), a local resident, was a member of the ill-fated polar expedition, officially called the **Lady Franklin Bay Expedition**, led by **Lieutenant Adolphus W. Greely** in the 1880s. The expedition was formed to establish one of a chain of international circumpolar meteorological stations. Relief ships failed to reach Greely's party camped at Cape Sabine. When the third relief vessel arrived in 1884 all but Greely and six others had perished from starvation, drowning, or exposure, including Whistler. The son of **Christian Whistler**, the body of the young soldier was returned to Carroll County and lay in state in the courthouse in August, 1884, for 24 hours.

Whistler's brother, Clarence, died in Australia on November 6, 1885, while holding the title of world champion wrestler. He went to Melbourne in October, 1885, to defend his title on November 3. He won the match and died three days later under mysterious circumstances.

CARROLL COUNTY HISTORICAL MUSEUM, on the first floor of the county courthouse, features the history of the Carroll County through exhibits and memorabilia. A vital part of the museum is its large Genealogy Library. Also featured in the museum are many photos of county settlers. The museum is open from 8:00 a.m. to 5:00 p.m. Monday, Tuesday, and Thursday; 8:00 a.m. to 12:00 noon Wednesday; and 9:30 a.m. to 5:00 p.m. Friday the year-round. Admission is free.

There are three structures in Delphi listed on the NRHP— **Barnett-Seawright-Wilson House** (1857), 203 East Monroe Street; **Niewerth Building** (1874), 124 East Main Street; and **Foreman-Case House** (c. 1851), 312 East Main Street.

Elsewhere in the county the **Adams Mill** (1846), off County Road 50E, in the Cutler area; **Burris House and Potawatomi**

**Spring** (c. 1840), Towpath Road, Lockport; **District School No. 3** (1874), northeast corner of County Road 750N and County Road 100W, in the Rockfield area; and the **Andrew Thomas House** (1869), West Main Street, Camden, are also on the NRHP.

Twenty six miles southwest of Lafayette, via IN 25 then west on IN 28, is WILLIAMSPORT (pop. 1,747), county seat of Warren County. The county was established March 1, 1827 and named in honor of **Dr. Joseph Warren** who died at the Battle of Bunker Hill. Williamsport was settled in 1829.

The **Kent and Hitchens House** (1854), 500 Main and 303 Lincoln Streets, Williamsport, and the **Andrew Brier House** (c. 1855), Old Highway 41, Carbondale, are listed on the NRHP.

Back on I-65 at Lafayette, it is 18 miles south to the IN 28 Exit and another eight miles east on IN 28 to FRANKFORT (pop. 15,221), county seat of Clinton County named in honor of **DeWitt Clinton**, the canal building governor of New York. The community was laid out in 1830; the county was established March 1, 1830.

The Shad-Wyck automobile, 1917-1918, was manufactured here by the Shadburne Brothers.

CLINTON COUNTY HISTORICAL MUSEUM, 301 East Clinton Street in Old Stoney, focuses on county history. Old Stoney was built in 1892, burned in 1922 and rebuilt in 1926. The museum is open 1:30 to 4:30 p.m. Sunday, April through December and by appointment at other times. Admission is free.

The **Clinton County Courthouse** and the **Old Frankfort Stone High School (Old Stoney)** (1892,1926), 301 East Clinton, are listed on the NRHP. The **Rosenberger Building** (c.1850), 83 Old Main Street, Colfax, is also listed on the NRHP.

Returning to I-65 at the IN 28 Exit, it is 16 miles south to LEBANON (pop. 12,456), county seat of Boone County. Lebanon was founded in 1831 and incorporated in 1838; the county, named in honor of frontiersman **Daniel Boone**, was established April 1, 1831. The founding fathers of the community were **James Perry Drake** and **George L. Kinnard**, two Indianapolis land speculators and community developers. The first county seat was located at **Jamestown**.

Lebanon attorney **Samuel M. Ralston** became Indiana's 27th governor and was serving in the United States Senate at the time of his death on October 14, 1925.

Northwest of Lebanon, on IN 47, six miles west of I-65, is THORNTOWN (pop. 1,468), home of **General Anson Mills**, the "Fighting Quaker" of Civil War fame and the western Indian campaigns. When Mills retired from the army he invented and manufactured the **Mills Woven Cartridge Belt** used by the armies of many nations. He had become a millionaire by the time of his death in 1903.

73

There are three structures in Boone County listed on the NRHP–the **Boone County Courthouse** (1911), Lebanon; **Thorntown Public Library** (1915), 124 North Market Street, Thorntown; and **Town Hall (Castle Hall)** (1902), 65 East Cedar Street, Zionsville.

PATRICK HENRY SULLIVAN MUSEUM, in Zionsville near Indianapolis, preserves the history and heritage of Boone County. It was a gift from writer, educator, poet, and historical researcher Iva Etta Sullivan, given in the memory of her great-grandfather Patrick H. Sullivan, who came to Boone County in 1823. Among its exhibits is a historical presentation of rural life in Boone County. The museum collections include early photographs and Indiana paintings, including an 1855 portrait of William Zion for whom Zionsville is named. The museum is open from 12:00 noon to 5:00 p.m. Tuesday, Thursday, and Saturday.

From Lebanon it is only 30 minutes to downtown Indianapolis.

Indianapolis is covered in Chapter 2.

Twenty miles south of Indianapolis and 90 miles north of Louisville, KY, on I-65 and US 31, is FRANKLIN (pop. 14,000), county seat of Johnson County. The town was laid out in 1822; the county, named in honor of **Indiana Supreme Court Judge John Johnson**, was established May 5, 1823.

The Baptists founded **Franklin College of Indiana** here in 1834. **Old Main** on the college campus, 600 East Monroe Street, dating back as far as 1847, and the college library, **Shirk Hall**, dating back to 1903, are listed on the NRHP.

A number of well-known persons have roots in Johnson County. Among them are **Roger D. Branigan** and **Paul V. McNutt**, governors of the state, and artists **William Merritt Chase, J. Otis Adams, Grant W. Christian**, and **Cecil Head**.

Sports figures from the county are pro basketball players **Jon McGlocklin, Thomas** and **Richard VanArsdale**, and the "Wonder Five"–**Wendell Ballard, Burl Friddle, Carlyle Friddle, John Gant, Robert "Fuzzy" Vandivier, Forrest "Woodie" Wood**, and their coach **Ernest B. "Griz" Wagner**. **George Crow** played for the Harlem Globetrotters, the New York Black Giants, and Milwaukee Braves baseball teams. Others in sports from Johnson County include **Bob Glidden**, national sports car driver, and **Ray LaBlanc**, 1992 Olympic hockey goalie.

Other well-known personalities from the county include authors **Harvey Jacobs**, *"We Came Rejoicing"* and *"Hugging the Heartland,"* and **M. F. Kennedy**, *"Schoolmaster of Yesterday;"* actors **Max Terhune**, popular in the 1930s, and **Brad Long**, who performed in the movie *"Hoosiers;"* and **Max Friedersdorf**, a White House advisor.

74

The Johnson County Museum in Franklin.

An automobile, the Continental, was built in Franklin from 1909 to 1914 by the Indiana Motor & Manufacturing Company.

JOHNSON COUNTY MUSEUM AND LOG CABIN, 135 North Main Street, focuses on Johnson County history through displays and exhibits. It is listed on the NRHP. The museum is open from 9:00 a.m. to 4:00 p.m. weekdays and from 10:00 a.m. to 3:00 p.m. the second Saturday of each month. It is closed on all county holidays. Admission is free.

In addition to those listed above, there are three buildings and a historic district in Franklin listed on the NRHP—**Herriott House** (1865), 696 East Monroe Street; **Johnson County Courthouse** (1881), Courthouse Square; **August Zeppenfeld House** (c. 1872), 300 West Jefferson Street; and the **Martin Place Historic District** (1850-1925), on the north and south sides of Martin Place between Graham Avenue and Water Street, 500, 498, and 450 North Main Streets. The **Van Nuys Farm** (1840-1920), on IN 144, Hopewell, is also listed on the NRHP.

It is 26 miles south on I-65 to COLUMBUS (pop. 31,200), county seat of Bartholomew County, named in honor of **General Joseph Bartholomew** who was wounded at Tippecanoe, established February 12, 1821. Columbus was settled in 1820 and

75

incorporated in 1854.

Columbus was the direct center of population (76,395,220) in the United States in 1900. The population of the town at the time was 9,000. A historical marker, placed by the *Indianapolis Star* and marking the exact spot, sits on the north side of IN 7 east of the city.

The Reeves automobile, 1896-1898; 1905-1912, was manufactured in Columbus by first The Reeves Pulley Company (1896-1910) and Milton O. Reeves (1911-1912). The Harper, 1907-1908, was built by the Harper Buggy Company.

**Milton Reeves** invented the first automotive variable speed transmission. His company, The Reeves Pulley Company, constructed a 30-foot wooden pulley that played a part in the construction of the Golden Gate Bridge, in the San Francisco Bay Area, California, and used a pulley-driven assembly line later copied by Henry Ford. The Reeves Motorcycle (1896) was the first automobile driven on the streets of Indianapolis. The car is displayed at the Speedway Museum.

In 1929, **Clessie Cummins** produced America's first diesel-powered automobile. In 1930, a Cummins diesel-powered racer was the first car to ever finish the Indianapolis 500 without a stop. Cummins Engine Company, one of Columbus's two Fortune 500 companies, incorporates in its world headquarters, located in downtown Columbus, the Cerealine Mill, which in the 1880s gave birth to the first flaked breakfast cereal in the United States.

An Army air base was established here in 1943 to provide fighter plane protection for Camp Atterbury and other war projects in the area. The site for the airfield was selected by **Captain Stratton Hammon** of the U. S. Corps of Army Engineers in August 3,1942. Construction began immediately and the field was turned over to the Army Air Corps on December 21, 1942. The first landing occurred September 18, 1942 when a lost Navy pilot touched down on the unpaved runway and stayed only long enough to get his bearings. The first official landing by the Army was on December 13, 1942 when an inspection team arrived; the first troops began arriving on February 3, 1943. The airfield was first known as the **Columbus Air Support Command Base**, then as the **Columbus Army Air Base**. The airfield was named **Atterbury Army Air Field** on April 21, 1943, named for **Brigadier General William Wallace Atterbury**, who served as Chief of Transport of the American Expeditionary Forces in Europe during World War I. The base trained glider pilots during the war and served as a troop carrier command. The first black bombardment group ever activated flying B-25s and B-26s was trained here during the war. After the war the air base was used as a training facility for the Air National Guard and Air Force reservists. The air base name was

An air museum has been established at the former Bakalar Air Force Base in Columbus.

changed in October, 1954 to eliminate confusion between the air base and Camp Atterbury. It was renamed **Bakalar Air Force Base** to honor **1st Lieutenant John Edmond Bakalar**, a P-51 fighter pilot, killed September 1, 1944 on a mission over France. Lieutenant Bakalar was a native of Hammond. It continued to serve as a training center for various missions until it was closed in January, 1970. The City of Columbus received title to the land occupied by the air base in 1972.

ATTERBURY-BAKALAR AIR MUSEUM is located at the Columbus airport, 4742 Ray Boll Boulevard. It was opened in November, 1992 and through its exhibits provides a history for the old air field as well as some of the units that served here. The museum is open from 10:00 a.m. to 4:00 p.m. Saturday, and from 1:00 to 4:00 p.m. Sunday and by appointment. For additional information, call the airport manager, (812) 376-2519. Admission is free.

A large part of the **Atterbury Reserve Forces Training Ground** covers the western section of the county with its main gate just outside EDINBOROUGH (pop. 4,779), just off US 31. Camp Atterbury, established in 1942, was named for General Atterbury, who was a native of New Albany. Atterbury was president of the Pennsylvania Railroad at the outbreak of World War I. He took a leave from his presidency of the railroad to serve

77

One of the exhibits in the Atterbury-Bakalar Air Museum in Columbus.

in the Army as an engineer. When the war ended, Atterbury stayed in Europe an additional year to help build several major railroads connecting several countries. Upon his return to the U.S. from military service, Atterbury returned to his position as president of the Pennsylvania Railroad and became active in politics.

Near the main gate at Camp Atterbury is its Veterans' Memorial built in 1992 and open to the public. Several old Army tanks are exhibited in the park area. The Memorial is located 2.5 miles off US 31.

The Veterans' Memorial at Camp Atterbury off US 31.

This small chapel  at Camp Atterbury was built during World War II by Italian and German POWs.

79

During World War II, thousands of Italian and German prisoners-of-war were confined at Camp Atterbury. The POWs were granted permission to construct a small chapel in their area. The World War II POW Chapel, which has been restored, is 1.8 miles west of the Memorial on paved road, then 1.2 miles north on a rough, gravel road.

Western film actors **Ken** and **Kermit Maynard** were born in Columbus. Other notables from the area include **Will Callahan**, who wrote *"Smiles "* and other popular songs of the World War II era, and **Eddie Blondell**, vaudevillian and father of actress Joan Blondell. **Ross** and **Don Barbour**, founders along with their cousin, **Bob Flanigan**, of the popular Four Freshmen singing group, graduated from Columbus High School.

In the literary field, Columbus was home to **Laura Long**, author of several titles in the Bobbs Merrill *"Childhood of Great Americans "* series, and **Melvin Lostutter**, whose novel *"High Fever "* was published by Harper's in 1935. **Margaret Anderson** moved from Columbus in 1912 and founded *"The Little Review,"* which first published the poems of Ezra Pound and, in serial, James Joyce's *"Ulysses"* (latter confiscated by the U.S. Postal Service). **Kent Cooper**, born in Columbus, became general manager of the Associated Press. He died in 1965.

**William H. Donner**, a Columbus native, made a fortune in tin plate and steel. Donora, Pennsylvania, is named in his honor. **George Doup**, now retired, was longtime president of the Indiana Farm Bureau and **Herschel Newsom** was National Master of the Grange.

**Irwin Union Bank** built in downtown Columbus in 1954 claims to be the first all-glass bank in the nation. The courthouse, built in 1874, is said to be the first fireproof building in Indiana.

BARTHOLOMEW COUNTY HISTORICAL MUSEUM, 524 Third Street, Columbus, is housed in the **McEwen-Samuels-Marr House**, 1864, 1875, listed on the NRHP. The museum presents the history of the county through exhibits, displays and memorabilia. It is open from 9:00 a.m. to 4:00 p.m. Tuesday through Friday. It is closed on holidays. Admission is free, donations are accepted. The genealogy library is open from 2:00 to 4:00 p.m. Tuesday and Thursday.

There are several structures in Columbus and the area listed on the NRHP. These include **Bartholomew County Courthouse** (1874), Third and Washington Streets; **Columbus City Hall** (1895), Fifth and Franklin Streets; **McKinley School (North Side School)** (1892), 17th Street and Home Avenue; and **James Marr House and Farm** (1871), northeast of Columbus on Marr Road. The **Columbus Historic District** (1821-1942), is bounded by the Pennsylvania Railroad tracks, Chestnut, 3rd, Washington, and Franklin Streets.

The Bartholomew County Historical Museum is housed in this building at 524 Third Street in Columbus.

Two small museums are located in the northeast section of Bartholomew County in HOPE (pop. 2,185). Hope can be reached by taking IN 46, 10 miles east of Columbus to IN 9, then north five miles.

THE YELLOW TRAIL MUSEUM, on the corner of Main and Jackson Streets, received its name from Elda Spaugh, who, in 1914, painted yellow bands on telephone poles marking the nearest major north-south, east-west highways from his garage in Hope. The museum contains local memorabilia and is open from 1:00 to 4:00 p.m. Sunday from May through October and at other times by appointment. Admission is free.

RFD-RURAL FREE DELIVERY-MUSEUM is located in the town square and is possibly one of the smallest museums in existence. Its artifacts are housed in a small building where visitors can view them through the plate glass windows.

Returning to Columbus and I-65 the route continues southward. Eighteen miles west of Columbus on IN 46 is Nashville (see Chapter 9).

At the US 50 exit 19 miles south on I-65, it is 12 miles east on US 50 to VERNON (pop. 329), county seat of Jennings

The Indiana Rural Letter Carriers Museum is located in the Hope town square.

County, established February 1, 1817. The county was named in honor of **Jonathan Jennings**, the first governor of Indiana. All of Vernon has been placed on the NRHP as a historic district.

**General John Hunt Morgan** and his Confederate raiders reached Vernon in July, 1863, and found the town heavily fortified and did not attack. The raiders did destroy a section of track of the O & M Railroad just east of unincorporated Hayden. Prior to the Civil War there were a number of active abolitionists who operated underground railroad stations from their homes to help fugitive slaves flee to safety.

HAYDEN (pop. 325), nine miles west of Vernon on US 50, can probably lay claim to producing the greatest number of professional baseball players for a town of its size–population 325. Five players from this small community reached the major leagues in the early part of this century–**Mike Simon** with the Pittsburgh Pirates; **Rolla Daringer** and **Forest More**, both with the St. Louis Cardinals; **Clifford Daringer** with the Detroit Tigers; and **Ray Ryan** with the Chicago White Sox.

This was not Jennings County only claim to baseball fame; Sunday baseball was. The Indiana state legislature, led by North Vernon's representative **Tom Brolley**, introduced the law legalizing Sunday baseball in 1909. Similar bills were quickly passed in other states. Brolley became nationally known as the "Father of Sunday Baseball."

Every Memorial Day, black and white checkered flags deck the graves of three famous professional auto race drivers, **Wilbur Shaw, Pat O'Connor,** and **Jim Hemmings,** buried in the Vernon City Cemetery. Shaw, a three-time Indy winner, was also president of the Indianapolis Speedway before his 1954 death in an airplane crash. O'Connor, born in the unincorporated town of Nebraska, three miles east of Butlersville on US 50, was a 1946 graduate of North Vernon High School. He raced in the Indy 500 five times beginning in 1954 and was predicted to win the 1958 Indy 500 but died in a 14-car pileup on the first lap. In 1962, Hemmings passed his rookie test giving him a chance to qualify for the Indy 500 but was killed that same year in a midget auto race in Marion, Ohio.

**Hannah Milhous,** mother of former President Richard Milhous Nixon, was born on a farm near Butlersville, nine miles east of Vernon on US 50. In 1971, a historical marker was placed near the site. President Nixon came to Jennings County and spoke to a large crowd on the lawn of the courthouse. His visit is commemorated in a display and plaque inside the courthouse.

**Jessamyn West,** a native daughter, is best known for her novel, *"Friendly Persuasion,"* set in Vernon and made into a movie of the same name in the 1950s that starred Gary Cooper.

**Ovid Butler,** founder of Butler University in Indianapolis, was born in Jennings County.

The **Vernon Historic District,** 1817-1907, on the NRHP, is one mile south of North Vernon on IN 3 and 7.

SEYMOUR (pop. 15,575) is just three miles off I-65 on US 50 enroute to the Jackson County seat. Seymour, platted in 1852 and incorporated in 1864, was named in honor of **John C. Seymour,** a railroad civil engineer. The town was founded by **Captain Meedy W.** and **Eliza P. Shields.**

Seymour is the home of rock singers **John Mellencamp,** born October 7, 1951, and **Larry Crane,** born October 8, 1956; and former governor **Edgar D. Whitcomb** (1969-1973). Whitcomb served in the Army Air Corps during World War II and was captured by the Japanese and held a prisoner for nearly two years. He wrote a book, *"Escape from Corregidor,"* about his POW experiences. Seymour is also the home of **Colonel Jim Sanders,** nephew of the late Colonel Harlan Sanders of Kentucky Fried Chicken fame. Jim Sanders was employed by the company who bought Harlan's business and traveled for three years representing the company at grand openings and other events.

Seymour was home of **Freeman Army Airfield,** an advanced flying school, from 1942 to 1947. The site was selected by

Major Leland S. Stranathan and Captain Paul T. Preuss, who grew up in Seymour, in April, 1942. On March 3, 1943, the War Department named the airfield in honor of an Indianan, Captain Richard S. Freeman, who was killed in a bomber crash in Nevada, February 6, 1941.

Captain Freeman, son of Ab Freeman of Winamac, Indiana, became famous for his "mercy flights," flying Red Cross supplies to earthquake victims in Chile in 1939. He later led a mercy mission to the leper colony near Molokai in the Pacific. Freeman, a 1930 West Point graduate, was founder and one time commandant of Ladd Field, Alaska. He participated in the goodwill mass flight of B-17 "Flying Fortresses" to Buenos Aires and flew with General Henry "Hap" Arnold, Chief of the U.S. Army Air Forces during World War II, on a mass flight of Martin bombers from Washington to Fairbanks, Alaska. Captain Freeman was awarded the Distinguished Flying Cross for meritorious service in flying and the Mackay Trophy for outstanding achievements in aviation engineering. At the time of his death, he was rated as a command pilot, navigator, pilot of multi-engine aircraft, and was considered an expert bombardier.

The War Department declared Freeman Field as surplus property in 1947 and 2,234 acres of the airfield were turned over to the City of Seymour. Freeman Airport and an industrial park development occupy a section of this land. The remaining 1,442 acres are leased for agricultural purposes.

It was in Seymour the world's first train robbery occurred. On October 6, 1866, John and Simeon Reno and another robber, Franklin Sparks, are said to have boarded the Ohio & Mississippi Railroad train as it left Seymour and in short order robbed the express car of some $10,000. This robbery occurred one-half mile east of the depot, near the present site of the Seymour State Police Post. On September 28, 1867, the Renos committed the world's second train robbery, and on May 22, 1868, they committed the world's third train robbery 14-miles south of Seymour. In this third robbery the Reno gang took an incredible $96,000 from the Adams Express Company car on the train. On July 10th, members of the gang attempted to rob the Adams Express Company a second time as the train arrived about 12 miles west of Seymour. Following the May 22nd robbery, several members of the gang fled to Canada.

There were six Reno children, four who turned bad and became known as the infamous Reno brothers—Frank, John, William and Simeon. Clinton and his sister, Laura Amanda, were never involved in their brothers activities. The parents, who lived near Rockford about a mile north of Seymour, were well-to-do Jackson County landowners.

The four brothers established what was probably the first organized gang in the nation, at a time when the country was

84

recovering from the Civil War. John and Frank deserted from the Army during the war and returned to their father's farm. They immediately began their illegal activities and created a reign of terror in Jackson County, southern Indiana and eventually into Illinois, Missouri, and Iowa. It is believed that at its peak the Reno gang may have numbered as many as 200 including counterfeiters, murderers, and thieves.

The Renos managed to build up an immunity in Jackson County through intimidation or connections with influential politicians. During this period, just after the war, it was not unusual to have 20 or more unsolved murders as well as robberies on the books each year. This violent period lasted from 1865 to 1869.

By early 1867, a group of the county's respected citizens decided they had enough and formed the vigilantes that dispensed swift justice for more than 20 years in Jackson County. This group, the Seymour Regulators or Southern Indiana Vigilance Committee numbering 50 to 200, were well organized and used numbers instead of names.

On July 20, 1868, the Seymour vigilantes hijacked the train taking three members of the Reno gang believed to have been involved in the July 10 robbery attempt to the county jail in Brownstown. The three outlaws, Val Elliott, Charles Roseberry, and Fred Clifton, were hanged from a tree about two miles west of Seymour where Second Street crosses the railroad and joins US 50. On July 24th three other members of the gang—Frank Sparks, John Moore, and Henry Jerrell— were arrested for the attempted train robbery on July 10th. The vigilantes also hanged them from the same tree two miles west of town as the other three. This crossing is still known as **"Hangman's Crossing"** by local citizens.

By October, 1868, Frank Reno and another gang member, Charles Anderson, had been extradited from Canada and were being held in the New Albany jail under federal protection. William and Simeon Reno were also awaiting trial in the same jail.

Saturday night, December 12, 1868 Seymour vigilantes broke into the New Albany jail and promptly hanged the four men from the jail rafters. This created an international incident prompting Great Britain to recall its ambassador from the U.S. As a result, Congress enacted laws guaranteeing that the federal government would safeguard all prisoners extradited from foreign countries to afford them a fair trial.

By this time the vigilantes had hanged three of the Reno brothers and seven members of their gang. No one was ever arrested or tried for any of these lynchings. Murder, however, became a rarity in Jackson County as a result. The last activity by the Jackson County vigilantes occurred in 1892 when they

This spot on Second Street west of downtown Seymour is believed to be the crossing where six members of the Reno gang were hanged by vigilantes.

hanged a lawbreaker.

John Reno escaped vigilante "justice." He was arrested, tried, and sentenced to 10 years in the Missouri State Prison in 1868. He died in Seymour in 1895. Frank, William and Simeon Reno are buried in the old City Cemetery at the corner of Ewing and Ninth Streets in Seymour. **Sara V. Ford Reno**, wife of Frank and later, John, who she divorced, died at the age of 86 in 1930. She was the last Reno to be buried in Seymour.

During World War II, a large Army Air Base training center, **Freeman Army Air Base**, was located here. It became one the first military helicopter training bases and was the nation's dissemination center for all types of captured enemy aircraft.

86

Today the site is an industrial park.

The **Farmers Club**, 1914, 105 South Chestnut Street, is listed on the NRHP.

Two other spots in Jackson County listed on the NRHP–the **Low Spur Archaeological Site** and the **Sand Hill Archaeological Site**.

There are three covered bridges in Jackson County worthy of note. The **Bell's Ford Bridge** on IN 258; **Medora Bridge**, one and a half miles east of Medora on IN 235; and the **Shieldstown Bridge**, over the East Fork of White River 3.6 miles east of Brownstown and .9 mile north of US 50. Bell's Ford Bridge is the only known Post truss bridge in existence.

Southwest of Seymour 10 miles on US 50 is BROWNSTOWN (pop. 2,704), county seat of Jackson County, established January 1, 1816. The county was named in honor of **General and President Andrew Jackson**. Brownstown was laid out in 1816.

JACKSON COUNTY HISTORICAL SOCIETY MUSEUM, 115 North Sugar Street, focuses on Jackson County history through its presentations. It is open from 1:30 to 4:00 p.m. Friday and Saturday during the spring and summer and at other times by appointment.

Back on I-65, it is 18 miles south and a mile east on IN 56 to SCOTTSBURG (pop. 5,068), county seat of Scott County. The county was established February 1, 1820 and named in honor of **Kentucky Governor Charles Scott**. Scottsburg was incorporated June 28, 1884. The county seat was moved to Scottsburg in 1874.

It is five miles south of Scottsburg on US 31 to the **Pigeon Roost Memorial** marking the site of the massacre of several white settlers by Indians on September 3, 1812. Three men, five women and 16 children were killed and thrown into the buildings the Indians had set on fire. **William Collings** kept up a steady fire from his cabin, killed three Indians, drove off the other marauders and helped several settlers to escape to safety.

Five miles south of the Pigeon Roost Memorial, on US 31, is HENRYVILLE (pop. 1,132), birthplace of **Colonel Harland Sanders**, founder of Kentucky Fried Chicken.

Twenty three miles east of Scottsburg, via IN 56, is MADISON (pop. 11,900) county seat of Jefferson County, established February 1, 1811. The county was named in honor of **President Thomas Jefferson**.

Madison, on the Ohio River, was settled in 1808 and incorporated in 1838. The entire community has been declared a Historic District, 1812-1900, and is listed on the NRHP.

Madison prospered in the early 19th century as a major river port, railway center, and supply town outfitting pioneers moving into the Old Northwest Territory.

87

This memorial marks the site of the Pigeon Roost massacre of 1812. Twenty-four settlers were killed here by Indian raiders.

**Hanover College**, seven miles west on IN 56 and 62, was founded in 1827 making it the oldest private four year college in the state.

The **Thomas Hendricks Library** (1903), on College Drive, and the **Crowe-Garritt House** (c. 1824), 172 Crowe Street, both in Hanover, are listed on the NRHP.

The Visitors Center is located at 301 East Main and is open

88

A native of Henryville, Harland Sanders, who became a Kentucky colonel, found a special way of preparing fried chicken. With his secret recipe he became famous for his Kentucky Fried Chicken outlets across the nation and beyond.

9:00 a.m. to 5:00 p.m. week days, 9:00 a.m. to 3:00 p.m. Saturday, and 10:00 a.m. to 3:00 p.m. Sunday, April through October.

MADISON RAILROAD STATION, 615 West Main, dates back to 1895 and was used as a passenger station until the 1930s. It has been restored to its Victorian splendor and is filled with railroad memorabilia.

Adjacent to the Railroad Station is the new JEFFERSON COUNTY HISTORICAL SOCIETY MUSEUM, filled with displays devoted to the history and art of southeastern Indiana. Here are found displays devoted to steamboating, the Civil War, the early Scot settlers—including a recreated stone cottage, and other exhibits about the past. A gift shop is located here as well. Both buildings are open from 10:00 a.m. to 4:30 p.m. weekdays and Saturday and from 1:00 to 4:00 p.m. Sunday April through November. From Thanksgiving to April 1 they are open 10:00 a.m. to 4:30 p.m. weekdays. An admission is charged.

Two other unusual buildings here are the JEFFERSON COUNTY COURTHOUSE AND JAIL, 300 block of East Main, and the FAIR PLAY FIRE COMPANY, 403 East Main. The courthouse was built in 1854-55 and just east of the courthouse is the old jail, completed in 1849. The old jail is listed on the NRHP. The fire house was built in 1875 as a trolley barn and has housed the fire company since 1888. The Italianate bell tower was added to support the large alarm bell. Atop the tower is the figure of a fireman, called "Little Jimmy," forming a weathervane. The Fair Play Fire Company, organized in 1841, is the oldest existing volunteer fire department in the state. Both facilities offer group tours by appointment.

MADISON—JEFFERSON COUNTY PUBLIC LIBRARY, 420 West Main, was the first public library established in the

Northwest Territory. The library includes an extensive collection of local history, photographs, and genealogy. It is open from 9:00 a.m. to 8:00 p.m. Monday through Thursday and from 9:00 a.m. to 6:00 p.m. Friday and Saturday.

SHREWSBURY HOUSE, 301 West First, was built by **Captain Charles L. Shrewsbury**, a riverboat entrepreneur. Designed by architect **Francis Costigan**, this Greek Revival home was completed in 1846. It is open from 10:00 a.m. to 4:30 p.m. daily, April through December. An admission is charged.

J.F.D. LANIER STATE HISTORIC SITE, 511 West First, was completed in 1844. Another residence was designed by Francis Costigan for financier **James Lanier** whose loans to the State of Indiana enabled the state to equip Union troops during the Civil War. It is open from 9:00 a.m. to 5:00 p.m. Wednesday through Saturday and from 1:00 to 5:00 p.m. Tuesday and Sunday. Admission is free, donations are welcome.

MASONIC SCHOFIELD HOUSE, 217 West Second, was built c. 1816 in the Federal style and is believed to be the first two-story tavern in Madison. The house has been restored by the Masonic Heritage Foundation and it is operated as a house museum. It is open from 9:30 a.m. to 4:30 p.m. Monday through Saturday and from 12:30 to 4:30 p.m. Sunday, April 1 through November 30. An admission is charged.

JEREMIAH SULLIVAN HOUSE, 304 West Second, was built in 1818 and is considered Madison's first mansion. It was owned by **Judge Jeremiah Sullivan**, a prominent figure in early Indiana history. It is an outstanding example of Federal architecture. The house is open from 10:00 a.m. to 4:30 p.m. weekdays and Saturday and from 1:00 to 4:30 p.m. Sunday, mid-April through October. It is open weekends only during November. An admission is charged.

DR. WILLIAM D. HUTCHINGS' OFFICE, 120 West Third, provides a glimpse into the life and work of a frontier doctor. This Greek Revival building was built in 1848 and was used by Dr. Hutchings until his death in 1903. It is open from 10:00 a.m. to 4:30 p.m. weekdays and Saturday, and 1:00 to 4:30 p.m. Sunday from mid-April through October. It is open weekends only during November. An admission is charged.

FRANCIS COSTIGAN HOUSE, 408 West Third, was the home built by the architect of the Lanier and Shrewsbury houses in 1851. It is open to group tours by appointment.

Eighteen miles west of Scottsburg on IN 56 is SALEM (pop. 5,290), county seat of Washington County. The county, named in honor of **President George Washington**, was established January 17, 1814; Salem was founded 1814 and incorporated in 1864.

The first courthouse was built in Salem in 1814 by **Colonel John DePauw** for the sum of $2,490. The prison was built for

90

$588 at the same time by **Marston Clark**, a cousin of the famous soldier George Rogers Clark. Entrance to this two-room jail was through a trap door in the roof. One of the cells was for criminals, the other for debtors.

Salem's direct involvement in the Civil War came when **General John Morgan** and his Confederate raiders attacked the city on July 11, 1863, burned the railroad depot and bridges on both sides of town, cutting off communications. Morgan threatened to burn the woolen mill and two flour mills unless he was paid $1,000 per building. After collecting the ransom for these three buildings the raiders left town.

Several Salem area residents have gained national fame. The most notable was **John Milton Hay** (1838-1905), secretary to President Abraham Lincoln, later his biographer, and the ambassador to Great Britain. He served as Secretary of State under Presidents William McKinley and Theodore Roosevelt from September 20, 1898, until his death July 1, 1905.

Two Salem natives became governors. **W. W. Durbin** became governor of Indiana; **Newton Booth** was elected governor of California. **Thomas Rodman** invented a cannon used during the Civil War and **Charles Knight** invented the sleeve valve motor, called the Silent Knight.

JOHN HAY CENTER, STEVENS MEMORIAL MUSEUM, PIONEER VILLAGE COMPLEX, 307 East Market Street, focuses on the history and heritage of the area. The John Hay House was built as a school in 1824 and acquired by **Charles Hay**, John's father, in 1837. This was the birthplace of John Hay

The John Hay Center is in this complex in Salem.

on October 8, 1838. The building has been restored and is furnished in the 1840 period. It is listed on the NRHP. The Stevens Memorial Museum was built in 1971 and features early-day law and dentist offices as well as hundreds of historic relics. Among these are Civil War mementoes, tools, agriculture items, furniture, clothing, and other historic items. Pioneer Village is an extension of the Stevens Memorial Museum and is reconstructed as a "living village" during the 1840 era. It contains a house, blacksmith shop, loom house, jail, barn, carriage house, carpenter shop, school, and church. The museum also houses the Washington County Historical Society genealogical and historical library. Not only does the library contain Indiana and local records, it also maintains data and records from other states. The Village and museum are open from 1:00 to 5:00 p.m. daily except Monday and holidays. An admission is charged.

Other structures in Salem listed on the NRHP include the **First Baptist Church** (1900), 201 North High Street; **Washington County Courthouse** (1880), town square; and **Washington County Jail and Sheriff's Residence** (1881), 106 South Main Street.

About 25 miles south and, just off I-65, east on IN 62 and on the Ohio River across from Louisville, Kentucky is JEFFERSONVILLE (pop. 26,000), county seat of Clark County. The county, named in honor of **George Rogers Clark**, was established February 3, 1801.

Jeffersonville, Clarksville, New Albany, and Corydon (see Chapter 10) are promoted as the "Sunny Side of Louisville" and home to outstanding figures such President William Henry Harrison, General George Rogers Clark, Governors Jonathan Jennings and Ashbel P. Willard, and U.S. Speaker of the House Michael Kerr.

Jeffersonville was settled about the same time because it became the county seat in June, 1801. Jeffersonville remained the county seat until 1812, when county government moved upriver to **Charlestown** but moved back to Jeffersonville permanently in 1878.

Forerunner of Jeffersonville was **Fort Finney**, near the present John F. Kennedy Bridge, built in 1787. This fort was renamed **Fort Steuben** and served as a militia post until about 1800.

Jeffersonville's early day growth centered around the steamboat industry. In 1819, several local businessmen financed the construction of the *United States,* a 700-ton vessel with the capacity to handle 3,000 bales of cotton. The Howard Shipyard was established in 1848 by **James Howard** and built boats for use on American rivers for over a century.

The **Big Four Bridge** or the "Bridge that goes nowhere," was built in the 1890s for the Cleveland, Cincinnati, Chicago &

St. Louis Railroad. Two major construction accidents cost the lives of 61 workers before the bridge was completed in 1895. In January, 1918, two interurban cars crashed, killing 20 passengers. The approaches have since been removed thus the bridge goes nowhere.

The January, 1937, flood created an estimated $18 million in damages to Jeffersonville, Clarksville, and New Albany.

HOWARD STEAMBOAT MUSEUM, 1101 East Market Street, is dedicated to riverboat history, the only one of its kind in the U.S. It is located in the elegant Victorian 22-room mansion built in the 1890s, when the steamboat era was flourishing, by **Edmonds J. Howard**, son of James Howard, founder of the Howard Shipyards. The Howard Home is listed on the NRHP and is famous for its original furnishings, 15 varieties of elegant hand-carved wood paneling and brass chandeliers. The museum houses a fascinating collection of navigational equipment, paddle wheels, and small replicas of steamboats, among other exhibits. The museum is open 10:00 a.m. to 3:00 p.m. Tuesday through Saturday, and 1:00 to 3:00 p.m. Sunday. It is closed on Mondays and on major holidays. An admission is charged.

The **Grisamore House**, 111-113 West Chestnut Street, built by **David** and **Wilson** in 1837, houses the Historic Landmarks Foundation and several private businesses. **William Henry Harrison** delivered a speech from the front porch during his 1840 presidential campaign. The house is listed on the NRHP.

The **Old Jeffersonville Historic District** (1815-1935), is bounded by Court Avenue, Graham Street, Ohio River, and I-65. The district boasts several distinctive Renaissance Revival commercial structures as well as a number of residential structures ranging from Federal to Victorian and several unique churches. It is listed on the NRHP.

The **Louisville Municipal Bridge** (1929), spanning the Ohio River between Jeffersonville and Louisville is also listed on the NRHP.

There are three structures listed on the NRHP in Charlestown, the county seat for 65 years. These include the **Thomas Downs House** (c. 1809), 1045 Main Street; **Benjamin Ferguson House** (1816), 673 High Street; and the **Watson House** (c. 1900), 1015 Water Street.

CLARKSVILLE (pop. 17,500), in Clark County between Jeffersonville and New Albany, is said to be the first American town in the Old Northwest. It was chartered in 1783 by the State of Virginia and named for **General George Rogers Clark**, who in 1778 and 1779 led the expedition that captured the forts of Kaskaskia, Cahokia, and Vincennes from the British and their Indian allies. In recognition for these victories, the Virginia Assembly in 1783 gave Clark and his troops a 150,000 acre land grant at the Falls of the Ohio River. One thousand acres were designated as the town of Clarksville, and Clark was appointed chairman of the town's board of trustees.

In 1803, Clark built a cabin overlooking the **Falls on the Ohio** and on October 26, that year witnessed the departure of the famous **Lewis and Clark expedition** to explore the Louisiana Purchase. **William Clark**, on that early historic expedition, was George's younger brother. While residing here, George Rogers Clark entertained visitors such as artist **John James Audubon** and a number of Indian leaders. In 1809, he suffered a stroke and fell into the fireplace, causing burns that necessitated the amputation of his right leg.

The George Rogers Clark **Homesite** is located at Harrison Avenue and Bailey in Clarksville.

A limestone reef which extends from the Clarksville shore into the Ohio River offers a spectacular display of 350 million-year-old fossils dating to the Devonian Era. This area has been designated as a National Wildlife Conservation Area and has been declared a National Natural Landmark. It is the newest Indiana State Park.

The Colgate-Palmolive plant here is located in the old Indiana reformatory. The Colgate clock, measuring 40 feet in diameter, is the second largest clock in the world and is a Southern Indiana landmark.

The **Old Clarksville Site** (1781-1809), in the Clarksville vicinity, is listed on the NRHP.

Adjacent to Clarksville is NEW ALBANY (pop. 37,300), county seat of **Floyd County**, established February 2, 1819. The county was probably named for **Davis Floyd**, the flamboyant politician who was the county's first circuit court judge.

New Albany was laid out in 1813 by **Joel, Abner, and Nathaniel Scribner**. The principal industry was shipbuilding and shipbuilders turned out many packet boats as well as famous steamboats with such names as *Eclipse, A. L. Shotwell,* and the *Robert E. Lee II*. By 1850, New Albany was the largest city in Indiana.

The site of New Albany was originally part of George Rogers Clark's grant from the Virginia legislature.

The Crown automobile, 1913-1914, and the Hercules, 1914, were built here by Hercules Motor Car Company .

Sociologist **Robert Stoughton Lynd** was born in New Albany in 1892. With his wife, **Helen Merrell Lynd**, he did a noted sociological study of Muncie published in 1929 as *"Middletown: a Study of Contemporary American Culture."*

FLOYD COUNTY MUSEUM, 201 East Spring Street, is located in an historic Carnegie Library building. The museum houses permanent exhibits depicting the pioneer period, the

This was once the home of New Albany businessman William Culbertson. Today this 1860s historic site is open to the public.

steamboat era, the Civil War and life along the Ohio River. The museum also offers changing art exhibits by local and regional artists. It is open from 10:00 a.m. to 4:00 p.m. Tuesday through Saturday. It is closed Sunday and Monday, all major holidays, and the first two weeks of August. Admission is free.

CULBERTSON MANSION, 914 East Main Street, was built by **William S. Culbertson**, one of Indiana's leading merchants and philanthropists, in the 1860s. Completed in 1869, the home reflects the affluent lifestyle of Ohio River towns during the post-Civil War period. Listed on the NRHP, the historic site is open from 9:00 a.m. to 5:00 p.m. Tuesday through Saturday and from 1:00 to 5:00 p.m. Sunday. It is closed on Monday. Donations are accepted.

SCRIBNER HOUSE, 106 East Main Street, was built in 1814 by **Joel Scribner**, one of the three brothers who founded New Albany. The house had been lived in by only three generations of Scribners before being purchased in 1917 by the Piankeshaw Chapter, Daughters of the American Revolution. The house is listed on the NRHP and is furnished with a collection of antiques, paintings, textiles and toys, many of which belonged to the Scribners. It is open only by appointment, (812) 949-1776 or 944-7330. An admission is charged.

95

Other New Albany listings on the NRHP include the **New Albany & Salem Railroad Station** (c. 1851), Pearl and Oak Streets, and the **Yenowine-Nichols-Collins House** (1832), 5118 IN 64. The **Mansion Row Historic District** (1814-1900), covers Main Street between State and 15th Streets and Market Street between 7th and 11th Streets.

There are two other buildings listed on the NRHP in Floyd County—the **Gabriel Farnsley House** (c. 1856), north of Bridgeport off IN 111, and **Jersey Park Farm** (1874), off Cunningham Sarles and Borden Roads in the Galena area.

This historical marker in Tippecanoe County is just across the road from the birthplace of Cartoonist John T. McCutcheon, born May 6, 1870. The most famous of his cartoons was his "Injun Summer," reminiscent of tales of Indian times in Tippecanoe County. His brother, George, who became a celebrated novelist was born a short distance south of the marker.

# Chapter 4
# West on I-70 (US 40)

Starting at the Ohio state line and driving west this route can take one through such places as Richmond, Fountain City, Liberty, Connersville, Centerville, Cambridge City, Milton, Hagerstown, Millville, New Castle, Middletown, Knightstown, Spiceland, Greenfield, Danville, Plainfield, Mooresville, Martinsville, Spencer, Gosport, Brazil, Terre Haute, Rockville, Clinton, Sullivan, and Shelburn. If you are interested in covered bridges don't miss a visit and tour of Parke County.

# Leadership in the Post War Years

As the country came out of the Civil War, population grew and Indiana had its share of growth and the problems that went with growth.

Governor Oliver P. Morton had survived the war and was in his second term, when, in 1867, he replaced Henry S. Lane in the U.S. Senate. Lieutenant Governor Conrad Baker served as acting governor through 1869. Baker was elected to the governorship on his record at the end of Morton's term.

The next five governors each served only one term.

Baker was replaced in 1873 by Democrat Thomas A. Hendricks who in turn was replaced in 1877 by Democrat James D. "Blue Jeans" Williams. Albert G. Porter, a Republican, was elected in 1881 but was replaced in 1885 by Isaac P. Gray from Union City. Gray was replaced in 1889 by Alvin P. Hovey of Mount Vernon. Hovey, a war hero, died in office on November 23, 1891. Ira J. Chase served out Hovey's term.

# Chapter 4
# West on I-70 (US 40)

It is 76 miles from the Ohio state line to Indianapolis and another 85 miles west from Indianapolis to the Illinois state line via I-70. Most of the historical sites along this route, however, are on US 40 which roughly parallels the interstate.

US 40 follows the early National Road across Indiana.

Entering Indiana from the east the first city is RICHMOND (pop. 38,800), county seat of Wayne County, established February 1, 1811. The county was named in honor of **General "Mad Anthony" Wayne**, hero of the battle of Fallen Timbers. Richmond, on US 40, was settled in 1806 by the Quakers.

The first motion picture projector and early television were invented by **C. Francis Jenkins**, a Richmond native. **Harry Henley** invented roller skates here. Richmond was the home of noted author and internationally known theologian **Dr. D. Elton Trueblood**, founder and president of Yokefellow Institute. Several well-known professional football stars—**Vegas Ferguson, Lamar Lundy, Paul Flatley**, and **Weeb Eubanks**—called Richmond home at one time or another. **Jerry Sturm**, born in Richmond in 1936, had a sucessful 11-year career in the NFL. A tackle and center, Sturm played with the Denver Broncos, the Houston Oilers and the Philadelphia Eagles.

**Hoagy Carmichael** recorded his hit song *"Star Dust"* in 1923 and **William Jennings Bryan** recorded his famous *"Cross of Gold Speech"* here in July of the same year.

Richmond was the home of many of the early automobiles–The Pilot, Crosley, E.I.M., Wescott, Wayne, Richmond, Rodefeld, Davis, and the Richmond Steam Runabout. The Crosley, 1939 to 1952, was built by Crosley Motors, Inc. in Richmond from 1939 to 1941 when the plant was moved to Marion where the car was built until it went out of production in 1952. The E.I.M., 1915, was manufactured here by the Eastern Motor Car Company. The Pilot, 1909-1924, was built by the Pilot Motor Car Company. The Richmond, 1902-1903, was manufactured by the Richmond Automobile & Cycle Company. The Wayne, 1905-1910, was built by the Wayne Works and the Westcott, 1912-1925, by the Westcott Motor Car Company. The Davis, 1908-1930, was designed and built by the George W. Davis Motor Car Company.

Henry Clay (1777-1852), campaigning against James K. Polk for the U.S. presidency, appeared in Richmond on October 1, 1842 and from a spot on the corner of 7th and A Streets is said to have addressed 20,000 persons. At the conclusion of his speech, he was presented a petition signed by 2,000 Quakers

Top photo: Wayne County Historical Museum features the Julia Meek Gaar collection. Photo below: The Indiana Football Hall of Fame is housed in this building. Both the museum and Hall of Fame are located in Richmond.

asking him to free his own slaves. He owned about 50 slaves at that time which he valued at $15,000. He was very indignant and told the person who had delivered the petition to go home and mind his own business.

**Earlham College** was founded here in 1847 by the Society of Friends (Quakers). On its campus is the JOSEPH MOORE MUSEUM featuring an Egyptian mummy and the fossilized remains of giant pre-historic mammals. Also exhibited is a prehistoric mastodon and allosaurus skeletons. Other exhibits include birds and mammals in natural habitat settings. The museum is open from 1:00 to 4:00 p.m. Monday, Wednesday and Friday, September through November and January through May, and from 1:00 to 5:00 p.m. Sundays the year-round. Admission is free.

WAYNE COUNTY MUSEUM (Julia Meek Gaar Historical Museum), 1150 North A Street, features the Julia Meek Gaar collection of curiosities from around the world, including an authentic Egyptian mummy; pioneer life exhibits; an early automobile collection of Richmond-made cars plus other exhibits of early area history. The Scott House, built in 1858 by Andrew Finley Scott, 126 North 10th Street, serves as an annex to the museum. It is listed on the National Register of Historic Places (NRHP). On the museum grounds is the Village Square that includes a blacksmith shop and livery stable, the Richmond Bakery and Palladium Printing Office, a two-story log house, and log school house. The museum is open from 9:00 a.m. to 4:00 p.m. Tuesday through Friday and from 1:00 to 4:00 p.m. weekends, March 4 through December 23. An admission is charged.

INDIANA FOOTBALL HALL OF FAME, 815 North A Street, features displays of football history and memorabilia from Indiana high school, collegiate and professional athletes. It is open from 8:30 a.m. to 4:30 p.m. weekdays March through August and from 10:00 a.m. to 2:00 p.m. weekdays September through February. Group tours are available weekends by special arrangement. An admission is charged.

The **Madonna of the Trail statue**, commemorating pioneer mothers of the covered wagon days, is the ninth link in the Great National Shrine erected by the Daughters of the American Revolution along the National Road Trail. There are only 12 statues linked along US 40 from Cumberland, Maryland, to Upland, California. The statue is located in Glen Miller Park, East Main and North 23rd Streets, in Richmond.

A historical marker in the 10th Street Park briefly tells the story of **Camp Wayne**, a Civil War training camp located on the old fairgrounds. The 57th, 74th, 84th, and 124th Regiments of the Indiana Volunteers were organized and trained here.

There are several buildings in Richmond included on the NRHP. These include **Bethel A.M.E. Church** (1854, 1892), 200

101

South Sixth Street; **Henry and Alice Gennett House** (1900), 1829 East Main Street; **Earlham College Observatory** (1861), National Road, Earlham College campus; **Abram Gaar House and Farm** (1876), 2411 Pleasant View Road; **Hicksite Friends Meetinghouse (Wayne County Museum)** (1865), 1150 North A Street; **Leland Hotel** (1928), 900 A Street; **Murray Theatre** (1909), 1003 Main Street; **Richmond Gas Company Building** (1855), 100 East Main Street; **Samuel G. Smith Farm** (1888), 3431 Crowe Road, west of town; **Starr Piano Company Warehouse and Administration Building** (1900), 300 South First Street; and the **Wayne County Courthouse** (1893), bounded by Third, Fourth, Main and South A Streets.

There are four historic districts here. These include the **East Main Street-Glen Miller Park Historic District** (1830-1937), encompassing both sides of East Main Street from 18th to 30th Streets; **Old Richmond Historic District** (1816, c. 1900), bounded by the C & O Railroad, South Eleventh and South A Streets, and the alley south of South E Street; **Richmond Railroad Station Historic District** (1853-1915), bounded by the Norfolk and Southern Railroad, North Tenth Street, Elm Place, North D Street, and Fort Wayne Avenue; and the **Starr Historic District** (1836-1900), bounded by North Sixteenth, E and D Streets, and the alley west of Noth Tenth Street.

Ten miles north of Richmond on US 27 is FOUNTAIN CITY (pop. 839), incorporated in 1834.

The LEVI COFFIN HOUSE, 113 US 27 North, was part of the legendary Underground Railroad for runaway slaves during the pre-Civil War period. The Federal-style brick home was built in 1839 and is a National Historic Landmark and enrolled on the NRHP. It is open from 1:00 to 4:00 p.m. Tuesday through Sunday June 1 through September 15 and from 1:00 to 4:00 p.m. weekends September 15 through October 31. An admission is charged.

The highest point in the state is in the northeast corner of Wayne County, just over a mile from the Randolph County line. The elevation is 1,257 feet.

About 20 miles south of Richmond, via US 27, is LIBERTY (pop. 1,844), county seat of Union County established February 1, 1821. The county was named for the union of American states.

Liberty was founded in 1822. Although **Brownsville**, northwest of Liberty, was the first county seat, it moved to Liberty in 1823. Brownsville dates back to 1815.

The railroad came to Liberty in 1860.

Several famous persons were born in Liberty and in Union County.

**Ambrose E. Burnside**, noted Union general and inventor of the Burnside Rifle, was born on a farm near Liberty, May 23,

Top photo: Madonna of the Trail statue in Richmond. Photo below: The Levi Coffin House in Fountain City.

1824. He graduated from West Point in 1847 but stayed in the army only a few years. He invented his breech-loading rifle in 1856 and established a factory in Bristol, Rhode Island. After the attack on Fort Sumter, Burnside assumed command of a Rhode Island regiment. He commanded a brigade at First Bull Run and the Army of the Potomac at Fredericksburg. He was commanding general of the Army of the Ohio when Morgan's Raiders were captured. Burnside achieved the rank of major general during the war. After the war he returned to Rhode Island and served as governor and United States Senator until his death in 1881.

Another general in the Union army came from Liberty. He was **Thomas W. Bennett,** born in Union County and practicing law in Liberty at the outbreak of the Civil War. He organized a company of volunteers, served as a captain in the 15th Indiana Regiment, and as a major of the 36th Indiana Regiment. As colonel of the 69th Indiana Regiment, he participated in the skirmishes and battles resulting in the capture of Vicksburg and in the Red River campaign. He attained the rank of brigadier general before the war ended and returned to Liberty after the war to practice law. President U.S. Grant appointed him as governor of Idaho Territory. He served as mayor of Richmond, Indiana, for eight years.

**Joaquin Miller** (1839-1913), famous as the poet of the Sierras, was born on his grandparents farm a few miles north of Liberty. He was given the name **Cincinnatus Hiner** by his Quaker parents, Hulings and Margaret Miller. He used his middle name until 1870 when a San Francisco poetess suggested that he adopt the name Joaquin from the title of a poem he had written about the Mexican bandit Joaquin Murrietta. His first book of poetry, "*Pacific Poems,*" was an instant success. His second volume, "*Songs of the Sierras,*" is generally considered his best work. He published a number of prose works—reminiscences, novels, and a play, "*The Danites,*" which was a box-office success on Broadway, on tour, and in London. He was a colorful character and traveled widely. He died at his Oakland, California, residence on February 17, 1913 and his ashes were scattered over the hillside where he lived.

Quaker **Oran D. Perry** was born in Liberty in 1838. Even though against his religious beliefs, Perry helped organize a military company soon after the outbreak of the Civil War. At the age of 25 he was promoted to the rank of lieutenant colonel of his regiment and witnessed the surrender of Vicksburg on July 4, 1863. By the time he left military service he held the rank of brigadier general.

**Dr. Paul Hawley** (1891-1965), of Liberty, became famous for his service during the two world wars. In World War I he served as a regimental surgeon. In World War II he was appointed Chief Surgeon of the Army in Great Britain and then the entire European Theatre of Operation, promoted to the rank of brigadier general in 1943. He was the most decorated doctor in military history.

One of James Whitcomb Riley's poems was *"Little Orphant Annie,"* based on his experiences as a boy of nine with **Mary Alice Smith**, a "bound" servant in the Riley household. Born near Liberty in 1850, Mary Alice endeared herself to the four Riley children with her stories of witches and goblins. On visits to Liberty, the poet was always asked for certain favorite poems and *"Little Orphant Annie"* was one of them. Mary Alice became Mrs. Leslie Gray and lived to be 84 years old.

Others from Union County to achieve success were **Zetti Bonnelle**, an actress who performed on Broadway; **Gene** and **Dudley Fosdick**, who played with several big name bands in New York; and **Teresa Maxwell Conover**, stage and movie actress.

The **Union County Courthouse** (1891), on Courthouse Square in Liberty, is listed on the NRHP.

TREATY-LINE MUSEUM AND PIONEER VILLAGE is located in unincorporated Dunlapsville, southwest of Liberty on a Dunlapsville Road. The museum is located in the old Liberty Township Grade School building in the village. Also on the grounds is the Quakertown General Store; the grist mill, originally erected along the Great Miami River in 1819; and five original cabins from the Whitewater Valley, featuring the Logan cabin built in 1804. The Village is open from 2:00 to 5:00 p.m. weekends, May through October.

West of Liberty 12 miles is CONNERSVILLE (pop. 17,023), county seat of Fayette County established January 1, 1819. A fur-trading post was established here by John Conner in 1808, and the city was laid out in 1813.

Once called "Indiana's Little Detroit" many cars were built in Connersville. The automobile industry in Indiana was on the verge of collapse when E. L. Cord first arrived in town in 1924.

Several early automobiles were built or assembled here with names such as the Amsted, the Howard, the Kelsey, the Lexington, and the McFarlan. The Amsted was built 1926-1927 by the Amsted Motor Company. The Howard was built from 1913-1914 by the Lexington-Howard Company that also built the Lexington from 1911-1918 then from 1918 to 1928 as the Lexington Motor Company. The Kelsey was built in 1913-1914 by the Kelsey Car Corporation and the McFarlan, from 1910-1928 by the McFarlan Motor Car Company. The Empire, 1912 to 1915, and the Van Auken Electric, 1914, also were built here. Also assembled here were the Auburn, 1929 to 1936; Cord, 1936 to 1937; Packard Darrin, 1940; and Pak-Age-Car, 1938 to 1941.

Several buildings in the county are listed on the NRHP and these include the **Canal House** (1842), 111 East Fourth Street,

Connersville; **Elmhurst** (1831), south of Connersville on IN 121; **William Lowry House** (c. 1825), Kniese Road, in the Bentonville vicinity; and **Thomas Ranck Round Barn** (c. 1904), north of Brownsville on CR 500N.

To return to US 40 or I-70 from Connersville drive north on IN 1 about 15 miles.

From Richmond west, via US 40, it is six miles to CENTERVILLE (pop. 2,284), the first county seat of Wayne county and the birthplace of **Oliver P. Morton**, Civil War governor of Indiana. **Dr. Charles Hufnagel**, pioneer heart surgeon and inventor of the first heart valve, resided in Centerville.

Two structures in Centerville are listed on the NRHP–the **Lewis Jones House** (1840), College Corner and Eliason Roads, and the **Oliver P. Morton House** (1848), 319 Main Street. Also on the NRHP is the **Centerville Historic District**, bounded by Corporation Line, Third and South Streets, and Willow Grove Road.

Eleven miles west of Centerville on US 40 is CAMBRIDGE CITY (pop. 2,407), settled in 1813 and platted in 1836.

HUDDLESTON FARMHOUSE INN MUSEUM, on US 40 West, was built in 1839-41 when the National Road was young. The museum includes the restored farmhouse, spring house, smokehouse, and barn. It is open from 10:00 a.m. to 4:00 p.m. Tuesday through Saturday and from 1:00 to 4:00 p.m. Sunday or by special appointment, May through August. It is closed on Saturday and Sunday (September through April), major holidays and the month of January. Donations are accepted.

MUSEUM OF OVERBECK ART POTTERY, downstairs in the Cambridge City Library, 33 West Main Street, houses the Overbeck Collection of pottery created by the Overbeck sisters, Margaret (1863-1911), Hannah (1870-1931), Elizabeth (1875-1936), and Mary Frances (1878-1955). The sisters established their pottery enterprise in their Cambridge City home, 520 East Church Street, in 1911. They won numerous awards for their work that has earned an important place in the history of American art. The museum is open from 10:00 a.m. to 12:00 noon and from 1:00 to 5:00 p.m. Monday through Saturday and by appointment for large groups. Admission is free.

The **Conklin-Montgomery House** (1838), 303 East Main Street, and the **Lackey-Overbeck House** (c.1830), 520 East Church Street, are listed on the NRHP.

A mile east on US 40 and two miles south on IN 1 is MILTON (pop. 729). Two miles south of Milton is **Beechwood (The Isaac Kinsey House)** (1871), on Sarver Road, listed on the NRHP.

It is a mile east on US 40 and three miles north on IN 1 to I-70 from Cambridge City. From I-70 it is another four miles north on IN 1 to HAGERSTOWN (pop. 1,950).

The home of Civil War Governor Oliver P. Morton in Centerville. It is a private residence today.

HAGERSTOWN MUSEUM, 96 1/2 East Main Street, is housed in what was once a public hall built in 1880. It features frescoed wall murals painted by local artist Charles L. Newcomb in 1913. Other exhibits focus on local and area history. The museum is open from 1:00 to 5:00 p.m. Tuesday through Sunday and other times by appointment. Donations are accepted.

The **Hagerstown I.O.O.F. Hall** (1863), Main and Perry Streets, is listed on the NRHP.

Driving west on IN 38 from Hagerstown about five miles is the county road leading north to MILLVILLE (unincorporated). North of Millville on Wilbur Wright Road to 100 N Road, east half a mile, then half mile north on 750 E is the re-created birthplace of **Wilbur Wright** (1867-1912), the pioneer of flight with his brother, Orville (1871-1948). He was born here April 16, 1867, son of **Bishop Milton and Susan (Koerner) Wright**. Orville Wright was born in Dayton, Ohio.

The Wright brothers became interested in aviation in the 1890s by Otto Lilienthal's gliders. Both were excellent mechanics and used a bicycle repair shop and factory for their early aircraft at Dayton (1892-1904). During this period they drew up tables of wind pressure and drift. On December 17, 1903, they made the first controlled, sustained flights in a power-driven aircraft at Kitty Hawk, North Carolina. They made four flights that day. The first, made by Orville, lasted 12 seconds. The

107

This marker on US 40 in Cambridge City identifies the location of the the home of General Solomon A. Meredith, commander of the Iron Brigade during the Civil War. Meredith was involved in Indiana politics.

The Wilbur Wright State Memorial, commemorating the aviation pioneer, is located northeast of Millville.

fourth, made by Wilbur, covered a distance of 852 feet in 59 seconds. They returned to Dayton and built several planes. In 1908, Orville made record-breaking flights in the United States while Wilbur repeated the feat in France to gain the brothers world fame. In 1909, the U.S. government accepted the Wright airplane for military use and the brothers established the Wright Company. The house where Orville was born and the bicycle repair shop and factory have been restored and moved to Greenfield Village, Michigan.

From Millville it is about six miles west on IN 39 to NEW CASTLE (pop. 18,500), county seat of Henry County, established June 1, 1822 and named for **Patrick Henry** of Virginia. New Castle was established in June, 1822.

Known as "The Rose City," the "American Beauty" rose was developed in a New Castle greenhouse. This rose won top honors at a National Flower Show.

The Maxwell-Briscoe auto, 1904-1925, was manufactured in New Castle and Tarrytown, New Jersey, by the Maxwell-Biscoe Motor Company from 1904 to 1913 when the company reorganized and moved to Detroit. The company was named for Jonathan Maxwell and Benjamin Briscoe who developed the car. The Lawter, 1909, was built by the Lawter Shredder Company.

**Frances M. Goodwin** (1855-1929) was a prominent sculptress. Her works can be found in the Indiana Statehouse, the

U.S. Capitol, Washington, D.C., and the Henry County Historical Society Museum. Another prominent artist from New Castle was **Helen M. Goodwin** (1865-1955).

**Herbert L. Heller,** another native, is the author of the multi-volume *"Historic Henry County."* His credentials are in education: professor at DePauw University and Baldwin-Wallace College, registrar of Hanover College, and Dean of Alaska Methodist University.

**Walter S. Chambers, Sr.** (1870-1950) worked as an editor, state legislator, and chairman of the Democratic Party in Indiana.

Twenty one persons were killed in the New Castle tornado of 1917. Other tragedies in Henry county include the cholera epidemic of 1833, the Dunreith train wreck in 1968, and the Kennard-Grant City tornado of 1974.

The citizens of the county displayed strong anti-slavery sentiment and many were abolitionists in the 1850s. The most famous of the hundreds of Henry Countians who fought for the Union cause during the Civil War was **Major General William Grose** (1812-1900). General Grose commanded the 36th Indiana Infantry Regiment during the Civil War. He was a successful attorney and served in the Indiana Senate.

**General Omar Bundy** (1861-1940), a native of New Castle, was a veteran of the Indian Wars, the Spanish-American War, the Philippine Insurrection, and a highly decorated officer during World War I.

**Brigadier General Bruce Harris** is another New Castle native. He served as Deputy Commanding General of the Signal Center at Ft. Gordon, Georgia; Deputy Assistant Secretary of Defense for Legislative Affairs, and Assistant Division Commander of the 9th Infantry Division at Ft. Lewis, Washington.

The **General William Grose House** (1870) 614 South 14th Street, today houses the HENRY COUNTY HISTORICAL MUSEUM. The home is listed on the NRHP. The museum contains the original furnishings when the Grose family resided here. Other exhibits preserve the heritage of the county and chronicle the changes in business, industry and the area. The museum is open from 1:00 to 4:30 p.m. Monday through Saturday. It is closed Sunday and on holidays. Admission is free.

New Castle is home of the INDIANA BASKETBALL HALL OF FAME MUSEUM, on Hall of Fame Court, east of IN 3. The Hall of Fame is a new $2.5 million facility that celebrates the history and excitement of Indiana high school basketball with displays of memorabilia, game films, and interactive exhibits. It was moved from Indianapolis in 1990. The Hall of Fame is open

Indiana's Basketball Hall of Fame Museum is located in New Castle.

from 10:00 a.m. to 5:00 p.m. Tuesday through Saturday and from 12:00 noon to 5:00 p.m. Sunday. It is closed Mondays, Thanksgiving, Christmas, and New Years. An admission is charged.

**Kent Benson**, a former Indiana "Mr. Basketball" and a member of Indiana University's NCAA championship in 1976, has been signed by the NBA Milwaukee Bucks and Detroit Pistons. He played high school basketball for New Castle Chrysler High School. **Steve Alford**, another Chrysler High School cage star, plays professionally with the NBA Dallas Mavericks.

The present court house, the third to occupy the court house square, was constructed 1865-69. Its claim to fame, other than its classic Victorian Italianate architecture, is that it is shown on the inside front cover of the 1948 best seller *"Raintree County."* The setting of the **Ross Lockridge, Jr.**, novel was Henry County. The author did much of his research in New Castle. The court house is listed on the NRHP.

**William O. Barnard** (1852-1939), a New Castle lawyer, served one term in the U.S. House of Representatives.

The **New Castle Archaeological Site**, on the grounds of the New Castle State Hospital, is also listed on the NRHP.

East of New Castle, just off US 36, is MOORELAND (pop. 479). In 1882, Miles Marshall Moore began selling lots to farmers who founded the town they named for Mr. Moore. The Stanley automobile was manufactured here in 1907 by the Stanley Automobile Manufacturing Company.

Former Mooreland resident **Crawford F. Parker** served as

111

Indiana Secretary of State and Lt. Governor of Indiana in 1957-1961. He was the Republican nominee for governor in 1960.

In the northwestern part of the county, on IN 236, is MIDDLETOWN (pop. 2,978). The town was laid out in 1829 and was named because of its location between New Castle and Anderson.

The LITTLE RED DOLL HOUSE, Rural Route 2, is a museum of dolls, stuffed animals, toys and antiques that fill a five room house. For information, call (317) 354-3453.

The **John W. Hedrick House** (1899), 506 High Street, is listed on the NRHP.

West of New Castle, just off IN 234, is SHIRLEY (pop. 919), platted in 1890 and named for Joseph A. Shirley, a railroad man.

The **Henry F. Whitlock House and Farm** (c. 1855), in the Shirley area is listed on the NRHP.

Returning to US 40 to the south it is a half dozen miles west from Cambridge City to LEWISVILLE (pop. 577), laid out in 1829 and named for the founder, **Lewis Freeman**.

**Marion Pierce**, while attending Lewisville High School (1957-61), scored 3,019 points in 94 games for a 32.1 point average, an individual record in the history of basketball for Indiana High Schools.

The **Guyer Opera House** (1902), has been restored for use for various programs. It is listed on the NRHP.

It is another 10 miles west on US 40 to KNIGHTSTOWN (pop. 2,325), laid out in 1827 and named for **John Knight**, one of the engineers involved in the construction of the National Road.

About mid-way between Lewisville and Knightstown, on the north side of the US 40, is a cement post marking the "Forty Mile" spot on the National Road where there was a large mudhole that created a number of wrecks during stage coach and wagon travel days.

Knightstown was hit hard in a smallpox epidemic in 1902.

**Charles A. Beard** (1874-1948), a graduate of Knightstown High School and Spiceland Academy, was known as the "Dean of American Historians" in his late years. He was a professor at Columbia University, a political scientist, and author of nearly 60 historical works.

**Clifford M. Hardin**, a Knightstown native, served as chancellor of the University of Nebraska and U.S. Secretary of Agriculture (1969-1971).

An early day automobile was manufactured in Knightstown—the Leader, 1906 to 1912 by the Leader Manufacturing Company. The car originated in McCordsville by the Columbia Electric Company in 1905.

Several scenes in the movie, *"Hoosiers,"* were shot at Knightstown Academy.

112

**Knightstown Academy** (1877), on Cary Street, is listed on the NRHP. Another NRHP structure is the **Elias Hinshaw House** (1877), 16 West Main Street. The **Knightstown Historic District** (1830-1936), is bounded by Morgan, Adams, Third, and McCullum Streets.

SPICELAND (pop. 940), two miles north of US 40 on IN 3, was platted in 1850 and named for the abundance of Spice Brush that grew in the area. It was the home of Spiceland Academy dating back to 1878.

A number of well-known personalities attended or graduated from the Academy. Among these:

**Howard Leigh** (1896-1981), an internationally famous lithographer, painter and archaeologist.

**Cortex A.M. Ewing**, considered one of the foremost politi-

This historical marker at Knightstown provides a brief description of the early-day National Road.

One of America's most beloved poets was James Whitcomb Riley shown here in his later years. (Photograph by Indiana Historical Society Library, Negative No. C5833.)

cal scientists in the United States. He served as a professor of government at the University of Oklahoma from 1928 until his death in 1962.

**William Lemuel Benedict**, professor at the University of Minnesota and head of the Section of Ophthalmology of Mayo

Clinic, Rochester, Minnesota, from 1917-1949.

Noted persons from the Spiceland area were **Elbridge Amos Stuart**, founder of the Carnation Milk Company in 1901 and **Gretchen Kiger Cryer**, broadway playwright, lyricist and recording artist.

Among other noted persons from Henry County are **James T. Hickman** (1867-1944), who invented such things as the strawberry box, camp stools and army cots, and a practical veneering machine; **Clessie Cummings**, founder of the Cummins Diesel Company at Columbus, Indiana, and credited with refining the diesel engine; **Howard McCormick** (1875-1943), a prominent artist and illustrator; **Helen Magner**, artist and illustrator who specialized in water colors; **Moses M. Hodson** (1855-1941) the rustic poet often referred to as "Mose the Miller;" **Luther G. Snyder**, first state geologist for Oklahoma; **Benjamin S. Parker,** poet, editor, legislator and diplomat; and one-time Henry County Circuit Court judge **Edward L. Jackson** (1873-1955) who became the 32nd governor of Indiana.

Continuing west on US 40 a dozen miles is GREENFIELD (pop. 11,299), county seat of Hancock County and birthplace of the Hoosier Poet **James Whitcomb Riley**. Greenfield was settled in 1828 and incorporated in 1850. Hancock County was established March 1, 1828 and named in honor of **John Hancock**, a signer of the Declaration of Independence.

James Whitcomb Riley was born one of six children to **Reuben** and **Elizabeth Marine Riley**. His father was a lawyer. The Riley children included John Andrew, 1844; Martha Celestia, 1847; James Whitcomb, October 7, 1849; Elva May, 1856; Alexander Humboldt (who died as a young man); and Mary Elizabeth, 1864. During his life time, he wrote more than 1,000 poems, the best loved were those written about his childhood. Among the collections of his verse are *"Rhymes of Childhood "* (1890), *"An Old Sweetheart of Mine "* (1902), and *"Knee Deep in June "* (1912). The Brandywine Creek flows through a memorial park in Greenfield and it was made famous by Riley's poem *"The Old Swimmin' Hole."* Before devoting himself completely to his poetry, he tried the careers of traveling actor, sign painter, and finally newspaperman. His father would have been more pleased if he had taken up law.

JAMES WHITCOMB RILEY BOYHOOD HOME AND MUSEUM, 250 West Main Street, contains some of the original family furniture. The home is listed on the NRHP. It is open from 10:00 a.m. to 4:00 p.m. Monday through Friday and from 1:00 to 4:00 p.m. Sunday, March 1 to December 22. An admission is charged.

The OLD LOG JAIL AND CHAPEL IN THE PARK MUSEUMS are located in Riley Park and are operated by the Hancock County Historical Society. The Old Log Jail dates back to 1853.

James Whitcomb Riley grew into manhood in this house in Greenfield. Today it houses the James Whitcomb Riley Museum.

These museums are only open on the weekends. For information, call (317) 462-7780.

The **Lilly Biological Laboratories** (1914), west of Greenfield off US 40, and the **Greenfield Courthouse Square Historic District** (1835-1935), bounded by North, Hinchman, South, and Pennsylvania Streets, are also listed on the NRHP.

From Greenfield both US 40 and I-70 run through Indianapolis (Section 2) and on the west side of the capital US 40 runs parallel to I-70 on the north.

The two highways enter Hendricks County southwest of Indianapolis. The county seat is DANVILLE (pop. 4,220) on US 36. (Chapter 3). The county, named in honor of **William Hendricks**, Indiana governor and senator, was established April 1, 1824; Danville was designated as the county seat and incorporated in 1835.

Danville once was the home of **Canterbury/Central Normal College** that graduated many Indiana teachers.

About 10 miles out of Indianapolis on US 40, is PLAINFIELD (pop. 9,191). The town was laid out in 1831 by Elias Hadley and Levi Jessup and incorporated in 1839.

It was here **Thomas Paine Westendorf**, an official at the Indiana Boys' School, wrote the song, *"I'll Take You Home Again, Kathleen."* His wife had gone to visit in New York and he wrote

116

The Society of Friends (the Quakers) have been meeting annually here in Plainfield since 1858. The Quaker records are stored in the Depository, built on this site in 1873.

the song for her.

The **Friends Meetinghouse** is identified with a historical marker on the grounds. The marker is visible driving east on US 40. The organization of the Society of Friends has meetings for worship and monthly, quarterly, and annual meetings. The Friends, also known as the Quakers, originated in England in the middle of the 17th century under George Fox.

The stage, screen and TV actor **Forrest Tucker** was born in Plainfield.

Thirteen miles west of Plainfield on US 40, is STILESVILLE (pop. 350). The **Melville F. McHaffie Farm** (1870-1872), on US 40 is listed on the NRHP.

Interstate-70 cuts across the northwestern corner of Morgan County, established on February 15, 1822. MOORESVILLE (pop. 5,493), laid out in 1824 by its founder Samuel Moore, is four miles off I-70 on IN 267.

The Indiana State Flag was designed by **Paul Hadley**, a well-known water color artist who lived in Mooresville for many years. The Daughters of the American Revolution sponsored a contest and prize for a design of a state flag. Hadley's design was selected by the General Assembly in 1917. Set on a field of blue, the torch in the center stands for liberty and understanding. The rays emanating from the torch represent the influence of both. The outer circle of stars represent the original 13 states of the United States, the inner circle of stars represent the next five states admitted to the union, and Indiana, the nineteenth state, is represented by the large star. The design is gold. Paul Hadley died in Richmond in 1971 and is buried in Crown Hill Cemetery in Indianapolis.

**John Dillinger**, who made headlines as a notorious bank robber in the early Depression years, stole a car in Mooresville July 21, 1923 and drove it 17 miles north of Indianapolis where he abandoned it. He was never arrested for this incident. The John Wilson Dillinger family moved from the Oak Hill section in Indianapolis to a farm in the Mooresville area when son John Herbert was in his early teens. The teenager entered high school in Mooresville. After he was killed by FBI agents in Chicago in July 1934, his body was claimed by his father and returned to the E. F. Harvey Funeral Home in Mooresville. The funeral was held at the home of his sister, Audrey Hancock, in Maywood and he was buried in the family plot beside his mother in Crown Hill Cemetery in Indianapolis.

The **Mooresville Friends Academy Building** (1861), 244 North Monroe Street, is listed on the NRHP.

The county seat of Morgan County is MARTINSVILLE (pop.11,311), south of I-70 some 15 miles on IN 39. The county, named for Virginian **Daniel Morgan**, an Indian fighter and Revolutionary War soldier, was established February 15, 1822. Martinsville was platted in 1833 and incorporated in 1905.

John Dillinger was arrested for an attempted robbery of a Martinsville grocery store in September, 1924. He often dated girls from Martinsville and played shortstop on the local baseball team. He was sentenced to concurrent terms of two to 14 years for attempted robbery and 10 to 20 years for conspiracy to commit a felony and sent to Indiana State Reformatory at Pendleton and later was transferred to Indiana State Prison in Michigan City. At the time of his 1924 arrest, Dillinger was considered somewhat of a talented athlete by some accounts. He was released from prison for this crime on May 22, 1933.

There are two structures in the Martinsville area listed on the NRHP–**Martinsville High School Gymnasium** (1924), 759 South Main Street, and **Cross School** (1856), Voiles and Townsend Roads.

Both highways cross Putnam County, named in honor of **Israel Putnam,** Indian fighter and general in the Continental Army, established on April 1, 1822. The county seat is GREENCASTLE (pop. 8,403) founded c. 1823 and incorporated in 1849.

It is home of **DePauw University** founded in 1832 by the Methodists. The university was initially called **Indiana Asbury College** but was renamed DePauw University in 1884 in honor of **Charles Washington De Pauw** of New Albany who donated over $300,000 to the school to keep it afloat.

John Dillinger, paroled from Indiana State Prison at Michigan City in May 1933, went on a robbery spree that lasted from June to September. He was arrested and sent to jail in Lima, Ohio. He was taken from jail by 10 escaped convicts from the

118

DePauw University in Greencastle was founded as Indiana Asbury College but was renamed for a benefactor in 1884.

Indiana State Prison who in the course of their escape, killed the sheriff on October 12, 1933. Eleven days later the gang robbed the Central Bank of Greencastle of $75,346.

There are several buildings in Greencastle listed on the NRHP–**East College of DePauw University** (1869-1882), 300 Simpson Street; **McKim Observatory** (1884), **DePauw University**, Depauw and Highbridge Avenues; **F. P. Nelson House** (1875), 701 East Seminary; **Lycurgus Stoner House** (1884), Manhattan Road; **William C. VanArsdale House** (1907), 125 Wood Street; and **Appleyard (Alexander Stevenson Farm)** (1843-1889), IN 240.

Returning from Newcastle on US 231, it is west two miles on US 40 to PUTNAMVILLE (unincorporated). The **Putnamville Presbyterian Church, (Putnamville Methodist Church)** (1834), on IN 243 is listed on the NRHP.

South of Putnamville 25 miles is SPENCER (pop. 2,732), county seat of Owen County, established January 1, 1819 and named for **Colonel Abraham Owen**, a Kentucky officer mortally wounded at the battle of Tippecanoe November, 1811. The town, platted in 1820, was named for **Captain Spier Spencer,** killed in the battle of Tippecanoe.

Hickam Field, the air base in Hawaii attacked by the Japanese on December 7, 1941, was named in honor of **Horace Hickam**, a pioneer military aviation authority, and a native of Spencer.

James **"Babe" Pierce**, a native of Owen County, starred in the last silent *"Tarzan "* movie, *"Tarzan and the Golden Lion,"* then became the radio voice of "Tarzan." Edgar Rice Burrough's daughter, Joan, was the radio voice of the character "Jane" and she and Babe Pierce were married in 1932. Burrough was the creator of "Tarzan."

The **Spencer Town Hall and Fire Station** (1898), 84 South Washington Street, and **David Enoch Beem House** (1874), 635 West Hillside Avenue, are listed on the NRHP. The **Ennis Archaeological Site** is also listed on the Register. The dig is in southeastern Owen County (the exact location is not given and it is not open to the public) and contains materials used by Indians for their tools and weapons as far back as 8000 BC.

"Spirit of The American Doughboy," a sculpture created by the late **E.M. Viquesney** (1876-1946), stands in the courthouse square in Spencer and is one of more than 140 such statues seen on courthouse lawns, parks and public squares throughout the nation. Viquesney copyrighted the design in 1920. He also created "The Infantry Trophy" for the U.S. Infantry Association.

Ten miles northeast of Spencer, via US 231 and IN 67, is GOSPORT (pop. 729), settled early in the 1800s, platted in 1829, and incorporated in 1865. Originally called Goss Port, it was a major port for shipping salt pork to New Orleans.

A stone bas-relief marker on the highway in Gosport commemorates the famous **Ten O'Clock Treaty Line** signed by William Henry Harrison and the leaders of the Pottawatomi, Delaware, Eel River, and Miami Indian tribes in 1809.

This treaty, signed at Fort Wayne, gave white settlers a section of what is now Indiana lying along the present Indiana-Illinois state line south to a point just west of Seymour, a few feet off US 50, in Jackson County. The boundary was established along the line of "a shadow cast by an Indian spear stuck in the ground at 10 o'clock in the morning." Surveyors frequently had to convince the Indians they were following such a line by setting up their instruments and placing a spear in the ground at that time in the morning.

The marker in Gosport was carved by **Frederic Hollis**, an Owen County artist and sculptor.

Northwest of Spencer, via IN 46 and 246, is PATRICKSBURG (unincorporated). **Governor Sam Ralston** grew up here.

Listed on the NRHP is the **Moffett-Ralston House** (1864), located 1.5 miles northeast of Patricksburg on Bixler Road.

Back on US 40 at Putnamville it is 15 miles west to BRAZIL (pop. 7,852), county seat of Clay County, established April 1, 1825. The county was named in honor of Kentucky **Senator Henry Clay**. The town became Brazil, after the South American country, in 1844 when a name was needed for a post office designation. The town was incorporated in 1866 and chartered in 1873.

The court house was moved from Bowling Green to Brazil in 1877.

**James Riddle "Jimmy" Hoffa**, the national labor leader, was born in Brazil in 1913. He began his union organizing efforts in 1932 and rose swiftly in the ranks of the International Brotherhood of Teamsters. By 1952, he became international vice president and five years later succeeded David Beck as president of the union. The Teamsters were expelled from the AFL-CIO in 1957 because of charges of corruption. Hoffa, under supervision by a three-man board of monitors, was reelected Teamster president in 1961. The following year he was indicted by a federal grand jury which charged he had accepted more than a million dollar in illegal payments from a Detroit truck company. A mistrial was declared in 1963. Hoffa resigned in 1971 and disappeared in 1975.

Other well-known personalities from the area are **Oliver Cromwell** (1774-1855), first Indiana statesman; **George Craig**, governor of Indiana, 1953-57; **Orville Redenbacher**, gourmet popcorn king; and **Colonel David Eberly**, first POW of the 1991 Persian Gulf War. **Johnnie "Scatman" Davis**, a musician and film actor, was born in Brazil in 1910.

In 1953 an unusual and extraordinary gift was presented to the people of Brazil, Indiana, by the country of Brazil, in South America. An exact size replica of the **Chafariz dos Contos (Fountain of Tales)** monument was given to the City of Brazil by the Republic of Brazil. The original sculpture is located in the ancient city of Oura Preto, Minas Garaes, Brazil. The gift was arranged by Brazilian President **Enrico Gaspar Dutro**. Dedication of the monument was held May 26, 1956 with the dedicatory address delivered by Brazilian Ambassador **Joan Muniz**. Governor **George Craig**, a Brazil (Indiana) native, and Mayor **Ted McCoy** accepted the gift for the City of Brazil. The monument is located in Forest Park on IN 59 South.

CLAY COUNTY HISTORICAL SOCIETY MUSEUM, 100 East National Avenue, is located in the old Brazil Post Office building and emphasizes county heritage. It is open from 1:00 to 4:00 p.m. weekends and on weekdays by appointment during the summer months. Admission is free.

HISTORIC PIONEER CABINS, in Forest Park, features two log cabins built around 1858 in Jackson Township in Clay County. These were dismantled log by log, moved to Forest Park, and restored around 1959. The west cabin is furnished to represent a typical home of that period. The east cabin is used to display artifacts. These are open from 1:00 to 4:00 p.m. weekends during the summer months. Admission is free.

**The Poland Presbyterian Church** (1869, 1893), on IN 42

and County Road 56S, Poland, east of I-70 at the IN 59 exit and east on IN 42 is listed on the NRHP. The religious heritage of Clay County is represented by the Poland Historical Chapel. It was organized by Presbyterians and dedicated in 1869.

From Brazil it is 18 miles to TERRE HAUTE (pop. 57,400), county seat of Vigo County, established on February 15, 1818. Fort Harrison, three miles north of Terre Haute, was built in 1811 and a settlement developed around the fort. The fort was successfully defended against an Indian attack in 1812 by Captain Zachary Taylor. The town was platted in 1816 and incorporated in 1832. Terre haute are the French words meaning "high ground."

Vigo County was named in honor of **Colonel Francis Vigo** (1740-1836), the financial backer of the expedition led by George Rogers Clark. Vigo's estate was eventually reimbursed for the loan of $8,616 to General Clark.

**Indiana State University** began here in 1870 as Indiana Normal College. **Rose-Hulman Institute of Technology,** an independent engineering school that ranks among the top three engineering schools in the country, was founded in 1874 as the Terre Haute School of Industrial Science by Chauncey Rose. In the small village of St. Mary-of-the-Woods, just north of Terre Haute, Mother Theodore Guerin and a tiny band of French nuns founded **Saint Mary-of-the-Woods College,** a women's liberal arts college, in 1840.

The National Road (today designated as US 40) from Washington, D.C. to Terre Haute was completed in 1838. By 1839, 12 stage lines operated over the National Road and it served as an important transportation link for the following two decades. The **Wabash & Erie Canal** reached Terre Haute in 1849 to open trade as far away as the eastern seaboard.

During the Civil War, Vigo was one of 30 counties that suffered violence at the hands of draft resisters. The Terre Haute newspaper presses were wrecked as a result of this violence.

Several strikes in Terre Haute have attracted nationwide attention. A nine month coal miners strike occurred in 1922. A general strike, involving as many as 26,000 persons, occurred in 1935 when a company that was struck imported 58 professional strikebreakers into its plant. The 600 workers at the Columbian Enameling & Stamping Company had been on strike since March 23 when the company sent for the strikebreakers on July 18, 1935. The general strike was called for July 22 and ended two days later. In the meantime the governor declared martial law and ordered 2,000 National Guardsmen into the city. In an incident, 1,800 strikers were tear gassed by the troops. Martial law was not lifted until February, 1936.

A high security federal prison was dedicated and opened in October, 1940.

The **Hulman Field Air National Guard Base** operates from the Hulman Regional Airport at Terre Haute. The 181st Tactical Fighter Group and 113th Tactical Fighter Squadron stationed here are to maintain combat readiness in support of tactical forces of the U.S. Air Force.

The Overland automobile, 1903-1929, was manufactured from 1903 to 1905 by the Standard Wheel Company in Terre Haute before moving to Indianapolis.

Several nationally known personalities are natives of Terre Haute. Probably the best-known is **Eugene Victor Debs** (1855-1926), the American Socialist Party leader.

Debs quit school when he was 15 years old and went to work for the railroad. In 1884, he served in Indiana legislature. He became involved in the labor movement and moved swiftly to a leadership role when he became the national secretary and treasurer of the Brotherhood of Locomotive Firemen. He resigned in 1892 and a year later formed the American Railway Workers Union, embracing all railroad workers, and then ordered a strike against the Pullman Company and the railroads in Chicago the next year. President Grover Cleveland ordered federal troops into Chicago to put down the strike against the railroads, alleging interference with the U.S. mail service. Debs was sentenced to a six month jail term for refusing to comply with a federal court injunction. He came out of jail a confirmed Socialist and ran for the U.S. presidency five times—1900, 1904, 1908, 1912, and 1920— as a Socialist candidate. During World War I he made a speech condemning the war and was convicted under the Espionage Law in 1918 and sentenced to 10 years in prison. His run for the presidency in 1920 was while he was in prison. The sentence was commuted on Christmas Day, in 1921, by President Warren Harding. Debs was inducted into the Labor Hall of Fame, Washington, D.C. in 1990.

The HOME OF EUGENE V. DEBS, 451 North Eighth Street, built in 1890 as Eugene Debs' residence until his death, is maintained as a historical museum. It is now surrounded by the campus of Indiana State University. The home is open from 1:00 to 4:30 p.m. Wednesday through Sunday. Admission is free. For other information, call (812) 232-2163. The Debs Home Museum is a State and National Historic Landmark.

Novelist **Theodore Dreiser** (1871-1945) was also born in Terre Haute. The family moved from Terre Haute in 1874. He began his writing career working for midwestern newspapers before going to New York where he wrote for magazines. His first novel, *"Sister Carrie,"* was released in 1900 and his second, *"Jennie Gerhardt,"* in 1911. He is best known for his novel *"An American Tragedy "* published in 1925.

**Paul Dresser** (1858-1906), the songwriter, was his brother. When he was 15 years old he was sent to St. Meinrad Academy

123

Socialist Eugene Debs ran five times for President. (Photograph by Indiana Historical Society Library, Negative No. C2283.).

to study for the priesthood. He grew restless and finally ran away, changed his name to Dresser, and joined a medicine show. In 1892 he joined a music publishing firm in New York and turned out such hits at the time as *"Just Tell Them That You Saw Me," "The Blue and the Gray,"* and *"On the Banks of the Wabash, Far Away,"* the Indiana state song. In his day, he was considered one of the most popular song writers in the country.

PAUL DRESSER HOME is owned and operated as a museum by the Vigo County Historical Society. It is open from 1:00 to 4:00 p.m. Sundays during the summer months. Open at other times by special arrangement, call (812) 235-9717 for information. Admission is free.

**Daniel Wolsey Voorhees** (1827-1897), as a U.S. Senator, was noted for his debating abilities. His defense of John Brown, John Cook and others for the attack on Harpers Ferry before the Civil War brought him national fame. He is buried in Highland Lawn Cemetery in Terre Haute.

**Colonel Richard W. Thompson** (1809-1900), Secretary

This was the Terre Haute home of Eugene Debs, the internationally-known American Socialist Party leader and labor organizer.

of the Navy under President Rutherford B. Hayes, was a native son and is also buried in Highland Lawn Cemetery.

**John Palmer Usher** (1816-1889), a prominent local attorney, became Secretary of Interior under President Abraham Lincoln.

**Colonel William E. McLean** was appointed to the eight-member tribunal near the end of the Civil War to courtmartial members of the Knights of the Golden Circle for treason, a case scholars study today for constitutional law.

**Thomas Henry Nelson** (1820-1896) was appointed ambassador to Chile by President Abraham Lincoln and served from 1861 to 1866. In 1869 President Ulysses S. Grant appointed Nelson ambassador to Mexico where he served until 1873.

**Cynthia Shepard Perry** is only the fifth black woman to be named a foreign ambassador in the history of the United States. She served as U.S. ambassador to Sierra Leone, West Africa under President Ronald Reagan and ambassador to Burundi under President George Bush.

**Major Orlando J. Smith** (1842-1908), a journalist and Civil War veteran, was the founder and first president of The Associated Press. He was born in Terre Haute on June 14, 1842.

**Charles Cruft** (1826-1883) was the only Terre Haute native to achieve the rank of brigadier general during the Civil War. He was wounded twice at the Battle Shiloh and saw action in several other campaigns.

**James Whitcomb** (1795-1852) was practicing law in Terre Haute when he was elected governor in 1843 and served two terms.

**Max Ehrmann** (1872-1945), the poet, was born in Terre Haute. A life long resident, Ehrmann was the author of world favorites, *"A Prayer"* and *"Desiderata."* Among others notables are **Claude Bowers** (1878-1958), historian and diplomat; **Janet Scudder**, sculptor; **Alice Fischer**, noted stage actress; **Lyman Abbott**, minister, author, and magazine editor; **Gilbert Wilson**, muralist; **Anthony "Skeets" Gallagher**, stage and screen comedian; and **Benjamin Sherman "Scatman" Crothers**, a singer and musician initially who appeared in numerous movies and TV shows.

**James Farrington Gookins** (1840-1904), a Terre Haute native, was one of the great painters of the latter 1800s, his works housed in museums throughout the world.

**Anton "Tony" Hulman** (1901-1977), a resident of Terre Haute, purchased the Indianapolis Motor Speedway from Eddie Rickenbacher in 1945. His name is synonymous with the Indianapolis "500" returning it to the grandeur of its heyday after several years of neglect. He also provided land for what became the Hulman Regional Airport.

**Leroy A. Wilson**, born February 21, 1901 in Terre Haute,

epitomized the "American Dream," rising from obscurity as a traffic clerk of the world's biggest company to become its president. Wilson, after 27 years with the company, became president of American Telegraph & Telephone Company (AT&T) in 1948. He died June 28, 1951 at the age of 50 and is buried in Highland Lawn Cemetery.

**Claude Thornhill**, band leader during the Big Band Era, was born in Terre Haute August 10, 1909.

**Ellen Church Marshall** of Terre Haute was the world's first airline stewardess.

Three Terre Hauteans gained national fame on the basketball court. **Terry Dischinger** won a gold medal as a starting forward with the U.S. Olympic team in 1960. He then went on to play for several NBA professional teams. Others include **Bobby "Slick" Leonard**, a star for the Minneapolis Lakers and Chicago Bulls; and **Clyde Lovellette**, a standout for the Boston Lakers after a sensational career at Kansas.

Baseball Hall of Famer **Mordicai "Three Fingered" Brown** pitched the Chicago Cubs to four pennants between 1906 and 1910. **Max "Scoop" Carey** (1890-1976), born Max Carnarius, held the National League record for career steals (738), which stood until broken by Lou Brock of St. Louis. Carey achieved many early records and was elected to the Hall of Fame in 1961. Other baseball greats from Terre Haute are **Tommy John**, who pitched in the World Series with the Los Angeles Dodgers in 1977 and with the New York Yankees in 1981; **Art Nehf**, who pitched in a dozen World Series games and when the New York Giants paid him $55,000 in 1919 the highest salary, at the time, ever paid by a team; and **Paul H. "Dizzy" Trout**, a pitcher in the major leagues during the World War II era and appeared in two World Series.

**Paul Moss** played two years in the National Football League, first with the Pittsburgh Pirates (later the Steelers) in 1933, then with the St. Louis Gunners that replaced the Cincinnati team in the NFL in 1934.

**Charles Bernard "Bud" Taylor** (1903-1962) was the bantamweight boxing champion of the world in 1927 and then vacated the title in 1928 to fight in the featherweight division. Known as "The Blonde Terror," Taylor was elected to the Helms Hall of Fame in 1956.

**Greg Bell** of Terre Haute won the gold medal in the long jump in the 1956 Olympic Games.

**Bryan Leturgez**, born August 3, 1962 in Terre Haute, participated in the 1992 Winter Olympics as the pusher for the U.S. bobsled team.

The infamous Bonnie and Clyde of the Barrows gang spent several days in hiding in Terre Haute in March 1934 after their wild escapes across Texas, Oklahoma, Kansas, Iowa, and Mis-

127

souri. They appeared openly in shops and restaurants during their stay.

HISTORICAL MUSEUM OF WABASH VALLEY, 1411 South Sixth Street, presents area history and heritage through exhibits and memorabilia. The museum is open from 1:00 to 4:00 p.m. Tuesday through Sunday. It is closed during the month of January. Admission is free.

SHELDON SWOPE ART MUSEUM, 25 South Seventh Street, features a permanent art collection and also presents traveling exhibits periodically. Among some of the works to be found here are by Grant Wood, Thomas Hart Benton, Edward Hopper, Mary Fairchild MacMonnies, Andy Warhol, and Marc Chagall. The museum is open from 10:00 a.m. to 5:00 p.m. Tuesday through Friday, and from 12:00 noon to 5:00 p.m. weekends. Admission is free.

CHILDREN'S AND SCIENCE TECHNOLOGY MUSEUM, 523 Wabash Avenue, in downtown Terre Haute, provides exhibits and and displays, both static and rotating, many of which provide hands-on experiences for children. It is open from 9:00 a.m. to 4:00 p.m. Tuesday through Saturday. An admission is charged.

TERRE HAUTE BREWERY AND CIVIL WAR MUSEUM, Ninth Street and Poplar (IN 42), includes the E. Bleemel Flour & Feed operated as a brewery during the period 1862 and 1874. The museum is located on the second floor of the General Store and contains detailed information about the brewery. Civil War items include Civil War prints and photographs as well as several oil paintings and a field journal owned by Captain George Farrington. This complex is open from 10:30 a.m. to 5:30 p.m. Monday and Tuesday and Thursday through Friday, from 12:00 noon to 4:00 p.m. Sunday. It is closed on Wednesday.

The following in Terre Haute are listed on the NRHP–**Allen Chapel African Episcopal Church** (1913), 224 Crawford Street; **Collett Park** (1890-1904), North Seventh Street and Maple Avenue; **Condit House** (1860), 629 Mulberry Street on Indiana State University campus; **Eugene V. Debs House** (c. 1885), 451 North Eighth Street (also designated a National Historic Landmark); **Paul Dresser Birthplace** (1859), First and Farrington Streets; **Fire Station No. 9** (1906), 1728 South Eighth Street; **Foley Hall** (1860-1897), St. Mary of the Woods College campus, off US 50; **Highland Lawn Cemetery** (1864-1940), 4520 Wabash Avenue; **Markle House and Mill Site** (1817, 1849), 4900 Mill Dam Road; **Old State Bank of Indiana (Memorial Hall)** (1834), 219 Ohio Street; **Sage-Robinson-Nagel House** (1868), 1411 South Sixth Street; and **Williams-Warren-Zimmerman House** (c. 1859), 904 South Fourth Street.

North of Terre Haute 25 miles, via US 41, is ROCKVILLE (pop. 2,785), county seat of Parke County. The county was

Billie Creek Village replicates a turn-of-the-century Indiana village in Rockville.

established on April 2, 1821 and was named in honor of **Judge Benjamin Parke**, attorney general for the Indiana Territory and a U.S. District Judge. Rockville was settled in 1823 and incorporated in 1854.

In 1820, the Wea Indians sold their last lands in Indiana at the mouth of Raccoon Creek in Parke County.

**Joseph A. Wright**, the 10th governor of Indiana, began his law practice in Rockville at the age of 20.

The county has the largest concentration of preserved covered bridges in the nation—32. Wooden bridges were first covered shortly after 1800 when builders discovered their bridges last far longer when the structural beams were protected from the weather. The trend, which started in the New England area, soon moved west with the pioneers to the Midwest.

Detailed maps, needed to find some of the back road covered bridges, are available at the old railroad depot, housing the Parke County Convention and Visitors Bureau, in Rockville. The Visitors Bureau is open 9:00 a.m. to 4:00 p.m. Monday through Saturday and 10:00 a.m. to 3:00 p.m. Sunday during the summer and 9:00 a.m. to 4:00 p.m. weekdays the year-round. Bridge hunters can follow one of five marked routes through the county, or can pick and choose among the bridges and other historic sites. Most bridges are still open to traffic. All are listed on the NRHP.

Parke County Incorporated hosts the annual Covered Bridge Festival (held 10 days in October) that draws over a million visitors annually. For schedules and other information write to

Two of the more than 30 covered bridges in Parke County are shown here. Above is perhaps on of the most photographed of the covered bridges, the Bridgeton bridge. Below is the Mansfield covered bridge in Parke County.

the Visitors Bureau, P.O. 165, Rockville, IN 47872 or call (317) 569-5226.

Covered bridges in the Rockville area: **Billie Creek Bridge** (1895), crosses Williams Creek; **Bowsher Ford Bridge** (1915), crosses Mill Creek; **Catlin Bridge** (1907), is on the Parke County Golf Course; **Cox Ford Bridge** (1913), crosses Sugar Creek; **Jackson Bridge** (1861), crosses Sugar Creek; **Marshall Bridge** (1917), crosses Rush Creek; **Mill Creek Bridge** (1907), crosses Mill Creek; **Narrows Bridge** (1882), crosses Sugar Creek; **Rush Creek Bridge** (1904), crosses Rush Creek; **State Sanitorium Bridge** (1913), crosses Little Raccoon Creek; and **Wilkins Mill Bridge** (1906), crosses Sugar Mill Creek.

Bridges in the Mecca area: **Harry Evans Bridge** (1908), crosses Rock Run Creek; **Mecca Bridge** (1873), crosses the Big Raccoon Creek; **Roseville Bridge** (1910), crosses Big Raccoon Creek; **Thorpe Ford Bridge** (1912), crosses Big Raccoon Creek; and **Zacke Cox Bridge** (1908), crosses Rock Run Creek.

Bridges in the Montezuma area: **Leatherwood Station Bridge** (1899), moved to Billie Creek Village in 1981; **Melcher Bridge** (1896), crosses Leatherwood Creek; **Phillips Bridge** (1909), crosses Big Pond Creek; **Sim Smith Bridge** (1883), crosses Leatherwood Creek; and **West Union Bridge** (1876), crosses Sugar Creek.

Bridges in the Bridgeton area: **Bridgeton Bridge** (1868), crosses the Big Raccoon Creek; **Conley's Ford Bridge** (1907), crosses the Big Raccoon Creek; **Crooks Bridge** (1856), crosses the Little Raccoon Creek; **Jeffries Ford Bridge** (1915), crosses the Little Raccoon Creek; **McAllister Bridge** (1914), crosses the Little Raccoon Creek; **Neet Bridge** (1904), crosses the Little Raccoon Creek; and the **Nevins Bridge** (1920), crosses the Little Raccoon Creek.

Bridges in the Mansfield area: **Big Rocky Fork Bridge** (1900), crosses Big Rocky Fork, and **Mansfield Bridge** (1867), crosses the Big Raccoon Creek.

Bridges in the Marshall area: **Beeson Bridge** (1906), moved to Billie Creek Village in 1980, and **Portland Mills Bridge** (1856), crosses Little Raccoon Creek.

In Rockville it is a mile east to BILLIE CREEK VILLAGE, a typical turn-of-the-century Hoosier village assembled from 38 historic buildings brought from throughout the county. A blacksmith is at work at the smithy shop, a horse-drawn wagon will transport visitors to the old farmstead. Among the other old buildings is the little red schoolhouse, log cabin and three covered bridges. The staff here dress in period costumes. A stone statue of Governor Joseph Albert Wright stands along side his home, moved to Billie Creek Village. The general store is open from 10:00 a.m. to 4:00 p.m. daily, except Christmas week. An admission is charged during all events weekends from Memorial

Day through Halloween weekend; free on week days except during school days and during the Parke County Covered Bridge Festival.

The PARKE COUNTY MUSEUM, on US 36, east off US 41 in Rockville, houses displays and memorabilia focusing on county history. It is open from 1:00 to 4:00 p.m. daily from Memorial Day to mid-October. An admission is charged.

The Parke County Museum, on US 36 in Rockville, is in a building dating back to 1839 and has seen many uses over time.

In Turkey Run State Park, north of Rockville, is the **Narrows Bridge** that spans a rocky gorge over Sugar Creek. Near the bridge on one of the Sugar Creek channels, **Captain Salmon Lusk**, who first built a grist mill on the creek in 1826, built a brick home for his family overlooking the creek in 1841. The home has been restored to the time period, complete with furnishings from the 1840s and 1850s. It is open by special arrangements for tours during the summer months.

The mill in Mansfield is a veritable museum of mechanical implements from earlier times. It is open from 12:00 noon to 5:00 p.m. Wednesday through Friday, and 9:00 a.m. to 5:00 p.m. weekends. Tours are free. The Mansfield Bridge, constructed by bridge builder Joseph J. Daniels, boasts the longest span in the country. It is 247 feet long and is a twin-span, burr arch bridge.

Another perfectly preserved water mill is found in Bridgeton, to the west. Here, the old **Weise Mill**, dating back to 1823, holds worn burr stones used to grind wheat, corn, buckwheat and rye, used by housewives for decades to bake bread and pies for the small town.

South of Rockville 11 miles on US 41 is CLINTON (pop. 5,267), scene of a bank robbery December 16, 1930. Led by **Herman K. Lamm**, a gang that included Walter Dietrich, later to become a member of the John Dillinger gang of bank robbers, robbed the Citizens State Bank of $15,567. Through several mishaps the robbers did not make a clean getaway and were captured during their escape just across the Illinois state line. Lamm and a fellow gang member were killed by law officers and another gang member committed suicide when the officers closed in on them. Lamm had designed a "timing" system for robbing banks, a system passed on in prison to John Dillinger by Walter Dietrich. Dillinger used the system successfully during his spree of bank robberies in 1933 and 1934.

South of Terre Haute 25 miles via US 41 and 150 is SULLIVAN (pop. 4,774), county seat of Sullivan County, established January 15, 1817. The county and city were named for Indian fighter **Daniel Sullivan**, an army courier killed by Indians while carrying dispatches for General George Rogers Clark. The county seat was platted in 1842.

A plaque at the Sullivan County Courthouse honors **Antoinette Leach**, the first woman in Indiana to practice law.

Sullivan is near the center of the Indiana coal mining district and scene of a gas explosion in 1925 that killed 51 miners.

**William Harrison Hays** (1879-1954), a politician and motion-picture executive, was born in Sullivan. He served as chairman of the Republican National Committee from 1918-21. He was appointed Postmaster General (1921-22) by President Warren G. Harding. As president (1922-45) of the Motion Picture Producers and Distributors of America, he administered

133

the motion-picture moral code—*The Hays Code*—which was promulgated in 1934 by agreement of the leaders in the industry.

SULLIVAN HISTORICAL SOCIETY MUSEUM, 10 South Court Street, focuses on local and county history in is exhibits and displays. It is open from 8:00 a.m. to 4:00 p.m. weekdays. It is closed weekends. Donations are accepted.

North of Sullivan five miles is SHELBURN (pop. 1,281). Near the town is Morrison Creek where in 1815 Lieutenant John Morrison and four of his soldiers were killed while they were sleeping.

Near unincorporated Fairbanks, west of Shelburn on IN 63, is the site of of an Indian ambush in which Lieutenant Henry Fairbanks and all but three of his detail of men were killed. The soldiers were transporting supplies to Captain Zachary Taylor at Fort Harrison.

South west of Sullivan is MEROM on the Wabash River at IN 54 and 63. It is home of the United Church of Christ Merom Conference Center. First established in 1859 as Union Christian College, it was one of the first co-educational, interracial colleges in the country. Merom is said to have been a busy port on the Wabash River in its earliest history.

The Wabash Valley Correctional Center north of CARLISLE (pop. 714) is a state maximum security prison. A medium security facility is planned at this same location in the future. Carlisle is 11 miles south of Sullivan just off US 41.

The **Sherman Building** (1916), 2-4 South Court Street, Sullivan, is listed on the NRHP. South west of Sullivan is Merom, on the Wabash River, that has two listings on the NRHP—**Union Christian Church** (1863), Third and Philip Streets, and **Merom Site and Fort Azatlan**, north of town. The other site in Sullivan County listed on the NRHP is the **Daugherty-Monroe Archaeological Site**.

# Chapter 5
# East/West on I-80/I-90

*This route is a quick one to drive through Indiana to Ohio and east or Illinois and west. Taking some exits along the way will provide visitors some unusual and interesting sights. For example, this is an excellent opportunity to get a glimpse of Amish life styles.*

# During the Period of Two Wars

As the 19th century was coming to a close, the nation would soon be facing war, twice in less than 20 years. Indiana was involved in both encounters.

In 1893, Claude Matthews of Vermillion County assumed the office of governor. He was a Democrat. A Republican, James A. Mount of Montgomery assumed the governorship in 1897 and served in this post through the Spanish American War. In 1901, Mount was replaced by a fellow Republican, Winfield T. Durbin of Anderson. Durbin was also replaced by a Republican, J. Frank Hanly of Warren County in 1905.

A Democrat, Thomas R. Marshall of Columbia City, was elected to the post in 1909 and was succeeded in office in 1913 by Democrat Samuel M. Ralston of Lebanon.

Two Republicans came next. In 1917, James P. Goodrich of Winchester was elected to lead the state. Warren T. McCray of Kentland assumed the post in 1921.

# Chapter 5
# The Indiana Toll Road

Interstates 80 and 90 run through the northernmost part of Indiana. I-90 is a toll way coming south from Chicago while I-80 comes across Illinois through Joliet and enters Indiana at Hammond. The two interstate highways join together about 20 miles into the state and become the Indiana Toll Road, completed in 1956. It is approximately 160 miles across the state from Hammond east to the Ohio state line.

I-80 and I-94 enter the state together and separate when I-80 and I-90 become the Indiana Toll Road. I-94 continues northeasterly to enter Michigan.

Gary and Hammond are the major cities in Lake County, established February 15, 1837. The county seat is CROWN POINT (pop. 16,455), settled in 1834, incorporated as a town in 1868, and as a city in 1911.

Entering Indiana I-90 also enters WHITING (pop. 5,630), settled in 1885 and incorporated in 1903.

The **Standard Oil Company** built one of the world's largest oil refineries in Whiting in 1889.

WHITING-ROBERTSDALE HISTORICAL SOCIETY MUSEUM, 1610 119th Street, provides local history, Standard Oil of Indiana artifacts, Whiting high school yearbooks, and early-day newspapers. Robertsdale is adjacent to Whiting. The museum is open from 1:00 to 4:00 p.m. Tuesday, Wednesday, and Saturday. For additional information call (219) 659-1432.

The **Whiting Memorial Community House** (1923), 1938 Clark Street, and **Hoosier Theatre Building** (1924), 1329-1335 119th Street, are listed on the National Register of Historic Places (NRHP).

Just east is EAST CHICAGO (pop. 36,000).

On January 15, 1934, **John Dillinger** and members of his gang robbed the bank in East Chicago of $20,376. In the commission of the crime, Patrolman Patrick J. O'Malley was shot and killed. It was believed Dillinger fired the fatal shot.

The **Marktown Historic District** (1888-1926), bounded by Pine, Riley, Dickey, and 129th Streets, is listed on the NRHP. This model community was built for employees of Mark Manufacturing in 1917, predecessor of Youngstown and LTV Steel.

GARY (pop. 140,600) was chartered in 1906 and was named for **Judge Elbert H. Gary** (1846-1927), who organized U.S. Steel Corporation in 1901 and served as the chairman of its board until his death. The land for the city was purchased by the steel company in 1905 and the city was chartered the following

137

J. Pierpont Morgan selected Elbert Henry Gary, born near Wheaton, IL, to head the Federal Steel Company in 1898 and then to organize U. S. Steel Corporation in 1901. Gary served two terms as a county judge early in his career and afterward was always known as Judge Gary.

year. The nation-wide steel strike of 1919 was brought on over notoriously long working hours in the mills and Judge Gary's adamant opposition to labor unions in the Gary mills. The strike failed but Judge Gary, under public pressure, was forced to shorten working hours in his mills. Gary is the second largest city in Indiana.

**Octave Chanute** made the first successful flight in a heavier-than-air craft in the Indiana Dunes in 1896. After many unsuccessful attempts, Chanute finally achieved success when his flying machine flew a distance of 489 feet. This feat made it possible for the Wright brothers' flight four years later. A commemorative marker has been established in Marquette Park in suburban Miller.

In 1923, the mayor, prosecuting attorney, and a judge in Gary were among 60 persons convicted and jailed in Gary for violating liquor laws.

In 1967, **Richard Hatcher** of Gary was elected the state's first black mayor and in November, 1982, Democrat **Katie Hall** of Gary became the first black woman from Indiana sent to the U.S. Congress.

Six persons were wounded by sniper fire in July, 1968, in Gary as a result of court-ordered busing.

The Gary Automobile Manufacturing Company built the Gary automobile in 1916-17.

The **Gary Land Company Building** (1906), Fourth Avenue and Pennsylvania Street; **Knights of Columbus Building** (1925), 333 West Fifth Avenue; **Miller Town Hall** (1911), junction of Miller Avenue, Old Hobart Road, and Grand Boulevard; **John Stewart Settlement House** (1925), 1501 Massachusetts Street; and **West Fifth Avenue Apartments Historic District** (1922-1928), bounded by Fifth Avenue from Taft

138

to Pierce Street, are listed on the NRHP.

HAMMOND (pop. 87,800), originally called Hohman for an early resident, was settled in 1851 and incorporated in 1884. Initially it served as an important site for slaughterhouses but today is a diversified industrial center. **George Hammond**, a Detroit butcher, arrived in the area and built a slaughterhouse in 1869. The massive plant was destroyed by fire in 1901.

Hammond native **Alvah C. Roebuck**, a watchmaker, teamed up with a salesman, Richard W. Sears, to form Sears Roebuck and Company in Chicago in 1892.

Hammond was the home of the nation's first professional football team, the Hammond Professionals or Pros or "Hippos" (for their monstrous front wall) in the American Professional League. The team played between World War I and 1926 or 1927. The National Football League succeeded the American Professional Football league in 1922. The Hammond team was a charter member of both leagues. One of the standouts on the Hammond team was **George Halas** who later became owner-coach of the team that became the Chicago Bears.

**Calumet College** was founded in Hammond in 1960.

The **State Bank of Hammond Building** (1927), 5444-5446 Calumet Avenue, is listed on the NRHP.

The communities of Gary, East Chicago, Whiting, and Hammond make up the Calumet Region in the upper part of Lake County because of the two Calumet Rivers. *Chalameau* was the French word meaning "little reed" and pipes with reed stems used by the French and Indians were called calumets.

Just south of Hammond is MUNSTER (pop. 20,671) on US 6. **Jacob Munster** opened a contract postoffice in a corner of his general store giving the town its name. Jacob, a storekeeper and farmer, was also involved in local politics serving as a town trustee, school board member, and road supervisor. He and his wife, Henrietta, had 12 children. The town of Munster was incorporated in 1907.

Three Corten steel figures representing Munster's history, an Indian, a farmer, and a steel worker, were erected in Rotary Park during the city's observance of the bicentennial.

South of Munster on US 30, near the Illinois state line, is DYER (pop. 4,906), settled in the late 1830s and incorporated in 1910. The town took its name from Mrs. Aaron N. Hart's maiden name. **Aaron Hart**, a Philadelphia publisher who moved his family here in 1861, is credited with reclaiming about 20,000 acres of swamp land for farming and settlement. At the time of his death in 1883 he owned 17,000 acres crossed by five railroads with five railroad stations on his land.

**George F. Davis** of Dyer won about 50 awards for his livestock and waterfowl exhibited at Chicago's 1893 Columbian Exposition.

East of Munster just off US 41 is HIGHLAND (pop. 24,947), settled first by Germans then by the Dutch. The Town of Highland was incorporated in 1910. The townsite was platted in 1882 as Clough Postal Station. A historical marker relating to the Dutch connection has been placed at 8941 Kleinman Road.

Wicker Park in Highland was established as Memorial Park in 1925 to commemorate the sacrifices made by World War I veterans. The land for the park, called Wicker Pasteur, was provided by three Highland men. **President Calvin Coolidge** came to Highland in 1927 to dedicate the park.

HIGHLAND HISTORICAL SOCIETY MUSEUM, Lincoln Center, 2450 Lincoln Avenue, focuses on local and area history. It is open Saturday mornings or by appointment, (219) 838-2962.

Returning to Hammond and continuing east on US 6 is HOBART (pop. 21,822), settled c. 1849 and incorporated in 1921.

HOBART HISTORICAL SOCIETY MUSEUM, 706 East Fourth Street, is located in the former Hobart Public Library building constructed in 1914 and dedicated February 11, 1915. It includes exhibits that focus on the history of the Hobart area and home life in the late 19th and early 20th centuries. Objects and exhibits date from fossils and ice age objects through Indian artifacts, furnishings brought to Hobart by covered wagon in the 1830s, and Civil War memorabilia. The Ballantyne Gallery includes a collection of wheelwright and woodworking tools as well as replicas of a blacksmith shop, a wheelmaking and woodworking shop, and an operating print shop. The museum is open from 10:00 a.m. to 3:00 p.m. Saturday and other times by appointment. Admission is free.

WOOD'S HISTORIC GRIST MILL (1838) located in Deep River County Park at 9410 Old Lincoln Highway, is listed on the NRHP. At Wood's Mill, visitors can see daily grinding demonstrations in which corn is stone ground between 4,000-pound millstones. Visitors may also purchase freshly ground flours and cornmeal. Mill museum exhibits include furniture and fashion displays depicting 19th century life. Adjacent to Wood's Mill is the Visitors' Center/Gift Shoppe, housed in a 1904 church building. Wood's Historic Grist Mill and the Visitors' Center/Gift Shoppe are open from 10:00 a.m. to 5:00 p.m. daily, May 1 through October 31. An admission is charged.

The **Hobart Carnegie Library** (1915), 706 East Fourth Street, and **Pennsylvania Railroad Station** (1910), 1001 Lillian Street, are listed on the NRHP.

Continuing east is Porter County, established February 1, 1836. The county seat is VALPARAISO (pop. 22,900), settled in 1834 and incorporated in 1865. The county was named for War of 1812 naval commander **David Porter**. Valparaiso is located south of the interstate highways just off US 30.

**Orville Redenbacher**, an agronomist at Valparaiso University, and **Charles Bowman** began a popcorn-growing business in Valparaiso in 1952 that has become popular across the nation.

The noted actress, **Beulah Bondi**, was raised in Valparaiso. At the age of seven she was performing as *"Little Lord Fauntleroy"* locally. She performed in a number of films and won an Emmy Award for her role in an episode of *"The Waltons."*

It is the home of **Valparaiso University**, northwest corner US 30 and IN 130, founded by the Methodists in 1859 as the Valparaiso Male and Female College. The school was closed briefly in 1870 because of financial problems but reopened by 26-year old Henry Baker Brown under an endorsement from the Methodists and Porter County. Under Brown's tenure the school became nationally known as the "poor man's Harvard." The death of Brown in 1915 and World War I created economic problems for the university effecting their programs and enrollment. The university was purchased by the Lutheran Church in 1925 and is open to students of all faiths. The Chapel of the Resurrection on campus today is the largest collegiate chapel in the world.

Among some of the well-known who have attended Valparaiso University were **Len Small**, an Illinois governor and newspaper executive; **George W. Norris**, noted U.S. senator from Nebraska; **Flem D. Sampson**, a Kentucky governor; and **Lowell Thomas**, world known broadcaster and world traveler.

A marker at 760 West Street (on the south side of the road) pinpoints the site of an 1863 Union infantry camp operated in Valparaiso.

HISTORICAL SOCIETY OF PORTER COUNTY/OLD JAIL MUSEUM, 153 South Franklin Street, is filled with a variety of historical artifacts ranging from the remains of a mastodon to examples of an art form called pictorial marquetry. Broncho John, a partner with Colonel William F. "Buffalo Bill" Cody in his internationally famous Wild West Show, left much of his memorabilia to the museum upon his retirement in Valparaiso. Beulah Bondi, the award-winning actress, also provided the museum with a few pieces. The museum is open from 1:00 to 4:00 p.m. Tuesday, Wednesday, and Friday.

There are several sites in Valparaiso listed on the NRHP. These include **Heritage Hall** (1875), South College Avenue; **Immanuel Lutheran Church** (1891), 308 North Washington Street; **Dr. David J. Loring Residence and Clinic** (1906), 102 Washington Street; **Porter County Jail and Sheriff's House**, House (c. 1860), Jail (1871), 153 Franklin Street; **Porter County Memorial Hall** (1893), 104 Indiana Avenue, and **David Garland Rose House** (c. 1860), 156 Garfield Street. Also listed on the NRHP is the Valparaiso **Downtown Commercial District** (c. 1870-1930), bounded by Jefferson, Morgan, Indiana, and

Napoleon Streets.

In the northern part of Porter County are Portage and Chesterton.

PORTAGE (pop. 32,500) was incorporated as a town in 1959 and took in the three small communities of Crisman, Garyton, and McCool. Settlement of the area began as early as the 1830s. An "Underground Railroad," assisting runaway slaves bound for Canada, operated here during the period leading to the Civil War.

In 1908, **Randall Burns** petitioned the county to establish a drainage ditch that would empty into Lake Michigan thus permitting the use of thousands of acres of swamp land in the Portage area. Opposition to this proposition delayed any action on the project until 1928 when the issue was resolved by the U.S. Supreme Court. Today, this channel is called "The Portage-Burns Waterway."

PORTAGE COMMUNITY HISTORICAL MUSEUM, 5250 US 6 in Countryside Park, Portage, focuses on local history. It is open from 11:00 a.m. to 4:00 p.m. Saturdays.

CHESTERTON (pop. 8,531) was platted in 1852 and incorporated in 1869.

Two miles north of I-95 on IN 49, and a half mile past the Indiana Dunes State Park Gatehouse, on the east side, is a marker that commemorates the Revolutionary War **Battle of the Dunes**, December 5, 1780.

**Beverly Shores, South Shore Railroad Station**, 1929 Broadway Avenue and US 12, Beverly Shores, is listed on the NRHP.

Driving from Porter County east is LaPorte County, established April 1, 1832. The county seat is LAPORTE (pop. 21,900), settled in 1830, incorporated as a town in 1835 and as a city in 1852. LaPorte is the French word for "the door." The city is south of the Indiana Toll Road on US 35.

A hospital for returning wounded Union soldiers was built at the southeast corner of 1st and C Streets in 1861-62. Called the "Butcher Shop," the hospital served veterans until after the Civil War. The original building still stands and serves as a private residential unit today.

Two training camps were established in the area during the Civil War—**Camp Colfax**, IN 2 and Colfax Avenue, and **Camp Jackson**, site of City Park on Park Street. Indiana's 9th Regiment trained at Camp Colfax and marched off to war in September 1861. The 28th Indiana Cavalry Regiment trained at Camp Jackson. It is claimed that three quarters of the able-bodied men of LaPorte volunteered for the Union army.

An unsolved mystery surrounds LaPorte's infamous **Belle Gunness**, believed to have murdered at least a dozen men. Her alleged last victim, A. K. Helgelein, is buried in Patton Cemetery

This historical marker in LaPorte identifies two Civil War training centers operated here.

at 1401 Rumely Street. The story begins in 1904 when either a meat cleaver or a sausage grinder fell from a kitchen shelf killing her second husband. Shortly after, Belle began advertising in lonely hearts columns seeking a fairly well-off husband. When men responded to her ad, she invited them to her McClung Road farm after they were first asked to convert their assets to cash. Several men appeared but soon disappeared. Helgelein arrived at the Gunness farm in late 1907 or early 1908 from the Dakotas. After a long period of time and no word from him, his brother wrote to Belle and was told that he had returned to Norway. On April 27, 1908, Mrs. Gunness drove into LaPorte and made out her will leaving her possessions to her children should they survive her or to a Norwegian orphanage in Chicago if they did not. Early the next morning, her farm burned to the ground and Belle Gunness and her adopted children were believed to have died in the fire. Ray Lamphere, her handy man, was arrested for murder and arson. Helgelein's brother read about the fire in a Chicago newspaper and hurried to LaPorte and managed to convince the sheriff to dig up the Gunness farmyard. They found the remains of A.K. Helgelein and 11 others. Several of the bodies contained quantities of arsenic in their stomachs. Convicted of arson, Lamphere, before his death from tuberculosis in prison at Michigan City, claimed that Belle Gunness did not die in the fire and that he had burned the house on her orders. No

Among the collections in the LaPorte County Museum is the W. A. Jones firearms collection, one of the finest in the world.

one is certain whether Belle died in that fire or not or the circumstances of the 12 deaths on her farm. Lamphere was buried in Rossburg Cemetery on US 20 and Wilhelm Rd.

The second kindergarten program in the United States was developed in LaPorte by **W. N. Hailmann,** a LaPorte school superintendent for whom Hailmann Elementary School was named.

In its early days the LaPorte Library Association sponsored a series of lectures featuring some of the intellectuals of the day including **Elizabeth Cady Stanton, Ralph Waldo Emerson,**

**William Loyd Garrison**, and **Charles Sumner**.

The first medical school in the midwest, called the LaPorte University and later the **LaPorte Medical College**, was founded here in 1842 by **Drs. Daniel Meeker, Gustav A. Rose, Franklin Hunt**, and **John B. Niles**, LaPorte's first attorney. The school claims **Dr. William W. Mayo**, whose sons Dr. Charles H. and Dr. William J. developed the famed Mayo Clinic in Rochester, Minnesota, was once a student.

**Meinrad** and **John Rumely**, two German immigrants, were founders of the Rumely Company in 1853 and manufactured corn shellers, horse drawn farm machines, and iron castings for the railroad shops. Later this developed into the gigantic Advance-Rumely Company, manufacturer of the famous **Rumely Oil Pull tractor** which helped to open the Great Plains to the cultivation of wheat. The brothers built their first successful threshing machine in 1857 which turned out to be popular with regional farmers and made the Rumelys modestly rich. By 1869, the company was the largest employer in the city. Allis-Chalmers acquired Advance-Rumely Company's assets in 1931.

The Munson automobile was produced here from 1899 to 1902 by the Munson Electric Motor Company.

During World War II, Allis-Chalmers manufactured anti-aircraft guns as well as harvesters and other farm equipment here.

LAPORTE COUNTY MUSEUM, in the LaPorte County Complex, houses some 80,000 items and artifacts relating to the county's history. Among the collections is the **W. A. Jones** collection of antique firearms and other weapons of over 1,000 pieces said to be one of the finest in the world. The museum is open from 10:00 a.m. to 4:30 p.m. weekdays and also from 1:00 to 4:00 p.m. the first Sunday of each month. Admission is free.

Three structures in LaPorte have been placed on the NRHP. These include the **Francis H. Morrison House** (1904), 1217 Michigan Avenue; **William Orr House** (1875), 4076 West Small Road; and **Pinehurst Hall** (1853), 3042 N. U.S. 35. The **Downtown LaPorte Historic District** (1850-1914), is bounded by State, Jackson, Maple, and Chicago Streets.

Seven miles south of LaPorte, via US 35, is KINGSLEY, site of one the largest ordnance plants in the world during World War II.

In the northwestern most part of the county, via US 35, is MICHIGAN CITY (pop. 36,000), settled in 1830 and incorporated in 1836. Located on Lake Michigan, the first lake shipment went through the "port" here in 1836.

The **Battle of Trail Creek** was fought here during the Revolutionary War. A historical marker commemorating this event is located at East 8th and Liberty Trail in Michigan City.

145

Dredging of the harbor began in 1837 and continued for years. In 1839, 10 vessels were stranded in the harbor. Many immigrants arrived in 1839 via lake steamers. The famous Rivers and Harbors Convention was held in Michigan City in 1847, attended by **Abraham Lincoln** on July 5th, gave impetus to the lake port project. By 1852 shipping over water was brisk and during a single week nine sailing ships took on cargo consisting of 20,000 bushels of grain, 2,300 barrels of flour and 30 barrels of pork.

President Lincoln's funeral train stopped here briefly enroute to Springfield, Illinois, in 1865. This hour-long stop occurred when the delegation from Chicago to meet the train were late in arriving in Michigan City.

Clarinetist **Benny Goodman** spent his boyhood days here.

One of many shipwrecks in Lake Michigan was the *Muskegon*, built in 1872, abandoned in 1910 and sunk deliberately in 1911 off Michigan City harbor. This shipwreck site is listed on the NRHP.

OLD LIGHTHOUSE MUSEUM, Heisman Harbor Road, Washington Park, was built in 1858 to replace the lighthouse built in 1837. Featured are a keeper's living room and bedroom, Fresnel Lens, stories of shipwrecks, shipbuilding tools, the stop of the Lincoln funeral train, and Michigan City history. It was also the site of the launching of the first submarines on the Great Lakes by **L. D. Phillips** in 1845. It is listed on the NRHP. The museum is open from 1:00 to 4:00 p.m. Tuesday through Saturday year-round. It is closed on Mondays and holidays. An admission is charged.

BARKER MANSION, in Barker Civic Center, 631 Washington Street, was built in 1857. The mansion was owned by **John H. Barker**, industrialist and philanthropist and president of the Haskell and Barker Car Co., the largest manufacturer of freight cars in the world. The Barkers added extensively to the home in 1900-1905 and the mansion has been placed on the NRHP. Their daughter, Catherine Barker Hickox, gave the mansion to the city as a gift. Today it is open for tours and the furnishing and art objects were the personal property of the Barker family. The mansion is open for guided tours at 10:00 and 11:30 a.m. and at 1:00 p.m. weekdays the year-round and at 12:00 noon and 2:00 p.m. on weekends from June 1 through October 31. An admission is charged.

The **Michigan City East Pierhead Light Tower and Elevated Walk (Michigan City Lighthouse)** (1904), on the east side entrance to Michigan City Harbor, is also listed on the NRHP.

Michigan City is the site of the **Indiana State Prison**. This maximum security prison facility carries out executions for the state. John Dillinger was imprisoned here in the 1930s. One of

President Lincoln's funeral train made an unscheduled stop in Westville in May 1865 enroute to Springfield, Illinois.

the most sensational escapes from the prison occurred September 26, 1933, when ten inmates broke out aided by parolee Dillinger. The ten were Harry Pierpont, John Hamilton, Charles Mackley, Russell Lee Clark, Walter Detrick, Joseph Fox, Edward Shouse, James Clark, James Jenkins and Joseph Burns. Those who eluded early capture participated on and off in crimes led by Dillinger.

South of the Indiana Toll Road, via US 421 about five miles, is WESTVILLE (pop. 2,887), site of the Westville Correctional Center. It was an unscheduled stop for President Lincoln's funeral train on May 1, 1865. A marker at the Monon Railroad

147

tracks five blocks south of the intersection of US 421 and IN 2 commemorates this event.

The **Everel S. Smith House** (1879), 56 West Jefferson Street, is listed on the NRHP.

Back on the Indiana Toll Road, it is 26 miles to SOUTH BEND (pop. 107,900), county seat of St. Joseph County. The county, named for the Biblical Joseph, husband of the Virgin Mary, was established April 1, 1830. From LaPorte, South Bend can also be reached via US 35 and US 20.

South Bend was settled c. 1820 as a post of the American Fur Company on the site of a French mission and trading post. It was laid out in 1830.

**Henry** and **Clement Studebaker** opened a blacksmith and wagon shop in South Bend in 1852 and their company, the H and C Studebaker firm, by 1875 claimed to be "the largest vehicle house in the world." With a brother, John, they helped to equip the Union army during the Civil War. By 1895, the Studebaker Brothers Manufacturing Company was making 75,000 horse-drawn vehicles annually.

By the turn of the century, Studebaker had begun to build chassis for budding automobile companies. In 1902, Studebaker built 20 electric runabouts, officially the company's first cars. They began building gasoline-powered automobiles in 1904 with a single cylinder and the next year added four cylinder models. The new Studebaker Corporation was formed February 14, 1911. By 1912 Studebaker ranked third in production and sales in the infant auto industry. The company discontinued making wagons in 1921. In 1925, the company produced 134,664 cars and trucks. In the 1920s and '30s the company won numerous awards for record-breaking and long-distance competitions. During World War II, Studebaker built trucks, airplane engines and the Weasel personnel carrier, which it also designed. The company's greatest auto sales year was 1950 with 335,000 units. In 1962, Studebaker introduced the Avanti, the most spectacular model ever produced by the company. The Avanti, designed by Raymond Loewy, had a glass fibre body, disc brakes on the front, and an optional supercharger. After suffering financial difficulties for years, the Studebaker Corporation ended automobile production in South Bend in 1963. The company stopped making automobiles completely in 1966. Many still remember such Studebaker models as the Champion, President, Commander, Land Cruiser, Dictator, Golden Hawk, Lark, and the Starliner. The Starliner has been hailed as one of the most beautiful cars ever made. The Erskine, 1926-1930, was also built by Studebaker.

The Avanti II has been built by the Avanti Motor Company since 1965. Several South Bend businessmen took over the plant from Studebaker and rejuvenated the car and its production.

148

This museum in South Bend preserves the history of the Studebaker brothers and their company.

STUDEBAKER NATIONAL MUSEUM, INC., 525 South Main Street, provides 114 years of Studebaker history. The historic collection provides the visitor with an insight into the country's transportation history. On display is a large collection of wagons, carriages, cars and trucks from the Studebaker family's conestoga wagon to the last car made in South Bend. The museum is open from 9:00 a.m. to 5:00 p.m. Monday through Saturday and from 12:00 noon to 5:00 p.m. Sunday. It is closed on Thanksgiving and Christmas. An admission is charged.

Other automobiles built in South Bend have been the Diamond, 1910-1912, by the Diamond Automobile Company; the Perfection, 1906-1908, by the Perfection Auto Works; the Ricketts, 1908-1909, by Ricketts Auto Works; the South Bend, 1914, by South Bend Motor Car Works; the Tincher, 1903-1908, by the Tincher Motor Car Company; and the Williams, 1905, by W. L. Cassady Manufacturing Company.

**James Oliver**, a Scotsman who arrived in South Bend in 1855, received his first patent on a hard-faced, chill-steel plow in 1868.

COPSHAHOLM HOUSE MUSEUM, 808 West Washington in the West Washington National Historic District, was the home of Joseph Doty Oliver, president of the Oliver Chilled Plow Works, and his family. Joseph Oliver was the son of James Oliver, inventor of the Oliver plow and founder of the company. The 38-room house was built in 1895-96 on three floors with a full basement and attic with nine bathrooms and 14 fireplaces. It was the first home in South Bend with electricity. The house

149

is listed on the NRHP. Visitors can take a guided tour of all three floors, or a 1st floor tour of the main rooms. Reservations are encouraged; groups of 10 or more must make a reservation, preferably two weeks in advance. Tour tickets are purchased in the Copshaholm Carriage House. The Carriage House and attached Leighton Gallery feature exhibitions and a gift shop. The tours begin about every 20 minutes and visitors should allow one and a half hours for the orientation and tour. Copshaholm is open from 10:00 a.m. to 5:00 p.m. Tuesday through Saturday; from 12:00 noon to 5:00 p.m. Sunday with the last tour beginning at 4:00 p.m. It is closed Mondays, the month of January and most major holidays. An admission is charged. There is no charge to the Carriage House and Gallery. Both are open from 10:00 a.m. to 5:00 p.m. the same weekdays and Saturday as the museum and 12:00 noon to 5:00 p.m. Sundays. Copshaholm is closed mid-January to mid-February and on major holidays. The museum is operated by the Northern Indiana Historical Society.

The Northern Indiana Historical Society, organized in 1867 to collect, preserve, and disseminate the heritage of the St. Joseph River Valley region, owns and operates two other museums. The ST. JOSEPH VALLEY CENTER FOR HISTORY and

The beautiful Copshaholm House in South Bend serves as a unique museum. The home was built in the late 19th century.

THE WORKER HOUSE MUSEUM (opened in 1994) are on the same eight acres of ground where Copshaholm is located. The History Center features changing and permanent exhibition galleries, a children's interactive gallery, an archival library, an auditorium and an outdoor amphitheatre. The Worker House Museum is a restored 1870's house which commemorates the many immigrants who came to the Valley in search of jobs and a new beginning. It includes historical gardens indicative of a worker house lifestyle. The hours these museums are in operation are the same as the Copshaholm.

**Notre Dame University** was founded in 1842 and St. Mary's College in 1844. The bishop of Vincennes granted 600 acres to **Father Edward Sorin** to establish a college here in 1842. At the time the site was called St. Marie des Lacs. The first student at Notre Dame was **Alexis Coquillard**, founder of South Bend. Women were first admitted to the university in 1972. The university has a noted law school and laboratories for research in botany, radiation, geology, metallurgy, and engineering and also operates important research institutes in the humanities. It is also noted for its sports teams, particularly football, as "The Fighting Irish." Many gridiron stars have come out of Notre Dame University to play the sport professionally.

The library building is a landmark on the Notre Dame University campus.

Knute Rockne (1888-1931) not only put Notre Dame on the football map but also revolutionized football theory during his 13 years as head coach (1918-31). In those years Rockne teams won 105 games, lost 12, and tied five. He had five undefeated, untied seasons. He stressed offense, developed the precision backfield, called the Notre Dame shift, and perfected line play. He was a great team motivator. Many football greats have come out of Notre Dame but none as famous as the backfield called the "Four Horsemen," composed of **Harry Stuhldreher, Don Miller, James Crowley,** and **Elmer Layden. George Gipp,** Notre Dame football great, died of a throat infection December 14, 1920 shortly after being named the university's first All-American. While a student at the university, Rockne played football and in 1913, with **Gus Dorias,** scored a sensational upset over a heavily favored Army team by throwing a forward pass, a legal but then unused football tactic. He served one year, 1914, as a chemistry instructor and assistant football coach at the university before being appointed head football coach. Knute Rockne was killed in an airplane crash near Bazaar, Kansas, March 3, 1931.

Visitors touring Notre Dame campus will be especially interested in the Stepan Center geodesic dome, the Athletic and Convocation Center, the library's 13-story marble mosaic facade, and Church of the Sacred Heart.

THE SNITE MUSEUM OF ART is located on the campus of the University. The Snite Museum of Art's collection, from ancient to contemporary, numbers some 19,000 pieces. There are particularly important works in the Butkin Collection of pre-Columbian art, the Reilly Collection of Old Masters through 19th century drawings, and the Fedderson Collection of Rembrandt etchings. The museum is open from 10:00 a.m. to 4:00 p.m. Tuesday through Saturday and from 1:00 to 4:00 p.m. Sunday and from 10:00 a.m. to 8:00 p.m. Thursday, when university classes are in session. It is closed on Monday and major holidays. Admission is free.

SOUTH BEND REGIONAL MUSEUM OF ART, 120 South St. Joseph Street, offers exhibitions of both regional and national significance in its three gallery space. The museum's permanent collection includes 19th and 20th century works of aesthetic and historical importance by Indiana and regional artists, 19th and 20th century works on paper by significant American artists and large scale sculpture by contemporary artists of the region. A docent program, co-sponsored with the Snite Museum of Art at the University of Notre Dame, develops and guides tours through both institutions. Tours are available for both children and adults. The galleries and museum shop are open from 11:00 a.m. to 5:00 p.m. Tuesday through Friday, and from 12:00 noon to 5:00 p.m. weekends. An admission is charged for all non-members.

The **University of Notre Dame Main and South Quad-rangles** (1913-1938), are listed on the NRHP.

A number of structures in South Bend are listed on the NRHP. Among these are the **Horatio Chapin House** (1857), 601 Park Avenue; **James A. Judie House** (1930), 1515 Jefferson Boulevard; **Kelly-Frederickson House and Office Building** (1892), 233 North Lafayette Boulevard and 314 West LaSalle Street; **Chauncey N. Lawton House** (1872), 405 West Wayne Street; **Samuel Leeper, Jr. House** (1888), 113 West North Shore Drive; **O'Brien Electric Priming Company** (1882), 2001 West Washington Street; **Old Courthouse** (1854), 112 South Lafayette Boulevard; **Palais Royale Building** (1922), 113-15 West Colfax Avenue and 201-09 North Michigan Streets; **Tippecanoe Place (Studebaker House)** (1901), 620 West Washington Street; and **Water Street/Darden Road Bridge** (1885), over St. Joseph River and Darden Road. Also included are two historic district—**Chapin Park Historic District** (1871-1910), bounded by the St. Joseph River, Main, Madison, Rex, Lindsey, and William Streets, and Leland and Portage Avenues, and **West Washington Historic District** (1850-1920), bounded by Main Street, Western and LaSalle Avenues, and McPherson Street.

Also on the NRHP is the Downtown South Bend Historic Multiple Resources Area that includes the **All American Bank Building** (1924), 111 West Washington; **Bertling Building** (1905), 228 West Colfax; **Blackstone-State Theatre** (1919), 212 South Michigan; **Cathedral of St. James and Parish Hall** (1894), 117 North Lafayette; **Central High School and Boys Vocational School** (1913, 1928), 115 North St. James Court; **Citizens Bank** (1913), 112 West Jefferson; **Colfax Theatre** (1928), 213 West Colfax; **Commercial Building** (1922), 226 West Colfax; **Farmer's Security Bank** (1915), 133 South Main Street; **Former First Presbyterian Church** (1888), 101 South Lafayette; **Hager Residence** (1910), 415 West Wayne; **W. R. Hinkle and Company** (1922), 225 North Lafayette; **Hoffman Hotel** (1930), 120 West LaSalle; **J.M.S. Building** (1910), 108 North Main; **John G. Kerr & Company** (1891), 121 West Colfax; **Knights of Columbus** (1924), 320 West Jefferson; **Knights of Pythias Lodge** (1922), 224 West Jefferson; **LaSalle Annex** (1925), 306 North Michigan; **LaSalle Hotel** (1921), 306 North Michigan; **Morey-Lampert House** (1896), 322 West Washington; **Morey House** (1909), 110-112 Franklin Place; **Northern Indiana Gas and Electric Company Building** (1915), 221 North Michigan; **Palace Theatre** (1921), 211 North Michigan; **Second Saint Joseph Hotel** (1868), 117-119 West Colfax; **South Bend Remedy Company** (1895), 220 West LaSalle; **Sommers-Longley Residence** (1910), 312-314 West

Colfax; **Third Saint Joseph County Courthouse** (1897), 105 South Main; and **Tower Building** (1929), 216 West Washington.

West of South Bend, on US 20, is NEW CARLISLE (pop. 1,439). On June 10, 1933, **John Dillinger**, who had been released from the Indiana State Prison at Michigan City on May 22, robbed the National Bank of New Carlisle of $10,000. Dillinger and **"Pretty Boy" Floyd**, a notorious killer and robber during this period, robbed the Merchants National Bank of South Bend of $18,000 on June 30, 1934.

Adjacent east of South Bend is MISHAWAKA (pop. 41,500), settled c. 1830 and incorporated in 1899. It was named for **Princess Mishawaka**, daughter of Shawnee Indian Chief Elkhart. The princess died in 1912 and is buried in the city's Lincoln Park.

Mishawaka is the home of **Bethel College**, founded in 1947.

The Kenworthy Motor Company built the Kenworthy, 1920-1922, and the American Simplex, 1906-1910, was built by Simplex Motor Car Company, both in Mishawaka.

HANNAH LINDAHL CHILDREN'S MUSEUM, 1402 South Main Street, Mishawaka, provides a "look at history" for children through exhibits of all kinds as well as hands on experience in such settings as a one-room school house and trying out various fire fighting equipment. A look into the lives of the Japanese may be experienced in the Japanese house. Local natural history is explored in Gallery Hall, where children can examine fossils, geodes, rocks, minerals, shells, and a facsimile Potawatomie Indian tepee. The museum is open from 9:30 a.m. to 12:00 noon and from 1:00 to 4:00 p.m. Tuesday through Friday and from 10:00 a.m. to 2:00 p.m. the second and fourth Saturday of each month. During June the museum is open from 10:00 a.m. to 2:00 p.m. Tuesday through Thursday. It is closed during July and August and all school holidays. Admission is free, donations are appreciated.

There are several structures here listed on the NRHP. These include the **Beiger House** (1909), 317 Lincolnway Road; **Dodge House** (1889), 415 Lincolnway East; **Eller-Hosford House** (1875), 722 Lincolnway East; **Kamm and Schellinger Brewery** (1853-1870), 100 Center Street; **Merrifield-Cass House** (1837, 1867), 816 Lincolnway East; and **Ellis-Schindler House** (1834), 900 Lincolnway East.

The **Studebaker Clubhouse and Tree Sign** (1926, 1938), 32132 IN 2, in the New Carlisle area northwest of South Bend, is also listed on the NRHP.

From Mishawaka the toll road continues east 15 miles to ELKHART (pop. 43,627) in Elkhart County.

Elkhart, originally called Pulaski for the Polish patriot **Count Casmir Pulaski** who joined George Washington's

Pulaski was the name of the village that became Elkhart in 1832. The name of the postoffice did not change for another seven years.

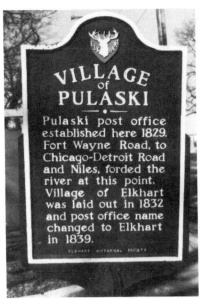

VILLAGE
of
PULASKI
—•—
Pulaski post office established here 1829. Fort Wayne Road, to Chicago-Detroit Road and Niles, forded the river at this point. Village of Elkhart was laid out in 1832 and post office name changed to Elkhart in 1839.

ELKHART HISTORICAL SOCIETY

Revolutionary War army and became a hero, officially got its current name March 14, 1839. The town was settled and platted in 1832 and incorporated in 1877. The land for the town was purchased April 21, 1831 by **Dr. Havilah Beardsley** for $800 from **Potawatomi Indian Chief Pierre Moran** and the sale was approved by President Andrew Jackson January 13, 1832. The original settlement was built around Island Park, an island at the conflux of the St. Joseph and Elkheart Rivers, and Indians described the island as being in the shape of an elk's heart.

By 1850, the Michigan and Southern railroad reached Elkhart.

**C. G. Conn** began production of band instruments in 1875 that became world famous. He was born in 1844 and arrived in Elkhart as a young boy when his father was appointed superintendent of schools. He received his patent for a rubber-rimmed mouthpiece for musical instruments in 1875 and that same year joined with Eugene Dupont to produce a "Four-in-One" valve trumpet. By the late 1880s, Conn developed the first American saxophone, metal clarinet, and double valve euphonium. He entered the political arena and served as mayor of Elkhart and was elected to Congress in 1892. He founded the town's newspaper, the *Elkhart Truth* in 1889, and while in Washington, D.C., purchased the *Washington Times*. In 1915, C. G. Conn sold his company to Charles Greenleaf. He was nearly penniless at the time of his death in 1931.

Dr. Miles Medical Company, makers of Alka Seltzer and One-A-Day multivitamins, was established in 1884 and its first

155

product was Dr. Miles Nervine medicine. At age 38, **Dr. Franklin Miles** founded the company bearing his name in 1884, nine years after he opened his medical practice in Elkhart. The first product to come out of the Miles Medical Company was "Nervine," his own preparation used in the treatment of a number of chronic illnesses. Dr. Miles served as president of the company until his death in 1929. The company, with several divisions, manufactures such products as One-A-Day multivitamins, Flintstones and Bugs Bunny vitamin brands and diagnostic instruments such as the Glucometer, the most widely used diabetes self-testing systems in the world.

**Wilbur Schult** began producing trailer homes in 1936 giving birth to the mobile home industry.

MIDWEST MUSEUM OF AMERICAN ART, 429 South Main Street, contains an impressive collection of 19th and 20th century works. Among a few of the noteworthy artists represented are Robert Henri, George Luks, Grandma Moses, Norman Rockwell, Alfred Stieglitz, and Grant Woods. The museum also presents a number of temporary shows annually. The museum is open from 11:00 a.m. to 5:00 p.m. Tuesday through Friday and from 1:00 to 4:00 p.m. weekends. An admission is charged.

NATIONAL NYC RAILROAD MUSEUM, 721 South Main Street, boasts a large collection from New York Central Railroad stations and rail cars in addition to three locomotives in the process of restoration. The three locomotives include a 3001 L-3a "Mohawk" steam engine, the only one of its kind still in existence; an E-8 diesel; and a GG-1 electric engine. Railroad buffs especially will not want to pass up this unique railroad museum. It is open from 10:00 a.m. to 2:00 p.m. Tuesday through Friday and from 10:00 a.m. to 3:00 p.m. weekends. Admission is free, donations are accepted.

"TIME WAS" DOWNTOWN ELKHART MUSEUM, 125-A North Main Street, offers a unique look back into the city's past through vintage photographs, back issues of the Elkhart newspapers, high school yearbooks from 1900, and city directories from 1864. Also on display are other publications and advertising memorabilia. It is open from 9:30 a.m. to 3:00 p.m. Thursday through Saturday.

RV/MH HERITAGE FOUNDATION/HALL OF FAME MUSEUM, 810 Benham Avenue, houses displays including memorabilia of recreational vehicles and manufactured housing industries, camping trailers, and the national industry Hall of Fame. The museum is open from 9:00 a.m. to 12:00 noon (EST) Tuesday, Wednesday, and Thursday.

RUTHMERE 1910 HOUSE MUSEUM, 302 East Beardsley Avenue, is furnished in authentic period furnishings and the home is considered to be a work of art with its mahogany paneling, silk upholstered walls, gilt, gesso, and painted ceilings

The Midwest Museum of American Art is housed in this former bank building in Elkhart.

The regal 1910 Ruthmere House serves as an Elkhart museum.

throughout. The house, built in 1908 by Albert R. Beardsley, one of the early organizers of Miles Laboratories, was named for his only child, Ruth, who died in infancy. Among some of the amenities is the green house, connected to the main house by a tunnel, and the garage equipped with an automobile turntable. The museum is open for guided tours at 11:00 a.m., 1:00 and 3:00 p.m. Tuesday through Friday with an added 7:00 p.m. tour on Wednesday. The library is open from 10:00 a.m. to 3:00 p.m. Tuesday through Friday. It is closed from December 15 through March 31, Memorial Day, July 4th, and Thanksgiving Day. An admission is charged.

S. RAY MILLER FOUNDATION ANTIQUE CAR MUSEUM, 2130 Middlebury Street, features approximately 40 antique and classic automobiles. Among these are the 1930 Duesenberg "J" Murphy once owned by Al Capone's lawyer, and the 1909 Sterling Model "K" Brass Car originally owned by World Champion Heavyweight Wrestler Frank Gotch. Many of the cars displayed were manufactured in Indiana, including Auburn, Cord, Duesenberg, Platt, Marmon Sixteen, Studebaker, Sterling, and Stutz, to name a few. The museum is open from 1:00 to 4:00 p.m. weekdays and from 12:00 noon to 4:00 p.m. the last complete weekend of each month. An admission is charged.

Many early day automobiles were manufactured in Elkhart. Among these were the Crow-Elkhart, 1909-1924, by Crow-Elkhart Motor Car Company; the Elcar, 1915-1931, and the Elkhart, 1908-1909, by Elkhart Carriage & Motor Car Company; the Huffman, 1920-1925, by Huffman Brothers Motor Company; the Mercer, 1910-1925; 1931, originally was manufactured in New Jersey but the 1931 car was built by Elcar Motor Car Company in an attempt to revive the car name; the Morriss-London, 1919-1925, was an assembled car built for export to England by Crow-Elkhart Motor Car Company that became the Century Motor Car Company; the Pratt-Elkhart, Pratt, 1911-1917, by Elkhart Carriage & Harness Manufacturing Company and the last two years by Pratt Motor Company; the Sellers, 1909-1912, by Sellers Automobile Company; the Shoemaker, 1906-1908, by Shoemaker Automobile Company; the Sperling, 1921-1923, by Associated Motors Corporation; the Sterling, 1909-1911, by Elkhart Carriage & Motor Car Company; and the Sun, 1915-1918, by Sun Motor Car Company.

The Elkhart structures listed on the NRHP include the **Albert R. Beardsley House** (1910), 302 East Beardsley Avenue; **Emmanuel C. Bickel House** (c. 1870), 614 Bower Street; **Buescher Bank Instrument Company Building** (1904, 1920, 1922, 1923, 1946), 225 East Jackson Avenue; **Green Block** (1895), 109-115 East Lexington; **Lerner Theatre (Elco Theatre)** (1924), 401 South Main Street; and **Mark L. and Harriett E. Monteith House** (1910), 871 East Beardsley Avenue.

The county seat of Elkhart County is GOSHEN (pop. 21,700). The county was established April 1, 1830 and is named for the Elkhart Indian tribe. Dunlap, just south of Elkhart on US 33, served as the county seat in 1830-31. Goshen became the county seat in 1831.

Amish settlers arrived in the county in 1841 and two years later the Mennonites arrived. The **Old Order Amish**, the most conservative sect of the Mennonite Plain People, are concentrated east of Goshen, in Elkhart and LaGrange counties, southwest of Goshen in the Nappanee-Bremen area. The other two areas of concentrations of Old Order Amish are found in Lancaster County, Pennsylvania, and in Holmes County, Ohio. The Amish who own automobiles and built churches are sometimes referred to as "church Amish" in contrast to Old Order Amish who hold their religious services in their home and are referred to as "house Amish." Pennsylvania German is the language used in most Amish homes.

The Amish broke away from the Swiss Mennonites led by Brethren **Bishop Jakob Ammann** because of the disagreements over church discipline in the 1690s and arrived in America in 1728. Families are divided into districts with about 150 members in each. Each district has a bishop, two preachers and a deacon. The bishop is the executive of the Amish government. His word on diverse matters is law.

The Amish shun materialism and rarely accumulate wealth. Modern conveniences such as television and radio are forbidden, as is electricity. Their mode of travel is usually by buggy or wagon. Clothing may be colorful, but the colors must be solid; no designs. The girls and women wear bonnets while the men wear wide-brimmed black hats that are exchanged for similarly style straw hats in the summer months. There are no buttons on outer garments; hooks and eyes are used for fasteners. They oppose military tradition and buttons, especially polished ones, that are associated with uniforms. It is for this reason that Amish men, who wear flowing beards, do not wear mustaches. At the time the sect was formed, many military men wore mustaches. The Amish do not dance, attend movies or stage shows. They neither smoke or drink. Amish schools emphasize reading, writing, and arithmetic, with some history and science on the side. A Bible lesson is taught daily.

Most Amish men registered as conscientious objectors during World War I and served as medics and in assignments behind the front lines. They declined to bear arms. Members are forbidden to go to war, swear oaths, or hold public office. Many volunteered for regular military service during World War II, however.

(Please note: Do not ask Amish people if you may take their photograph. Consenting to be photographed violates their reli-

Most Amish continue to use the horse and carriage as their mode of transportation. Several Amish vehicles are parked alongside automobiles in a bank parking lot here. Below the Amish have a large parking lot for their horses and carriages at this Shipshewana shopping center.

gious code, and you will make them very uncomfortable.)

The best way to see the Northern Indiana Amish Country and experience the Amish culture is to drive the 90-mile Heritage Trail, a loop over state and county roads in Elkhart and LaGrange counties. From the Indiana Toll Road, Heritage Trail begins at Exit 92 interchange. The Elkhart County Visitors Center is off IN 19 on Caravan Drive where visitors may obtain information on the area's attractions. The Heritage Trail is accessible from all highways—IN 13, 15, and 19 and US 20 and 33 as well as I-80/I-90.

From the Elkhart County Visitors Center the Heritage Trail heads east from Elkhart to BRISTOL (pop. 1,203) on IN 120 and Bonneyville Mill, then on to MIDDLEBURY (pop. 1,665) for shopping or an Amish family-style meal at a local restaurant.

Continuing east through the Amish countryside the next stop is SHIPSHEWANA (pop. 466) on IN 5, noted for its world-famous auction and flea market. The settlement was named for **Potawatomi Indian Chief Shipshewana**. Chief Shipshewana was one of the hundreds of Indians forced to move to Kansas in 1838.

It is here one will see many Amish carriages coming and going along the roads or parked at the railings at many places of business. There are numerous shops here featuring Amish-made arts and crafts.

One of many small shops offering Amish-made crafts in Shipshewana.

161

MENN-HOF MENNONITE-AMISH VISITORS CENTER, north of the intersection of US 20 and IN 5, through multi-image presentations, historical environments, and colorful displays the visitor is taken on a journey inside the unique world of the Mennonites and Amish. The Mennonites emerged in 1525 and the Amish broke from the Mennonites in 1693, but they have cooperated in many ways. Thousands of men and women of the faiths were imprisoned, tortured and executed for their religious beliefs. Today there are some 750,000 Mennonites and Amish scattered throughout 57 countries. A tour of Menn-Hof will help

This historical marker describes one of the farms in Amish Country as well as the Amish settlement in northern Indiana.

162

The Menn-Hof Mennonite-Amish Visitors Center.

This is a typical scene in Indiana's Amish Country.

explain their past. The center, operated by the Mennonites and Amish-Mennonites of northern Indiana, is open from 10:00 a.m. to 5:00 p.m. Monday, Wednesday through Saturday; from 10:00 a.m. to 7:00 p.m. Tuesday during the summer. Hours are seasonally adjusted. Allow a minimum of one hour for a tour. The last tour begins a half hour before closing. Admission by donation.

From Shipshewana the Trail continues through some of the most picturesque parts of Amish Country to Goshen.

The Trail continues from Goshen to NAPPANEE (pop. 4,722) and a historic working Amish Farm open to the public.

From Nappanee the Trail returns northward to WAKARUSA (pop. 1,281) and back to I-80/I-90. The BIRDS EYE VIEW MUSEUM is located in Wakarusa and focuses on community history through unique exhibits. It is open from 8:00 a.m. to 5:00 p.m. weekdays and from 8:00 a.m. to 12:00 noon on Saturday. An admission is charged.

**Goshen College** was founded in Goshen by the Mennonites in 1894.

The buildings in Goshen listed on the NRHP include the **Elkhart County Courthouse** (1870), Courthouse Square; **Goshen Carnegie Public Library** (1901), 202 North Fifth Street; and the **William N. Violett House** (c. 1854), 3004 South Main Street. The **Goshen Historic District** (1831-1909), is bounded by Pike, Railroad, Cottage, Plymouth, Main, Purl, the Canal, and Second Streets.

South of Goshen about 11 miles, via IN 15, is SYRACUSE (2,579), platted in 1837 and incorporated in 1874.

**Charles Hoeflinger** of Mishawaka robbed the State Bank of Syracuse on April 19, 1933. He was arrested and convicted of the robbery and sent to the Indiana State Prison.

SYRACUSE-TURKEY CREEK MUSEUM, 115 East Main Street, contains local and area history and features the Mier Car built in 1905 by Sheldon Harkless of Syracuse. The museum is open from 1:00 to 5:00 p.m. weekdays.

Back to the Elkhart area.

BRISTOL (pop. 1,203) is one mile south of the toll road, east of Elkhart on IN 15.

ELKHART COUNTY HISTORICAL MUSEUM, 304 West Vistula Street, Bristol, includes 13 rooms of displays that focus on the county's history, a genealogy library and archives, and historical society and museum programs. The museum, housed in the Rush Memorial Center, is open 1:00 to 5:00 p.m. Sunday, 6:00 to 8:00 p.m. Tuesday, 10:00 a.m. to 5:00 p.m. Wednesday, 12:00 noon to 3:00 p.m. Friday.

**St. John of the Cross Episcopal Church, Rectory, and Cemetery** Rectory (1830), Church (1847), 601 and 611 East Vistula Road, and **Bonneyville Mills** (1832), 2.5 miles east of Bristol on CR 131, are listed on the NRHP.

The Elkhart County Historical Museum is housed in this former school building in Bristol.

Howe was named for the founder of Howe Military School that dates back to the late 19th century.

Returning to the Indiana Toll Road at Elkhart, it is 17 miles east to LaGrange County, established April 1, 1832. The county and county seat, LAGRANGE (pop. 2,164), are named for Lafayette's home near Paris, France. Lafayette distinguished himself as a major general in General Washington's army during the Revolutionary War. The town was platted in 1836 and incorporated in 1855. LaGrange is eight miles south of the I-80-90 toll road on IN 9.

LAGRANGE HISTORICAL SOCIETY MUSEUM, on Poplar Street south of US 20, focuses on county history. The museum is open from 2:00 to 4:00 p.m. Sundays.

Four murals in the LaGrange Courthouse, depict the history of the town and county.

The **LaGrange County Courthouse** (1878), on Detroit Street, is listed on the NRHP.

The town of HOWE (pop. 550), two miles south of the toll road on IN 9, originally was called Lima and served as the county seat from 1832-1844. LaGrange was named the county seat in 1844. Lima's named was changed to Howe in honor of **John B. Howe** who founded the Howe Military Academy here in 1884.

In Howe, the **Samuel P. Williams House** (1843), 101 South Street, is listed on the NRHP.

The unincorporated village of MONGO, a shortened form of the Indian name Mongoquinon, northeast of LaGrange, is the home of the **Olde Store (John O'Ferrel Store)** (1832), West and 2nd Streets, listed on the NRHP.

Twenty miles south of LaGrange on IN 9 is ALBION (pop. 1,637), county seat of Noble County. Noble County, named in honor of Indiana's **U.S. Senator James Noble**, was established March 1, 1836; Albion was laid out in 1847.

Noble County produces more than 50 percent of the world's marshmallows. Plants are located in Ligonier and Kendallville.

The **Noble County Courthouse** (1888), on Courthouse Square, and **Noble County Sheriff's House and Jail** (1875), West Main and Oak Streets, are listed on the NRHP.

**Gene Porter Stratton's Cabin,** called THE CABIN IN THE WILDFLOWER WOODS, on the shores of Sylvan Lake was built in 1914. The two-story cabin was designed by Mrs. Porter. Listed on the NRHP, the cabin is located five miles west of Kendallville on US 6 and three miles north on IN 9 near Rome City. The home is open from 9:00 a.m. to 5:00 p.m. Tuesday through Saturday with the last tour beginning at 4:30 p.m. It is closed Mondays and from January 1 to March 15. Admission is free; donations are accepted.

ROME CITY (pop. 1,319), off IN 9, is about mid-way between LaGrange and Albion.

Fourteen miles northwest of Albion, on IN 5 just off US 6, is LIGONIER (pop. 3,134). It is about a dozen miles south of

The Cabin in the Wildflower Woods on Sylvan Lake was owned by author Gene Porter Stratton, who loved these kinds of settings for her writing.

Shipshewana via IN 5. The town was founded by Isaac Cavin in May, 1835 and named for his hometown in Pennsylvania.

Among the early settlers were many Jewish immigrants from Germany. Among the first members of the Jewish community were Frederick Strauss and Solomon Mier who arrived in 1854. By the 1880s, the Jewish community included virtually all of the city's merchants, bankers, and professionals, as well as most of the city's wealth.

The Mier Carriage & Buggy Company built the Mier (the

The community of Ligonier is proud of its Jewish heritage.

Runabout) automobile, 1908-1909 here. The company was owned by Solomon Mier.

LIGONIER HISTORICAL MUSEUM, 503 Main Street, is housed in the former Ahavas Shalom Reform Temple dating back to 1889. The museum focuses on the heritage of the city and area. It is open from 1:00 to 4:00 p.m. Tuesday, Saturday and Sunday. Admission is free, donations are accepted.

STONE'S TAVERN MUSEUM, three miles south of Ligonier at the junction of US 33 and IN 5, presents the Stone's Trace Pioneer Crafts Festival with Stone's Trace Regulator's Rendezvous one weekend every September. On the grounds is a museum, 1839 Stage Coach Inn, woodshop and herb garden.

There are three individual listings on the NRHP in the Ligonier area. These include **Ahavas Shalom Reform Temple** (1889), 503 South Main Street; **Jacob Straus House (Louis**

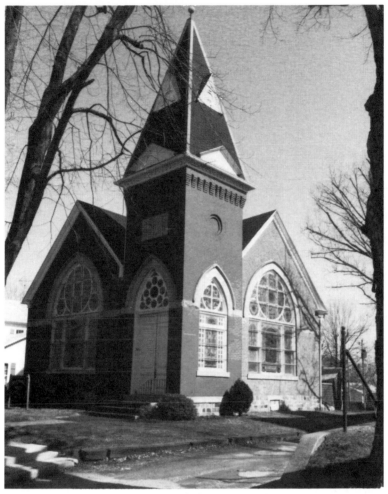
Ligonier's historical museum is housed in this former synogogue.

**Levy House)** (1899), 210 South Main Street; and **Stone's Trace** (1839), in the vicinity of US 33 and IN 5. The **Ligonier Historic District** (1835-1937) is bounded by the Conrail right-of-way, Smith, Union, College, and Grand Streets.

Sixteen miles east of Ligonier, just off US 6, is KENDALLVILLE (pop. 7,299).

The **Iddings-Gilbert-Leader-Anderson Block** (1891-1895), 105-113 North Main Street, Kendallville, is listed on the NRHP.

The last eastern county through which the Indiana Toll Road runs in Indiana is Steuben County. ANGOLA (pop. 5,486)

169

Stone's Tavern, south of Ligonier, is one of the buildings in the Stone's Trace Historical Society Museum complex.

is the county seat.

The county, named in honor of **Baron Friedrich von Steuben** who served under George Washington in the Revolutionary War, was established May 21, 1837. Angola was platted in 1838 and incorporated as a town in 1886.

Tri-State University was founded as Tri-State Normal School in 1884 by a group of Angola citizens. Tri-State is a private, nondenominational university with an enrollment of between 1,100-1,200 students.

HERSHEY MUSEUM is located in the basement of the General Lewis B. Hershey Hall on the West Campus. The museum focuses on local history. It is open weekdays by appointment, (219) 665-4141.

The **Steuben County Courthouse** (1868), and **Steuben County Jail** (1877), 201 South Wayne, in Angola, are listed on the NRHP. **The Free Church** (1876), Old Road 1 North, in the Angola area; **William L. Lords House** (c. 1848), Clear Lake Road; and **Enos Michael House** (c. 1850), 200 East Toledo Street, Fremont, are also listed on the NRHP.

It is 10 miles east on US 20 to the Indiana-Ohio state line. From I-80/I-90 at the I-69 intersection it is 13 miles to the state line.

# Chapter 6
# South on I-69

*There are many side roads to visit on this route through Indiana. For example, after leaving Fort Wayne there are several trips west of the interstate that offer differing kinds of history—for example, the Dan Quayle Museum in Huntington and then a little further west the birthplace of Gene Stratton Porter, one of the state's well-known authors. There are numerous opportunities on the east side of the interstate as well all along the route.*

# Roaring '20's and the Depression

The "war to end all wars" had come to an end and Americans feeling "good again" enjoyed good times during most of the Roaring '20s.

Warren McCray was elected to the governorship in 1921 but in the spring of 1924 was convicted of mail fraud and ousted from office April 30 to serve a 10 year prison sentence. Emmet F. Branch filled out his unexpired term.

Republican Ed Jackson, heavily supported by the powerful Ku Klux Klan, took over the governorship in 1925. It was the KKK that brought down several politicians in the state by exposing corruption in government.

Voters sent Harry G. Leslie, a Lafayette Republican, to the State House in 1929. It was the year of the Wall Street Crash and subsequent panic.

During the Great Depression Indianans trusted their leadership to Democrats.

They sent Paul V. McNutt to the Indianapolis State House in 1933. In 1937, it was M. Clifford Townsend of Grant County who was given the reins of state leadership.

Just as World War II loomed on the horizon, Democrat Henry F. Schricker of Knox became governor in 1941.

# Chapter 6
# South on I-69

It is 170 miles from I-80 and I-90 (the Indiana Toll Road), south on I-69, to Indianapolis. Several side trips are included to extend this mileage.

From the east west Interstate it is eight miles south and two miles east on US 20 to ANGOLA (pop. 5,486), county seat of Steuben County. (See Chapter 5 for more details.)

Returning to I-69 and continuing south it is 19 miles to Auburn Junction. The city is a mile east on IN 8.

AUBURN (pop. 8,122) is the county seat of DeKalb County, established May 1, 1837. The county seat was named in honor of **General Johann DeKalb** of the French army, who died fighting in the Revolutionary War. Auburn was settled in 1836 and was the original county seat.

**Brothers Frank and Morris Eckhart** became interested in the new invention, the automobile, in 1900. In 1903 they introduced their car, the Auburn named for their hometown, at the Chicago Auto Show. In 1919, the Eckharts sold their interest in the **Auburn Automobile Company** to an investor group from Chicago.

In their attempt to save the floundering company, the investors engaged **Errett Loban Cord** to run the business in 1924. Two years later, Cord owned the controlling interest in the company and became its president. In 1926, Cord purchased the **Duesenberg Motors Company** of Indianapolis in bankruptcy court. He renamed this company Duesenberg, Inc., and established it as a subsidiary of Auburn Automobile. In 1929, Cord introduced the Cord L-29, the first production automobile with front wheel drive, and the Duesenberg Model J. All 480 Model J Duesenbergs were handcrafted with a custom designed body tailored for the owner.

Cord introduced the celebrated Auburn Speedsters and Cords 810's during the Depression hoping these two models would save the company from collapse. He failed and the assembly line closed in 1937.

E. L. Cord was credited with saving the floundering Indiana automobile industry in the 1920s when he salvaged and then expanded much of the business in Connersville. He died in 1974.

The AUBURN-CORD-DUESENBERG MUSEUM is housed in the former Administration Building of the Auburn Automobile Company, 1600 South Wayne Street. Over 140 makes representing nearly every thing the automotive industry has

The Auburn-Cord-Duesenberg Museum in Auburn.

offered the world are on display. The administration building, dating back to 1930, is listed on the National Register of Historic Places (NRHP). The museum is open from 9:00 a.m. to 6:00 p.m. daily, except on Thanksgiving Day, Christmas, and New Year's Day. An admission is charged.

Another automobile, the DeSoto, was manufactured in Auburn from 1913 to 1916 by the De Soto Motor Car Company. The car manufacturer was taken over by Chrysler Corporation in Detroit. The IMP (1913-1914) was built by the W. H. McIntyre Company of Auburn. W. H. Kiblinger Company designed and built the Kiblinger, 1907-1909, and the McIntyre, 1909-1915. The Model, 1903-1909, was built by the Model Gas Engine Company from 1903 to 1906 when the company, now the Model Automobile Company, moved to Peru in 1906. The Zimmerman, 1908-1914, was built by the Zimmerman Manufacturing Company of Auburn.

The **Downtown Auburn Historic District** (1870-1936), bounded by East and West Fourth, North and South Cedar, East Twelfth, and North and South Jackson Streets, and **Eckhart Public Library and Park** (1911), 603 South Jackson Street, are listed on the NRHP. The **William Cornell Homestead** (c. 1863), southwest of Auburn on IN 427, is also listed.

Three miles west and one mile south of Auburn is GARRETT (pop. 4,751).

174

GARRETT HERITAGE PARK MUSEUM, on North Randolph Street north of the railroad crossing, features railroad memorabilia. It is open from 4:00 to 8:00 p.m. Friday, 1:00 to 6:00 p.m. Saturday, and 1:00 to 5:00 p.m. Sunday.

There are several structures listed on the NRHP in the area. These include the **Samuel Bevier House** (1905), CR 52 and CR 11; **Joseph Bowman Farmhouse** (1875), CR 19 and CR 40; **Brechbill-Davidson House** (1889), IN 8 and CR 7; **Brethren in Christ Church** (1882), CR 7; **Orin Clark House** (1870), CR 48 and CR 3; **DeKalb County Home Barn** (1908), CR 40; **William Fountain House** (1854), IN 8; **Gump House** (c. 1854), IN 8; **J. H. Haag House** (c. 1875), CR 54; **Edward Kelham House** (1870), CR 48; **Keyser Township School 8** (1914), East Quincy Street; **Charles Lehmback Farmstead** (1911), CR 15; **Mountz House** (1896), 507 East Houston Street; **Henry Peters House** (1910), 201 North Sixth Street; **Rakestraw House** (c. 1915), CR 19; **Henry Shull Farmhouse Inn** (1839), CR 11-A; and **John Wilderson House** (1909), 1349 South Cowen Street. Also listed is the **Garrett Historic District** (1875-1926), bounded by Railroad, Britton, Warfield and Hamsher Streets and Third Avenue.

At Spencerville, in the southeastern part of the county, the **Spencerville Covered Bridge** (1873), CR 68 at the St. Joseph River is another listing on the NRHP.

Twenty miles south of the Auburn Exit is FORT WAYNE (pop. 175,100), county seat of **Allen County**, established April 1, 1824. The county was named in honor of **John Allen** who had been in the army that relieved the siege of Fort Wayne in 1812. Allen was killed a short time after at the River Raisin Massacre.

Fort Wayne emerged from a chief town of the Miami Indians that was settled in the mid to late seventeenth century. The French founded a trading post here in 1680 and built **Fort St. Philippe (also called Post Miami)** in 1722. A second **Fort Miami** was constructed by the French in 1750 that remained in their control until 1760, when it was surrendered to the British. Indians controlled the fort briefly in Pontiac's Rebellion of 1763. British troops at the time were under the command of **Ensign Robert Holmes** who was lured out of the stockade by his Indian sweetheart and killed. The British recaptured the fort a short time later.

**General Josiah Harmar,** commanding American troops, was sent to the area to establish a post at Miami Town in 1790. Four days later, October 19, troops under command of **Colonel John Hardin** were attacked by Indians led by **Little Turtle**. **Major John Wyllys** and sixty of his men were slaughtered and Harmar's remaining command was forced to retreat. A year later **General Arthur St. Clair** led a second American army to the area only to be defeated by Little Turtle's Indians.

The task of ousting the Indian threat fell to **General "Mad" Anthony Wayne**, a Revolutionary War hero. Wayne defeated Little Turtle when he was sent to build a stockade in 1794. He chose a site for the American fort at today's intersection of Clay and Berry Streets. The chief engineer on the project was **Lieutenant John Whistler** and the fort was occupied on October 21, 1794. It was **Colonel John Hamtramck**, the post's commandant, who named the fort in honor of General Wayne.

Little Turtle emerged as the leader of the Indians in several treaty negotiations between 1795 and 1811. His most notable

A re-enactor's head is covered in the smoke of his flintlock rifle fire at a demonstration at the old fort at Fort Wayne.

176

words were uttered following the conclusion of negotiations of a treaty when he said, "I will be the last to sign this treaty, but I will be the last to break it." The Indian chief was invited to the national capital by Presidents Washington and Jefferson.

A new Fort Wayne was built in 1798 near the present-day location of Number 1 Fire House on East Main Street. John Whistler was responsible for its construction under **Colonel Thomas Hunt**. The new fort was not completed until 1800. **Tecumseh** and his brother, **Prophet**, visited Fort Wayne in 1807 and 1808 when **Captain Nathan Heald** was commandant. The area was the scene of sporadic Indian fighting for a dozen years beginning in 1800.

**William Wells**, the white son-in-law of Little Turtle, served as Indian agent at Fort Wayne from 1799 to 1809. While he served with Little Turtle in the defeats of Harmer and St. Clair, Wells became chief scout for General Wayne. Little Turtle and Wells played an important role in assisting the army in dealing with the Indians in the area. Little Turtle died in Wells's home in Fort Wayne on July 14, 1812 and was buried with military honors at the fort. A month later, Wells was killed by Potawatomis while assisting in the evacuation of Fort Dearborn.

The last Indian fighting in the vicinity of the fort occurred late in 1813 with the massacre of several of **Major Joseph Jenkinson's** men ambushed while moving supplies on the St. Mary's River to the fort.

Fort Wayne was rebuilt again in 1813-16 by now **Major John Whistler**, who had been given command of the post. His son, **George Washington Whistler**, a West Point graduate, became a famous railroad designer and builder, and his son, **James Abbott McNeill Whistler** (1834-1903), became a noted painter whose work includes the portrait of his mother, Anna McNeill.

The fort was closed as a U.S. military garrison on April 19, 1819.

The town of Fort Wayne began to develop in the early 1820s. It was incorporated as a town in 1829 and as a city in 1840.

Next to the Historical Museum parking lot, on Berry Street, is a historical marker noting the site of the first church building in Fort Wayne–the **First Presbyterian Church**–built in 1837. The First Presbyterian Church was organized July 1, 1831. The Roman Catholics were early arrivals in Fort Wayne and earlier were missionaries to the Indians in the region. The city is also known for its heritage and leadership in Lutheranism.

The first Jewish congregation in Indiana was organized here in 1848.

**John Chapman** (1774-1845), better known as **Johnny Appleseed**, wandered for over 40 years up and down Ohio, Indiana, and western Pennsylvania, visiting his forest nurseries

177

to prune and care for them and to aid hundreds of settlers in establishing orchards of their own. His ragged dress, eccentric ways, and religious turn of mind attracted attention, and he became a familiar figure to settlers. He was protecting newly planted saplings from some errant cows when he was overcome by exertion at one of his orchards north of Fort Wayne. He was buried along the St. Joseph River on the Archer farm, the site long forgotten. Many legends were told of him after his death. A historical marker has been placed atop the hill in present-day John Appleseed Park.

Ground breaking for the **Wabash & Erie Canal,** 1832-1874, occurred in Fort Wayne on February 22, 1832. Usually the canal was 50 feet wide and six feet deep and ran from Toledo, Ohio, to Evansville, Indiana. The canal and so-called packet boats, pulled by teams of two to six horses or mules, traveled six to eight miles per hour. Passengers were charged at three cents per mile on a packet boat; two and a half cents on freight boat. The first section of the canal to be completed was the leg to Huntington, then called Flint Springs, in 1835.

Another character noted in Fort Wayne's history is **Jean Baptiste Richardville,** chief of the Miami Indians who persuaded his Indians to cede the last of their territory to the U.S. government. The Indians felt he had betrayed them and he collected large sums of money from the sale of reservation lands. He died in 1841, a wealthy man, in his large brick house built for him by the government four miles south of city. In 1846, most of the remaining Miami Indians in the area, now refusing to work or integrate in the society, were moved to Kansas and later to the Oklahoma Territory. They were loaded on canal boats in Fort Wayne to begin their trek to Kansas and were led by **Chief Francis La Fontaine,** a son-in-law of Chief Richardville. He died enroute home in Lafayette.

The first railroad service, from Crestline, Ohio, was established in 1854 by the Ohio & Indiana Company. The Fort Wayne & Chicago line was established in 1856.

Although Allen County residents did not support President Lincoln, they rallied to the Union cause during the Civil War. Some 5,000 men were recruited for service and 500 died as a result of the war. The mustering and training center was at **Camp Allen,** just across the West Main Street bridge, along the St. Mary's River.

One of the regiment's organized at Camp Allen was the 30th Indiana Infantry, led by **Sion Bass.** He was killed at the battle of Shiloh in 1862. Bass's mother-in-law, **Eliza E. George** (1808-1865), who was known as "Mother George" on the battlefields, became a nurse serving on Union front lines in Mississippi, Tennessee, Georgia, and North Carolina. She died May 9, 1865 in Wilmington, North Carolina, of typhoid. She lived in Fort

178

Wayne before going off to war.

**Henry Lawton**, a student at Fort Wayne Methodist College, became a hero during the Civil War. As a captain in Company A, 30th Indiana Infantry, he received the Congressional Medal of Honor for heroism displayed in the battle of Atlanta, August 3, 1864. After the war, Lawton remained in the Army and served with distinction during the Indian wars. **Geronimo**, the wily Apache war chief, surrendered to Lawton after leading the Army on a wild chase in the southwest. Lawton achieved the rank of general before being killed December 9, 1899 in the Philippine Insurrection. A park in Fort Wayne is named in honor of this hometown hero.

During World War II an Army Air Corps base was established on the south side of the city. Named in honor of **Paul Baer**, a World War I ace, the airfield housed more than 2,000 airmen, who were training as fighter pilots. A training center was established at the railroad yards, near present-day McMillen Park, for Army locomotive engineers until 1943 and then became a German prisoner-of-war camp, called **Camp Scott**. It was closed in 1945.

The first professional baseball game in the world was played on May 4, 1874 when the **Fort Wayne Kekiongas** defeated the **Cleveland Forest Citys** 2 to 0. The National League was formed in 1871 when several baseball teams got together to organize. Among the first franchises was the Fort Wayne team. The Kekiongas had a miserable season in 1874 and disbanded midway in the schedule to be replaced in the National League by the Brooklyn Trolley Dodgers.

The first professional baseball night game was played in Fort Wayne in 1883. The playing field was illuminated by the new Jenney Arc Lights, invented by **James Denney** who had perfected the arc light about the same time Thomas Edison perfected the incandescent light. One of the players in this first night game was **Pearl Zane Grey**, who became famous for his numerous western novels.

There are three schools of higher learning in Fort Wayne—**Concordia Senior College**, founded in 1839; **Indiana Institute of Technology**, founded in 1930; and **St. Francis College**, founded in 1890.

Among some of the entertainment figures from Fort Wayne include actress **Carole Lombard**, born Jane Peters in 1908; humorist **Herb Shriner**; actress **Marilyn Maxwell**, a favorite on Bob Hope shows; and film and TV actress **Shelley Long**, who became well-known in her role on the popular TV series, *"Cheers."* Carole Lombard, a popular radio personality and sensuous film actress, was married to the popular actor Clark Gable. She was killed in a airplane crash in 1942 following her appearance at an Indianapolis bond rally.

179

Mother George (Mrs. Eliza E. George) was known to thousands of Union soldiers as she served as a nurse on the front lines during the Civil War as related in this historical marker.

The musical comedy *"Hellzapoppin,"* by **Chic Johnson** and **Ole Olsen**, premiered at the Palace here in 1936.

In 1931 the Zollner Piston Company relocated in Fort Wayne from Minneapolis. Fred Zollner, son of the founder, organized the **Zollner Pistons** professional basketball team. In 1946 the Zollner Pistons won the world's championship. The team was sold later and today is known as the **Detroit Pistons**.

The world's first contained washing machine went on the market in 1871 by Fort Wayne's Horton Washing Machine Company.

While James Jenney invented the arc light in Michigan, he came to Fort Wayne to market his new invention. He formed the Jenney Electric Company in 1881 and began selling urban lighting systems and in 1884 the company was contracted to provide the outdoor lighting for the New Orleans World's Fair. Another famous inventor to join the Jenney Electric Company was **Marmaduke Marcellus Slattery** who is best known as the father of the theory of alternating current. By 1911, the financially plagued company, by then called the Fort Wayne Electric Company, was bought out by the newly formed General Electric Company.

Another Fort Wayne native was **Samuel Foster** who was the "inventor" of the woman's shirtwaist or blouse in 1884 that became famous during the Gibson Girl era.

In 1911 native **George Jacobs** invented a method of coating electrical wiring, creating the magnet wire industry.

**Homer Capehart**, who became a well-known U.S. Senator, operated a small phonographic manufacturing company in Fort Wayne in the 1920s. By the late '20s, his engineers had developed a record-changing mechanism that lifted the records, turned them over and stacked them after they were played. The invention was sold to the Wurlitzer Company who made the juke box a world-wide product in the 1930s.

**Philo T. Farnsworth**, who brought his newly formed television manufacturing company to Fort Wayne and bought out Capehart, invented television in 1938. The company began to manufacture the first mass-produced televisions in 1940.

**Austin Armer**, leading a team of Magnavox engineers, invented the speaker system commonly known as stereophonic sound in the 1950s. In 1979, Magnavox engineers developed the first video games under the brand name of Odyssey.

In 1970, **Bowmar Incorporated** invented the world's first hand-held calculator, the "Bowmar Brain."

Modern day crime figures have made themselves known in Fort Wayne.

In 1930, **George R. "Machine Gun" Kelly** and members of his gang robbed the Broadway State Bank on the corner of Broadway and Taylor Street. In 1933, Kelly and other members of his gang kidnapped a wealthy Oklahoma oilman and after collecting a $200,000 ransom, released him unharmed. Kelly was captured in September 1933 and ultimately sentenced to life in prison. He died at Alcatraz in 1954.

Badman **John Dillinger** often was a visitor in Fort Wayne but never created any problems with the law. One of his trusted henchmen, Homer Van Meter, who had grown up in Fort Wayne's Bloomingdale district, robbed a train when he was only 19. Van Meter was a constant companion of Dillinger and was killed in a police ambush shortly after Dillinger was shot and killed by federal agents in Chicago in July 1934.

HISTORIC FORT WAYNE, 211 South Barr Street, is a full scale, authentically reconstructed military garrison as it ap-

The Historical Museum, on East Berry Street, is one of several to be found in Fort Wayne.

peared in 1816. Visitors can share in the daily life of accurately costumed civilian and military personnel as they relive the lives of actual 1816 residents. It is open from 10:00 a.m. to 5:00 p.m. Wednesday through Sunday, from mid-April through the end of October. An admission is charged.

THE HISTORICAL MUSEUM, 302 East Berry Street, is located in the old City Hall, built in 1893. A major attraction in the museum is "the Calaboose," the old city jail. Opened in 1984, "The Calaboose" represents the evolvement of the city police force through the lawless years to the present time. Other exhibits focus on city and county heritage. The museum is open from 9:00 a.m. to 5:00 p.m. Tuesday through Friday, and 12:00 noon to 5:00 p.m. weekends. An admission is charged.

Across the street, at 303 East Berry Street, is the GTE TELEPHONE MUSEUM. It is open from 10:00 a.m. to 4:00 p.m. Tuesday through Saturday. Admission is free.

The FIREFIGHTERS MUSEUM is located in an old fire station at 226 Washington Boulevard.

The CATHEDRAL MUSEUM is in the lower level of MacDougal Memorial Chapel on the grounds of the Cathedral of Immaculate Conception, on South Calhoun Street between East Jefferson Boulevard and East Lewis Street. The museum is open from 12:00 noon to 3:00 p.m. the second and fourth Sundays of the month. It is closed on holidays.

182

The LINCOLN LIBRARY AND MUSEUM, 1300 South Clinton Street in the home office of Lincoln National Life Insurance Company, houses one of the largest Abraham Lincoln collections found anywhere. The collection includes more than 20,000 books and pamphlets, thousands of manuscripts, 6,000 portraits, artifacts and family relics. It is open from 8:00 a.m. to 4:30 p.m. Monday through Thursday, and 8:00 a.m. to 12:00 noon Friday. Admission is free.

THOMAS W. SWINNEY HOMESTEAD, 1424 West Jefferson Boulevard, dates back to 1844. It is the center of Old Fort Settlers, a group dedicated to preservation of pioneer lifestyles and crafts. A two-story log cabin has been moved on the site. Tours by appointment. An admission is charged.

Worthy of a tour is the ALLEN COUNTY COURTHOUSE, 1 Main Street. Built in 1902 the building was designed by Brentwood Tolan and is characterized by a revolving copper statue surmounting a great dome over facades representing major historical figures. It is open from 9:00 a.m. to 5:00 p.m. weekdays. Admission is free.

FORT WAYNE MUSEUM OF ART, 311 East Main Street, features over 1,200 works of art by such well-known artists as Picasso, Matisse, Hopper, Wood, Renoir and Warhol as well as five traveling exhibitions annually. It is open from 10:00 a.m. to 5:00 p.m. Tuesday through Saturday and from 12:00 noon to 5:00 p.m. Sunday. An admission is charged. Admission is free to the public on the first Sunday of the month.

There are numerous structures in Fort Wayne listed on the NRHP. These include:

**Allen County Courthouse** (1902), 715 South Calhoun Street; **Johnny Appleseed Memorial Park**, Swanson Boulevard at Parnell Avenue along Old Feeder Canal; **John H. Bass Mansion (Brookside)** (c. 1902), 2701 Spring Street; **Blackstone Building** (1927), 112 West Washington Street; **Cathedral of the Immaculate Conception** (1860), Jefferson and Calhoun Streets; **William S. Edsall House** (1840), 305 West Main Street; **Embassy Theater and Indiana Hotel** (1928), 121 West Jefferson Street; **Engine House No. 3** (1893), 226 West Washington Boulevard; **Fairfield Manor** (1928), 2301 Fairfield Avenue; **Robert M. Feustel House** (1927), 4101 West Taylor Street; **Fort Wayne City Hall** (1893), 308 East Berry Street; **Fort Wayne Printing Company Building** (1911), 114 West Washington Street; **Journal-Gazette Building** (1928), 701 South Clinton Street; **Harry A. Keplinger House** (c. 1893), 235 West Creighton Avenue; **Kresge-Groth Building** (1926), 914 South Calhoun Street; **Lindenwood Cemetery** (1884, 1895), 2324 West Main Street; **Hugh McCulloch House** (1843), 616 West Superior Street; **Louis Mohr Block** (1891), 119 West Wayne Street; **John Claus Peters House** (1885), 831 West

Wayne Street; St. Mary's Catholic Church (1887), 1101 South Lafayette Street; St. Paul's Evangelical Lutheran Church (1889), 1126 South Barr Street; Schmitz Block (1888), 926-930 South Calhoun Street; Christian G. Struntz House (Sponhauer House) (1887), 1017 East Berry Street; Thomas W. Swinney House (1845), 1424 West Jefferson Street; Trinity Episcopal Church (1866), 611 West Berry Street; and Wells Street Bridge (1884), Wells Street at St. Mary's River. Also listed is the West End Historic District (1840-1934), bounded by Main, Webster, Jefferson, Broadway and Jones Streets, and St. Mary's River, as well as the Horney Robinson House (c. 1845), 7320 Lower Huntington Road in the Fort Wayne area.

Elsewhere in Allen County, the Craigville Depot (1879), Ryan and Edgerton Roads, in the New Haven area, and Fisher West Farm (c. 1860), 17935 West Road, in the Huntertown area, are both listed on the NRHP.

West of Fort Wayne some 20 miles on US 30 is COLUMBIA CITY (pop. 4,911), county seat of Whitley County.

WHITLEY COUNTY HISTORICAL MUSEUM, 108 W. Jefferson Street, occupies the home of former Vice President Thomas Riley Marshall (two terms under President Woodrow Wilson). The home was built in 1864 for John Rice and extensively remodeled in 1895 to suit the tastes of Thomas Marshall and his bride, Lois. It is listed on the NRHP. Throughout the home, visitors may view furniture, books, photographs, letters, and other personal items that belonged to the Marshalls. The museum is also filled with historic treasures of Whitley County. Items of local interest document pre-history of approximately 10,000 years past. Primitive Clovis points, which served as the early Indians only weapons, are displayed beside the bones of their prey. A highlight in the museum is an authentic "Mayflower Cup," a small cedar cup fashioned by Pilgrim hands during the Mayflower's historic voyage. Many of the items exhibited focus on the county's history. The museum is open by appointment, (219) 244-6372. Admission is free.

Driving south from Fort Wayne it is seven miles from the intersection of US 30 and I-69 to the US 24 Exit off I-69.

It is 21 miles south on US 24 to HUNTINGTON (pop. 16,202), county seat of Huntington County, established December 21, 1834. The county and city of Huntington were named for Samuel Huntington, a lawyer, governor of Connecticut, and a signer of the Declaration of Independence. The town was settled in 1831 and incorporated in 1848. Before 1831 it was called Wepecheange (place of flints).

Jean Baptiste Richardville, who once lived here, became the principal chief of the Miami Indians following the death of Little Turtle. Frances LaFontaine, the last principal chief of

This historical marker at Huntington provides background on Chief Richardville, last great chief of the Miamis.

the Miami Indians died in Lafayette in 1847 enroute home from Kansas where he had led his people. The 368-pound chief is buried in **Mt. Calvary Cemetery** on IN 5. **The Chief Richardville House and Miami Treaty Grounds** (1833-1841), west of Huntington on US 24 and IN 9, are listed on the NRHP.

Service to Huntington on the Wabash & Erie Canal was inaugurated on July 4, 1835. The first train arrived in Huntington on November 13, 1855.

This area was the home of one of the most active figures— **Lambdin P. Milligan**—in the Knights of the Golden Circle, an organization engaged in subversive activity against the Union in the Civil War. Milligan, a Huntington lawyer, was arrested with **Dr. William A. Bowles** of French Lick, **Horace Heffren** of Salem, and **Stephen Horsey** of Shoals in 1864 by Army authorities for fomenting rebellion. Heffren turned State's evidence accusing the other three with a plot to kidnap Indiana **Governor Oliver P. Morton** and hold him hostage during an insurrection planned for August 16, 1864. President Lincoln had suspended the writ of habeas corpus in cases where military officers held persons for offenses against the armed service. Milligan, Bowles, and Horsey were tried by a military commission, convicted of treason, and condemned to be hanged. They were taken out of the state by friends before the sentence could be carried out. The case, **Milligan, ex parte,** was finally decided by the U.S. Supreme Court in 1866. The high court held that civilians might be tried by a military tribunal only where civil courts could not function because of invasion or disorder. It ruled that there were limitations of martial law and that the Army had overstepped its authority because there were Federal courts operating in Indiana at the time and they alone might try the case. Milligan died in 1899 and is buried in Mount Hope Cemetery on US 24.

Other locals of note: **Lessel Long,** a Union soldier in the Civil War, was author of *"Twelve Months at Andersonville Prison."* Attorney **James R. Slack** served in the Union Army and attained the rank of brigadier general.

**John R. Kissinger** of Huntington, while serving as an army private in Cuba in 1900, submitted to the yellow fever tests of Dr. Walter Reed, head of the Yellow Fever Commission. Using the knowledge gained in these experiments, W. C. Gorgas was then able to rid Cuba and the Canal Zone of the disease by eradicating mosquitoes and preventing their contact with patients. Kissinger's health was so impaired by these experiments he received a lifetime pension from the government.

**Ed Roush,** who served in the U.S. Congress, was the founder of the 911 emergency number system used nationwide today.

**Chris Schenkel,** ABC-TV sports announcer, began his career announcing high school sports as a student in Huntington.

**Lt. Colonel Helen Purviance** was called the "Doughnut Girl" while serving with the Salvation Army on the front during World War I. She introduced doughnut production at Moniters, France, October 19, 1917.

**H. Allen Smith,** author of 40 books, lived in Huntington in his early years.

U. S. Vice President in the George Bush administration **J. Dan Quayle** is a native of Huntington. The QUAYLE MUSEUM, corner of Warren and East Tipton Streets, opened in June, 1993, and contains Quayle family memorabilia. The museum is open from 10:00 a.m. to 4:00 p.m. Dan Quayle served in both the House of Representatives and the U. S. Senate before his election as the 44th Vice President of the United States.

**Huntington College** was founded in 1897 by the Church of the United Brethren in Christ.

HUNTINGTON COUNTY HISTORICAL MUSEUM, on the fourth floor of the Huntington County Courthouse, focuses on county and local history. It is open from 1:00 to 4:00 p.m. Tuesday through Friday. Admission is free. The courthouse contains the nation's only surviving original GAR (Grand Army of the Republic) room on the second floor.

186

Dan Quayle, who served as vice president under President George Bush is a native of Huntington and one of several Indianans who have served as a vice president of the United States.

The Dan Quayle Center and Museum opened in his hometown of Huntington in 1993.

VICTORY NOLL, MOTHERHOUSE OF OUR LADY OF VICTORY MISSIONARY SISTERS, 1900 West Park Drive, is housed in a Spanish-Byzantine building atop a beautifully landscaped hill overlooking the river. It was founded in 1925 by Bishop Noll of the Roman Catholic Diocese of Fort Wayne. Visitors by appointment, (219) 356-0628.

GOOD SHEPHERD CHURCH OF UNITED BRETHREN (formerly the Monastery of St. Felix), 1280 Hitzfield, is a complex of Spanish Mission architecture. As the St. Felix Friary it was the home of Capuchin monks. Visitors by appointment, (219) 356-3789.

The structures in Huntington listed on the NRHP include the **German Reformed Church** (1903), 202 Etna Avenue; **Hotel LaFontaine** (1920), 200 West State Street; **John and Minerva Kline Farm** (1865), 2715 East 400 North; **Moore/Corlew Building** (1845), 400 and 410-418 North Jefferson Street; **Samuel Purviance House** (1859), 326 South Jefferson Street; **Taylor-Zent House** (1898), 715 North Jefferson Street; and **William Street School** (1895), 521 William Street. Elsewhere in the county, the **Guyer Opera House** (1902), on US 40, Lewisville, is also listed on the NRHP.

The house built by **Enos Taylor** on North Jefferson was constructed of bricks individually wrapped and shipped from Italy. It is considered one of the best examples of Romanesque architecture in Indiana.

West of Huntington, one mile south on IN 105 is ANDREWS (pop. 1,243), birthplace of **Ellwood Patterson Cubberly**, a nationally known educator. He graduated from Indiana University in 1891, taught at Vincennes, then became president of that school. Later he joined David Starr Jordan, the first president of Stanford University in California, in the development of a School of Education at the University. In 1938, Cubberly and his wife presented Stanford with enough money for the construction of a building for the School of Education.

From Huntington, it is 19 miles west on US 24 to WABASH (pop. 12,127), county seat of Wabash County, established March 1, 1835. The county and town were named for the **Wabash River** and the Indian word for " white water." Wabash was settled in 1834 and incorporated in 1854.

About a half dozen miles east of Wabash, north off US 24 is the birthplace of **Gene (Geneva Grace) Stratton-Porter**. She was born one of 12 children of a farmer and his invalid wife on the Hopewell Farm, August 17, 1873. Her father believed his oldest son living at home, Leander also called Laddie, would take over the farm but the young man drowned. The family moved to Wabash in 1874 where the mother died a short time later. Several members of the family, including Leander, are buried in the Hopewell Church cemetery. In 1884, Geneva Stratton met

188

The Hopewell Church, east of Wabash, served the rural area where noted Indiana author Gene Stratton Porter grew up as a young girl. Her father preached in this church and farmed land just across the road.

The Stratton family plot in the Hopewell Church cemetery. Several members of the family are buried here.

**Charles Darwin Porter**, 12 years her senior, and they were married in 1886. She wrote a dozen novels, several short stories, non-fiction books and poetry beginning in 1901. Among the best known of her novels are *"Freckles," "Girl of the Limberlost,"* and *"Keeper of the Bees."* Her novel, *"Laddie, A True Blue Story,"* written in 1913, was centered on her brother Leander.

A plaqued boulder near the corner of Market and Allen Streets in Wabash marks the **Site of the Signing of the Treaty of Paradise Springs**. The 1826 treaty between the U.S. and the Miami and Potawatomi Indian nations opened the area to white settlement.

The Wabash & Erie Canal arrived in Wabash in 1835 and with it the story of the near riot by two opposing group of Irish workers. About 300 of the canal construction workers were from northern Ireland with a like number from County Cork. The two groups had been feuding for some time when, on July 12, 1835, they drew battle lines and were about ready to commit mayhem on each other when the militia arrived to restore the peace.

Wabash was one of the first cities in the world to use electricity for public lighting when, on March 31, 1880, four carbon lamps atop the dome of the courthouse were lighted. On the courthouse square is the 35-ton statue of *"Lincoln of the People,"* by Charles Keck of New York. The courthouse is open from 8:00 a.m. to 4:00 p.m. weekdays.

190

The Wabash County Historical Museum is housed in this buidling just behind today's county courthouse.

Country Singer **Crystal Gayle**, born Brenda Gail Webb, graduated from Wabash High School.

The Champion automobile, 1916-1917, was built by the Champion Automobile Equipment Company in Wabash.

WABASH COUNTY HISTORICAL MUSEUM is housed in Memorial Hall, dedicated in 1899 as a tribute to veterans of American wars. It has a large collection of historical artifacts of Wabash County. It is open from 9:00 a.m. to 1:00 p.m. Tuesday through Saturday the year-round. Admission is free.

There are several NRHP listings in Wabash including the **James M. Amoss Building** (1880), 110 South Wabash Street; **First Christian Church** (1865), 110 West Hill Street; **Honeywell Memorial Community Center** (1940), 275 West Market Street; **Solomon Wilson Building** (1883), 102 South Wabash Street; **Downtown Wabash Historic District** (c. 1840 c. 1920), bounded by Hill, Wabash, Canal, and Miami Streets; and **Wabash Residential Historic District** (1840-1930), bounded by Norfolk Southern Railroad and Union Street, Wabash and Miami Street, Main Street, and Halliday Street.

LAGRO (pop. 549) on US 24 six miles east of Wabash at the

191

intersection of IN 524 is site of the **Kerr Lock** on the **Wabash & Erie Canal**. The lock, on Washington Street just off US 24, is one of the few remaining well-preserved locks of the canal. The side walls are in excellent condition and may be viewed at no cost. A CCC camp and World War II prisoner-of-war internment center were located near the Salamonie Reservoir.

Eleven miles south of Wabash on IN 13 is unincorporated SOMERSET where a monument marks the grave of **Frances Slocum**, kidnapped as a child and raised by Miami Indians. She was kidnapped during the Wyoming Massacre in Pennsylvania in 1778 and brought to the Peru area. She lived with the Indians as an Indian for 60 years and refused to return to her white family who eventually found her. She died in her adopted land.

Thirteen miles north of the intersection of US 24 and IN 13 at Wabash is NORTH MANCHESTER (pop. 5,998), home of **Manchester College**, moved from Roanoke, Indiana, to North Manchester in 1889, affiliated with the Church of the Brethren. The athletic field at the college was once the site of a Potawatomi village. The **Manchester College Historic District** (1889-1940), 604 College Avenue, is listed on the NRHP.

North Manchester was the birthplace of **Thomas R. Marshall** (1854-1925), former governor of Indiana (1909-1913) and Vice President of the United States under Woodrow Wilson (1913-1921). His was the expression, "What this country needs is a really good five cent cigar." Marshall moved to Columbia City in Whitley County when he was 20 years old and made his home there.

**Lloyd Cassel Douglas**, while pastor of the Zion Lutheran Church on Main Street from 1903 to 1905, was author of *"The Robe"* and *"The Big Fisherman."*

**Grace Van Studdiford** (1875-1927), a noted light opera singer, also lived in North Manchester.

Other structures listed on the NRHP in North Manchester include the **Lentz House (Hotel Sheller)** (1881), Walnut and Second Streets; **Noftzger-Adams House** (1880), 102 East 3rd Street; **North Manchester Planing and Band Saw Mill** (1876, 1898), 705 West Main Street (mill) and 706-708 West Grant Street and 202 North High Street (houses); and **North Manchester Covered Bridge** (1877), South Mill Street at the Eel River.

Elsewhere in Wabash County the **Roann Covered Bridge** (1877), north of ROANN (pop. 584) on CR 700W, is listed on the NRHP. Roann is nine miles north of Wabash on IN 15 and two miles west on IN 16.

In late January, 1934 the State Exchange Bank in Roann was robbed by **Merritt R. Longbrake**, who became one of the FBI's "most wanted" criminals.

Returning to I-69 at Fort Wayne, by taking US 27 and 33

192

from Fort Wayne south it is 22 miles to DECATUR (pop. 8,649), county seat of Adams County, established March 1, 1836. The county was named in honor of **President John Quincy Adams**. Decatur was platted in 1836.

Gene Stratton-Porter and her husband, Charles Darwin Porter, lived in Decatur for a short period and it was here their daughter, Jeanette, was born.

**David Lawrence Anspaugh**, a well-known film and TV producer-director, was born in Decatur September 24, 1946. He served as location director for the *"Super Train"* series; associate producer of *"Fighting Back"* and *"Vampire,"* two movies for TV; director and producer of the *"Hill Street Blues "* series for three years; and directed episodes on *"St. Elsewhere "* and *"Miami Vice"* as well as the TV special, *"The Last Leaf,"* starring Art Carney. He also directed the film, *"Hoosiers."* He has won numerous awards for his films.

Two noted sculptors, **David Smith** and **Ralph "Bud" Hurst**, were born in Decatur. Their works became famous worldwide. Smith was born in 1906; Hurst in 1918.

Author **Frederick Shroyer** is a native son, born October 28, 1916. He wrote *"Wall Against the Night,"* *"It Happened in Wayland,"* and *"There None Embrace."*

**Dr. Frank Charles Mann** served as director of experimental medicine and pathologic anatomy at the famed Mayo Clinic. He is credited with playing an important role in making the Mayo Foundation of the University of Minnesota a major center of training for academic medicine. He was best known for his studies on physiology and experimental pathology of the liver.

The **John S. Bower House** (1905), 104 Marshall Street, is listed on the NRHP.

Twenty miles south on US 27 is GENEVA (pop. 1,430), location of the **Limberlost State Historic Site** where Gene Stratton-Porter began her career as an author and naturalist. The Porters built a home near **Limberlost Swamp** in 1895. The swamp is said to have come by its name from the fate of **Limber Jim Corbus**, who went hunting in the swamp and never returned. When the locals asked where Jim Corbus was, the familiar answer would be "Limber's lost!" The swamp was drained in 1913.

During the 18 years she lived at the Limberlost, Mrs. Porter wrote six novels and five nature books, including the bestsellers, *"Freckles,"* *"Girl of the Limberlost,"* and *"The Harvester."* During her writing career, she wrote 12 novels, seven nature books, a book for children, two books of poetry, one book of essays, and numerous magazine articles.

The Porters built a 14-room home in the Limberlost. They were living in Rome City, Indiana, when, in 1920, Mrs. Porter's doctor advised they relocate to a better climate. The family

193

This was the home of Gene Stratton Porter near Limberlost Swamp where this noted author began her writing career.

moved to California where she continued to write. She was killed in an automobile accident in California in 1924.

LIMBERLOST STATE HISTORIC SITE, one block east of IN 27 in Geneva, preserves the white cedar log home of Gene Stratton-Porter and her family. The home was designed to blend with the area's magnificent surroundings. The Gene Stratton Porter cabin is listed on the NRHP. This is one of 17 sites in the Indiana State Museum System. It is open from 9:00 a.m. to 12:00 noon and from 1:00 to 5:00 p.m. Wednesday through Saturday, and from 1:00 to 5:00 p.m. Sunday. It is closed on Monday, Tuesday and some holidays. Donations are requested.

Geneva was the hometown of **Bob Juday**, who qualified for the 1924 Olympic team. He was an excellent athlete, played basketball, and participated in track events. In 1919, he won the Indiana high school high jump championship and in 1923, broke the U.S. Junior AAU record and held the title for five years. In 1924, he won the U.S. AAU championship qualifying him for the Olympic team.

Four miles north of Geneva is BERNE (pop. 3,301), home of the largest Mennonite Church in the country. Berne was founded in 1852 by Mennonite immigrants from Berne, Switzerland.

194

Berne was originally settled by 70 Mennonite immigrants who came directly from Switzerland in 1852.

The First Mennonite Church in Berne is the largest Mennonite church in the country.

This is Amish country where one can view the life style and heritage of this religious group.

From I-69, Berne can be reached off the US 224 Exit at Markle by taking IN 116.

**Robert "Bob" Dro**, a native of Berne, achieved significant

195

This is one of the exhibits in the Swiss Heritage Village just outside of Berne.

fame as a basketball star. He was inducted into Indiana's Basketball High School Hall of Fame, named a Big Ten Basketball All-American, named a Look Magazine All-American, and inducted into Indiana University's Athletic Hall of Fame.

Just outside of Berne to the north is SWISS HERITAGE VILLAGE. This is a Pioneer Village with beautiful gardens and a wild life preserve. The restored authenic buildings consist of a one-room brick school house, a church from the oldest congregation in the state, a half-timber house of 1848, a cheese house with a cheese maker's residence, a summer kitchen, the smoke house, and a hand-made commercial cider press, with the main beam 30 feet long and the screw 12 feet long. Restoration of other buildings is underway (1993). The Village is open from 10:00 a.m. to 4:00 p.m. Monday through Saturday and from 1:00 to 4:00 Sunday, June through August and open by appointment September and October.

Driving south on I-69 from Fort Wayne to the US 224 Exit, it is 13 miles from Markle to BLUFFTON (pop. 8,705), county seat of Wells County, established May 1, 1837. The county was named in honor of Indian agent **William Wells**, son-in-law of Chief Little Turtle. Bluffton was settled in 1836 and incorpo-

196

rated in 1851.

**Dr. Charles C. Deam**, the first State Forester, operated a drug store in Bluffton in the early 1900s. Starting as a hobby, Dr. Deam compiled the most comprehensive collection of plants and inventoried almost every species and variety of plants found in Indiana. His work has been used as the "bible" of botany by nationally known schools of agriculture and science, including Purdue University and Indiana University. Dr. Deam lived at 305 Wayne Street (not open to the public) in Bluffton.

**John Dillinger** was arrested in Ohio September 23, 1933 where he confessed that he had robbed the bank at Bluffton earlier.

WELLS COUNTY HISTORICAL MUSEUM, 420 West Market Street, is housed in the 1883 Stewart-Studabaker 3-story Victorian home. The museum contains over 10,000 catalogued items relating to Wells County history, culture, industry, business, and genealogy. Exhibits range from a 1902 curved dash Oldsmobile to the furniture and fixtures of the one-time bank of Uniondale in Wells County. The building is listed on the NRHP. The museum is open from 1:00 to 4:00 p.m. Wednesday and Sunday, June to August, and from 1:00 to 4:00 p.m. Sunday, April to November. Groups by appointment. It is closed Easter, Mothers Day, and Fathers Day. Admission is free.

The Wells County Historical Museum is housed in this 1883 Victorian home in Bluffton.

NRHP listings in Wells County, all in Bluffton or the surrounding area, include **Bethel Methodist Episcopal Church** (1900), southeast of the community; **John A. Grove House** (1891), 521 West Market Street; **Wells County Courthouse** (1891), 100 West Market Street; and **Villa North Historic District** (1891-1915), 706-760 and 707-731 North Main Street.

Back on I-69 it is 23 miles south and six miles west on IN 18 to MARION (pop. 36,000), county seat of Grant County, established April 1, 1832. The county was named in honor of **Moses** and **Samuel Grant** who died fighting Indians in southern Indiana. Marion, named in honor of **Francis Marion**, the "Swamp Fox" of Revolutionary War fame, was settled in 1826.

Marion has been selected as the site of the Quilters Hall of Fame. It is to be housed at 926 S. Washington Street, for many years the home of noted quilt designer Marie D. Webster. Mrs. Webster operated a mail-order quilt business, Practical Patterns, from this home. Her designs were featured in *Ladies Home Journal* in 1911.

Indiana's first commercial railroad made its headquarters in Marion.

Marion was the setting of the 1959 movie, *"Some Came Running."* The film received two academy award nominations.

The discovery of natural gas in 1887 in EATON (pop. 1,806) catapulted the tranquil farm town of Marion into a booming city, tripling the population in three years and redoubled in the next ten years. The gas boom ended just before World War I.

Marion is home of **Indiana Wesleyan University**, formerly Marion College, founded in 1920.

**Willis Van Devanter** (1859-1941), an Associate Justice on the U.S. Supreme Court from 1910 to 1937, was born in Marion. He practiced law in Indiana from 1881-84 when he moved to Wyoming and  became chief justice of the Wyoming supreme court in 1889, serving until 1897. He served as Assistant Attorney General and U.S. circuit court judge before his appointment to the U.S. Supreme Court. He was one of the four conservative justices who opposed most of President Franklin D. Roosevelt's New Deal.

**Captain George W. Steele Jr.**, who crossed the Atlantic Ocean by air four years before Charles A. Lindbergh accomplished the feat in 1927, was born in Marion.

**Caleb B. Smith**, President Lincoln's Secretary of the Interior, served as a local judge; Composer **Cole Porter**, studied music here; and **Kenesaw Mountain Landis**, first commissioner of organized baseball and an associate justice on the U.S. Supreme Court, practiced law in Marion.

Actor **James Byron Dean** was born February 8, 1931 to **Winton** and **Mildred Wilson Dean** in a house at the corner of Fourth and McClure Streets in Marion. The house has been

James Dean with his parents, Winton and Mildred Dean, in Marion in 1931, became a film actor. (Photograph courtesy of Fairmount Historical Museum, Inc.)

razed but a plaque marks the site. James Dean went to live on a Fairmount farm at the age of nine with an uncle and aunt, **Marcus** and **Ortense Dean Winslow**, after his mother's death on July 14, 1940. His mother is buried in Grant Memorial Park cemetery in southwest Marion.

America's first compact automobile, the Crosley, was built in Marion.

The **Aaron Swayzee House (Swayzee Love House)** (1855), 224 North Washington Street, and **J. Woodrow Wilson House** (1916), 723 Fourth Street, Marion, are listed on the NRHP.

**West Ward School** (1902), 210 West North Street, Gas City, is also on the NRHP.

**Taylor University**, founded in 1846, was lured to UP-LAND (pop. 3,335), on IN 22 southeast of Marion, in 1893.

Twenty miles east of Marion on IN 18 is MONTPELIER (pop. 1,995). **John Dillinger** and **Harry Copeland** robbed the First National Bank of Montpelier of $10,110 on August 4, 1933.

Nine miles south on I-69 from the Marion exit and six miles west on IN 26 or seven miles south from Marion on IN 9 and east on IN 26 is FAIRMOUNT (pop. 3,286), home of several prominent Americans. Among these personalities are **Mary Jane Ward**, author of *"The Snake Pit"* and *"A Little Night Music,"* among others; actor **James Dean**, who achieved fame for his roles in *"East of Eden"* and *"Rebel Without a Cause;"* cartoonist **Jim Davis**, creator of "Garfield;" **Phil Jones**, an award winning CBS news commentator; and **Robert C. Sheets**, director of the U.S. National Hurricane Center.

Among others who have achieved distinction are **Captain David L. Payne** who is credited with the founding of the State of Oklahoma because of his agitation as early as 1881 to open the Territory to settlement; **James R. Life**, who originated the idea of guiding ships and missiles electronically; **Dr. James A. DeWeerd**, was one of the youngest college presidents at the time he was named president of Kletzing College, Iowa, at the age of 33; **Dr. Thomas E. Jones**, served as president of Earlham College and Fisk University and was known for his writing abilities; **Alvin Seale**, a scientist who wrote over 140 publications and served as director of the Steinhart Aquarium in San Francisco, California, for 20 years; and **Dr. James A. Huston**, author, military historian, and teacher.

Perhaps the late James "Jimmy" Dean draws the greatest attention to Fairmount at the present time. About a mile north of town is Park Cemetery where the actor is buried. A mile north

The Fairmount Historical Museum features a large James Dean memorial exhibit. He gained fame as an actor in the film "East of Eden." He was killed in an auto accident in California.

It was at Fairmount High School that James Dean became interested in acting, inspired by a teacher. (Photograph courtesy Fairmount Historical Museum, Inc.)

of the cemetery is the Back Creek Friends Church where funeral services for Dean were held October 8, 1955, and a mile further north is the Winslow farm. Neither the church or the Winslow farm home are open to the public. He attended high school in Fairmount, played on the school basketball team, and was involved in plays and debates.

James Dean returned to visit Fairmount friends and relatives in February, 1955. He finished shooting *"Giant,"* the third blockbuster movie in his brief career and Warner Brothers was lining up his next film, *"Somebody Up There Likes Me,"* to be shot in 1956 in a six film deal over the next nine years. The only major film released before his death was *"East of Eden,"* with Julie Harris.

On the afternoon of September 30, 1955 at the intersection of California Highways 466 and 41 near Cholame east of Paso Robles, James Dean, driving a sports car, crashed into a limousine driven by a 23-year old student. Neither the limo driver or Dean's passenger, mechanic Rolf Wentherich, were seriously injured but the young actor died enroute to the hospital from his injuries. Dean and his mechanic were driving to Paso Robles for a car competition.

FAIRMOUNT HISTORICAL MUSEUM, 203 East Washington Street, features a large James Dean memorial exhibit along with area history. Exhibits of other local celebrities are also displayed. The former house of J. W. Patterson, in which the museum is housed, is listed on the NRHP. The museum is open from 10:00 a.m. to 5:00 p.m. weekdays and Saturday and from 12:00 noon to 5:00 p.m. Sunday, March through November. Admission is free but a dollar donation is suggested.

When the first settlers arrived in 1830 they called their settlement **Pucker**, a name that stuck for 20 years. In 1850, the name was changed to Fairmount for **Fairmount Park** in Philadelphia.

The town gained national attention in 1887 when the Fairmount Mining Company struck gas on a site now occupied by Fairmount Wire Products, Inc. It was a major strike and the well was called "Jumbo" and it was claimed to be the greatest producer in Indiana. In the fall of 1888, a fire started at the well that created such a blaze that people came from miles around to witness it. The well had a short life and was closed down in less than 20 years.

**Milton Wright**, father of Orville and Wilbur Wright, inventors of the airplane, is said to have founded the first telephone company in the community. It is claimed that **Elwood Haynes** of Kokomo developed his automobile from a wrecked vehicle invented by three Fairmount men—**Orlie R. Scott, Charles T. Payne**, and **Nathan A. Armfield**—in their shop at 215 East Washington Street. The trio forgot to install any kind of brakes on their horseless carriage and wrecked their vehicle on its test run. The men were ready to give up on their idea when Scott sold the wreck to Haynes who later was credited as being the inventor of the first automobile.

Southeast of Fairmount, near Matthews, the **Cumberland Covered Bridge** (1877), on CR1000 over the Mississinewa River, is listed on the NRHP.

East of Fairmount on IN 26 is HARTFORD CITY (pop. 7,622), county seat of Blackford County, established February 18, 1839. The county was named in honor of **Judge Isaac**

202

**Newton Blackford** of Indiana's Supreme Court and the U.S. Court of Appeals. Hartford City was settled in 1832, laid out in 1839 and incorporated in 1857.

BLACKFORD HISTORICAL MUSEUM, 321 North High Street, focuses on Blackford County heritage and history. It is open from 1:00 to 4:00 p.m. on Sunday. Admission is free.

The **Blackford County Courthouse** (1894), off IN 3, and **First Presbyterian Church** (1893), 220 North High Street, are both listed on the NRHP.

Twenty three miles east on IN 26 is PORTLAND (pop. 7,074), county seat of Jay County, established March 1, 1836. The county was named in honor of **U. S. Supreme Court Chief Justice John Jay** of New York. Portland was founded in 1835 and incorporated in 1843. It was the birthplace of **Elwood Haynes** (1857-1925), inventor of the first successful clutch-driven automobile. His birthplace, on Commerce Street a block north of Fire Station #1, is identified with a historical marker.

Haynes was also a successful scientist and inventor especially in the field of metallurgy. While only a boy of 15 he invented an apparatus for making gas and later invented the basic cobalt-based alloys known as Stellite alloys. He also invented stainless steel. He graduated from Portland schools and in 1883-84 served as principal of Portland High School and in 1885-86 taught science in Portland's Eastern Indiana Normal

The only concrete bow-string-truss bridge in Indiana is this one over the Salamonie River in Portland.

Two museums in Portland are the Jay County Society Museum (above) and the privately owned Studebaker Museum (below).

School. He was named manager of the Portland Natural Gas and Oil Company in 1886 and served in that capacity until 1890 when the family moved to Greentown. He became famous as the inventor of the first successful automobile while a resident of Kokomo.

Portland was also the birthplace of actor **Leon Ames,** born Leon Wycoff January 20, 1902. He appeared in over 100 motion pictures.

JAY COUNTY HISTORICAL SOCIETY MUSEUM, 903 East Main Street, houses a collection of historic artifacts and memorabilia relating to the county. It is open only by appointment by calling Orville Freeman (219) 776-2551 or Roseamond Scott (219) 997-6749.

THE STUDEBAKER MUSEUM, 929 West Main Street, is a private museum owned by George Reitenour, the noted auto racer. He named his 1936 Studebaker racing car "The Spirit of Jay County." The museum is open by appointment only by calling (219) 726-4678.

The South Meridian Street bridge over the Salamonie River is the only concrete bow-string-truss bridge in the state of Indiana. It was built in 1913 following the design of local engineer O. O. Clayton.

South of Portland, off US 27, is the **Treaty Marker,** identifying the boundary line established by a treaty with the Miami Indians in 1818.

**Floral Hall** (1891), West Votaw and Morton Streets, and **Jay County Courthouse** (1919), on US 27, are listed on the NRHP. Also listed on the NRHP is the grouping of **Religious Buildings at Trinity (St. Marys of the Woods Convent, Holy Trinity Church, Rectory and School)** (1845-1885), northeast of Portland.

In the west part of Jay County is DUNKIRK (pop. 3,180), home of THE GLASS MUSEUM, 309 South Franklin Street, featuring over 5,000 pieces of glass from 105 factories. Among the exhibits are leaded glass windows, hand blown and hand-pressed glass creations. The museum is open from 10:00 a.m. to 5:00 p.m. Tuesday through Saturday, and from 1:00 to 5:00 p.m. Sunday, May 1 through November 1. It is closed on Monday. Special tours can be arranged, (317) 768-6809.

At the intersection of Highland Avenue and North Main Street in Dunkirk is a memorial in honor of union organizer **Benjamin Rubrecht** who was active in the glass industry in the early part of this century. At one time there were seven glass factories in Dunkirk as a result of the gas boom of the 1880s. The community was first called Quincy and was laid out in 1837.

West of Portland, four miles north on US 27 and west CR 80, is PENNVILLE (pop. 798) on IN 1. There are a number of old buildings and other attractions along this route. Unincorporated

BALBEC is north of Pennville and is the site of an old station on the Underground Railroad. A restored cabin and a historical marker here pinpoint the site of the station.

Back on I-69 at the exit to Fairmount it is 18 miles south to IN 332 and east on IN 332 is MUNCIE (pop. 73,300), county seat of Delaware County, established April 1, 1827. The county was named in honor of the **Delaware Indians**. Muncie, originally called Munseytown, was platted in 1827 and incorporated in 1847. It was given its present name in 1845.

North on Minnetrise Boulevard, between Crane and Walnut Streets, is the site of a Delaware Indian Munsee clan's early village. In March, 1806, the Indians burned **John A. Christian** at the stake, an Indian martyr of the Christian faith.

Muncie expanded rapidly after the natural gas boom in the 1880s. Many industries located in this and other regional communities because of low cost fuel.

It is home of **Ball State University**, opened in 1899 as Eastern Indiana Normal University. It changed ownership several times and each time was given another name until 1918 when the Ball family, including five brothers, acquired the school and presented it to the state.

BALL STATE UNIVERSITY MUSEUM OF ART is located in the central portion of the Fine Arts Building, Riverside at Warfield, on the Ball State University campus. An unusual aspect of this collection, is that a written explanation about the artist, the style, the period, and other facts of interest accompany the works of art. The collection includes more than 9,500 originals including paintings, sculpture, prints, ancient glass, and other decorative arts from such masters as Rembrandt, Jean Honore Fragonard, Edgar Degas, and Alexander Calder. Some of the pieces date back 5,000 years. The museum is open from 9:00 a.m. to 4:30 p.m. Tuesday through Friday and from 1:30 to 4:30 p.m. weekends. It is closed Monday and Easter, Fourth of July, Thanksgiving, Christmas Eve and Day and New Year's Eve and Day. Admission is free.

MUNCIE CHILDREN'S MUSEUM, 306 South Walnut Plaza, is a totally hands-on museum with 18 interactive exhibit areas featuring natural sciences, physical sciences, and natural history. Children may explore an ant hill, experiment with magnets, discover the properties of water, and pretend to be a paleontologist. Future plans call for moving the museum to larger quarters to provide for updating existing exhibits as well as additional exhibits. All ages are welcome with a focus on the age group of pre-school to the fifth grade. The museum is open from 10:00 a.m. to 5:00 p.m. Tuesday through Saturday, and from 1:00 to 5:00 p.m. Sunday, year-round. It is closed on Monday and holidays. An admission is charged.

MINNESTRISTA CULTURAL CENTER, 1200 North

Photo above: Muncie Children's Museum provides unique experiences for pre-schoolers and school children to the fifth grade. Photo below: The beautiful and modern Minnestrista Cultural Center provides a view of history, art and science of east central Indiana.

Minnestrista Boulevard, is located on 20 landscaped acres on the banks of the White River in downtown Muncie. The center exhibits the history, art and science of east central Indiana. All exhibits are changed on a periodic basis. The center is open from 10:00 a.m. to 5:00 p.m. Tueday through Saturday, and from 1:00 to 5:00 p.m. Sunday. It is closed on Monday. An admission to the galleries is charged.

In 1908, Muncie was placed under martial law for two weeks during a strike of traction workers in the trolley system.

An automobile, the Inter-State, 1909-1918, was built by the Inter-State Automobile Company whose name changed in 1914 to the Inter-State Motor Company. The Sheridan, 1920-1921, was built by the Sheridan Motor Car Company and the Stratton, 1909, was built by the C. H. Stratton Carriage Company. The Rider-Lewis, 1908-1910, was manufactured by the Rider-Lewis Motor Car Company and the Princeton, 1923-1924, by Durant Motors, Inc.

Listed on the NRHP in **Muncie–Boyce Block** (1860), 216-224 East Main Street; **Hamilton Township Schoolhouse No. 4** (1897), IN 67; **J. C. Johnson House** (1897), 322 East Washington Street; **Margaret and George Riley Jones House** (1903), 315 East Charles Street; **Masonic Temple** (1926), 520 East Main Street; **Moore-Youse-Maxon House** (c. 1860), 122 East Washington Street; **Muncie Public Library** (1903), 301 East Jackson Street; **Roberts Hotel** (1921), 420 South High Street; **Francis T. Roots Building** (1895), 115-119 East Charles Street; **F. D. Rose Building** (1926), 121 East Charles Street; **John Valentine House** (1918), 1101 Riverside Avenue; and **Dr. Samuel Vaughn Jump House** (1855), southeast of town on IN 2.

The **Emily Kimbrough Historic District** (1880-1930), bounded by Monroe, East Washington, Hackley, and East Charles Street; **Old West End Historic District** (1827-1922), bounded by the White River and Washington Street, Liberty Street, Howard Street, and Orchard Place and Kilgore Avenue; and **Wysor Heights Historic District** (1880-1930), bounded by Highland Avenue, White River, North Elm Street, and North Walnut Street, are also listed on the NRHP.

In the northeast part of Delaware County, just off IN 67 is ALBANY (pop. 2,625). The Albany Automobile Company built the Albany car here in 1907-1908.

East of Muncie on IN 32 approximately 18 miles is WINCHESTER (pop. 5,559), county seat of Randolph County, established on August 10, 1818. The county is said to be named for **Randolph County, North Carolina,** or **Thomas Randolph,** a casualty of the Battle of Tippecanoe. Winchester, believed to be named for War of 1812 veteran **Brigadier General James Winchester,** was settled in 1819. Where the county and county

208

seat names came from officially remain a mystery.

**Robert Wise**, award winning film director for such hits as *"West Side Story"* and *"Sound of Music,"* was born in 1914 in Winchester. He lived here until he was eight years old when his family moved to Connersville.

The RANDOLPH COUNTY MUSEUM, 416 South Meridian Street, is housed in the former Cary Goodrich residence, constructed in 1859. The museum focuses on county history. It is open from 2:00 to 4:00 p.m. Sunday.

The WINCHESTER HISTORICAL MURAL hangs in the first floor corridor of the Randolph County Courthouse and depicts the important names and places in the county's history. There are 26 faces incorporated in the artwork by local artist Roy Barnes and includes such personalities as two governors, Isaac Gray (1880-81, 1885-89) and James P. Goodrich (1917-21); U.S. Senator James Eli Watson (1916-33); film director Robert Wise; and bio-chemist Wendell M. Stanley. Among the important places is the Winchester Speedway.

An interesting story is related to the Soldiers and Sailors Monument in the courthouse square. The 67-foot monument was dedicated July 21, 1892 with Governor Ira Chase delivering the dedicatory remarks. The story began in 1888 when the last will and testament of James Moorman, a 66 year old Quaker, left $2,000 of his estate to erect a monument to honor the Union

The Randolph County Museum is housed in this former 1859 Winchester residence.

This Soldiers and Sailors Monument in Winchester has an interesting history of its own.

veterans of Randolph County. As a Quaker, Moorman was supposed to be a "conscientious objector" but everyone believed had he been younger he would have joined the Union forces during the Civil War. Now that $2,000 had been contributed for a monument, one had to be built and the state legislature passed a measure permitting the county commissioners to spend $25,000 for such a project. The county appropriated the money in March, 1889. After some dispute over the design of the monument it was finally built and dedicated three years later. The cost to the county, after deducting the $2,000 Moorman gift, was $23,659 and Winchester could then boast it had the second largest veterans' memorial in the state.

For those with a sweet tooth it should be noted that Winchester is site of Wick's Pie Factory, south of Washington Street at Greenville Avenue, home of the famous patented Sugar Cream Pie.

**Silver Towne**, near the east city limits of Winchester, is known nationally by numismatists for its gold and silver coin collections.

Nearby are Indian earthworks called **Fudge Mound**, excavated in 1929. Skeletons, spear points, and copper bracelets were among some of the findings in this dig.

The **General Asahel Stone Mansion** (1872), 201 West Orange Street, Winchester, is listed on the NRHP.

About two miles west of Winchester, on IN 32, is the world famous **Winchester Speedway**, established in 1914 by **Frank Funk**. The state's second oldest racetrack, Winchester Speedway is hailed as the world's fastest half-mile track.

UNION CITY (pop. 3,908), nine miles east of Winchester on the Indiana-Ohio state line, was platted on the Indiana side in 1849. The portion of the town in Ohio was first platted in 1838.

For a time, Union City played a role in the emerging automobile business. The Union City Body Company, founded in 1898, provided the bodies for several autos including such early arrivals as the Haynes, Apperson, Essex, and Duesenberg. The Union Automobile Company built the Union here from 1902 to 1905.

The **William Kerr House** (c. 1896), 501 North Columbia Street, and **Union City Passenger Depot** (1913), on Howard Street, are listed on the NRHP. The Depot houses the Art Association of Randolph County whose collections include works by noted Indiana printmaker **Frederick Polley**. Polley was a native of Union City.

North of Winchester on IN 28 is RIDGEVILLE (pop. 993), birthplace of **Wendell Meredith Stanley**, who shared the 1946 Nobel Prize in chemistry with J. H. Northrop and J. B. Sumner for his isolation of crystalline forms of viruses. The famous biochemist was born in 1904 and received his education at Earlham College in Richmond, IN, and the University of Illinois.

**Ridgeville College**, one of the state's pioneer educational institutions, operated from 1867 to 1900.

The Victor Automobile Company built the Senator car here in 1906-1910.

RIDGEVILLE-KITSELMAN MUSEUM, INC., 110 East First Street, provides exhibits and displays focusing on Ridgeville history and its noted citizens. It is open from 2:00 to 4:00 p.m. Sundays the year-round and at other times by appointment, (317) 857-2598. An admission is charged.

The Ridgeville-Kitselman Museum focuses on the history of Ridgeville and its more illustrious citizens.

In the southeastern most part of Randolph County is unincorporated ARBA, once the largest settlement in the county. The village's history dates back to 1815 when the Friends' established a meetinghouse here. The village was not platted until 1855. It is site of a newer Friends' meetinghouse today.

North of Arba about four miles is SPARTANBURG, another unincorporated village settled by the Friends. The Friends established the **Union Literary Institute** here in 1845, which was chartered by the state in 1848. This school served primarily young blacks with an elementary and secondary-level education until shortly after the Civil War.

West of Spartanburg, via US 36, is LYNN (pop. 1,250). This small town was devastated by two tornadoes that struck in March, 1986. While no one was killed or injured, 24 homes were destroyed and 260 other buildings were damaged creating losses of more than $4 million.

The Washington Township Library and Museum is located in Lynn. For information, please contact the librarian.

The return to I-69 via IN 32 takes one through Muncie and to Daleville within two-three miles from the city limits of ANDERSON (pop. 60,400), county seat of Madison County. The county, established July 1, 1823, was named in honor of **Presi-**

212

**dent James Madison**. Anderson, occupying the site of a former Delaware Indian village, was platted in 1823 and incorporated in 1838. Called Andersontown until 1853, Anderson was named in honor of **Chief Kikthawenund**, an important Delaware Indian leader, whose name in English translated to **Captain Anderson**. When approached by Chief Tecumseh to join in the fight against white settlers, Captain Anderson declined. Captain Anderson lived in a log cabin located at a site at the present Eight Street and Central Avenue intersection.

The town's first "boom" occurred with the construction and opening of the Central Canal, a branch of the Wabash & Erie Canal, in 1837. The second "boom" came in 1851 with the establishment of rail service to Anderson, provided by the Indianapolis & Bellefontaine Railroad.

Anderson's first fire was in 1851 and all but destroyed the business section around the public square.

Anderson's Shadyside Park was acquired by the city in 1923 and dedicated in July that year as a memorial to the veterans of all wars.

213

The discovery of natural gas in the region in the late 1880s created a major "boom" to Anderson and other communities in a wide area in this part of Indiana. The first gas well here was opened March 31, 1887.

The first street railway, drawn by mules, was completed September 6, 1888 and the first electric street railway was completed in 1892.

On December 31, 1936, members of the United Auto Workers of America went on strike at General Motor's Guide Lamp division shutting down all General Motor operations in Anderson. Governor Townsend declared martial law and sent troops in to keep the peace. The strike was settled when a nationwide agreement was reached giving workers the right to bargain collectively.

Several automobiles have been built in Anderson. Among these were the Lambert, 1891, 1904-1917, by the Buckeye Manufacturing Company and the Laurel, 1916-1920, built by the Laurel Motors Corporation. The Madison, 1915-1918, was built by the Madison Motor Company and the Real, 1914-1915, by the H. Paul Prigg Company. The De Tamble was built here from 1909 to 1913 after moving from Indianapolis in 1909.

**Anderson College** was founded in 1917 by the Church of God.

**Carl D. Erskine**, pitcher for the Dodgers for 12 seasons, was

The Alford House/Anderson Fine Arts Center is housed in this former 1870 residence of a local banker.

born and raised in Anderson. Upon graduation from high school he attended Anderson College. During his professional baseball career, Erskine won 122 games and lost 78. He participated in five World Series, appearing in 11 games. He retired from the Dodgers in 1960 and today is a banker in Anderson.

Anderson is the hometown of **Sandi Patti,** nationally-known gospel music singer. With over ten million recordings sold, she has been awarded five Grammy Awards and 32 Dove Awards (the Gospel Grammy equivalent) through 1992. She began her professional singing career in 1979.

The GRUENEWALD HOUSE. 626 North Main Street, be-

The Gruenewald House in Anderson dates back to 1860.

This historical marker adjacent to the Gruenewald House describes the history of this historic Anderson structure.

gan as a modest two-story brick house in 1860 and the front sections of the house were constructed between 1870 and 1875. It is listed on the NRHP. The house is open for tours from 10:00 a.m. to 3:00 p.m. Tuesday through Friday, April 1 to mid-December. For additional details call (317) 646-5771.

ALFORD HOUSE/ANDERSON FINE ARTS CENTER is located at 226 West Historical Eighth Street. The Alford House, built c. 1870, was the private residence of Neal C. McCullough, founder of the Citizens Banking Company. Constructed of bricks made from clay excavated from the basement site, the original house consisted of a formal parlor and dining room on the first floor, and three bedrooms and a ballroom on the second floor. Since 1967 the Alford House, donated to the people of Anderson by Nellie Alford Hill, has been home to the Anderson Fine Arts Center. Today it features three spacious exhibition galleries and a theatre area that is also used for meetings, luncheons, and temporary exhibits. The Fine Arts Center is open from 10:00 a.m. to 5:00 p.m. Tuesday through Saturday and 2:00 to 5:00 p.m. Sunday, September through July. Admission is free.

Nearby **Mounds State Park** has numerous prehistoric

mounds. The Moravians operated an Indian mission in the area in 1801-06.

The **Anderson Bank Building** (1928), 931 Meridian Street; **Carnegie Public Library** (1905), 32 West 10th Street; **Mounds State Park**, three miles east of town on IN 32; **West Central Historic District** (1880-1934), bounded by Brown-Delaware, 10th, John, and 13th Streets; and **West Eighth Street Historic District** (1870-1910), bounded by 7th, 9th, Jackson, and Henry Streets, all in Anderson or the area, are listed on the NRHP.

The **George Makepeace House** (1850), 5 West Main Street, Chesterfield, is also listed on the NRHP.

On July 17, 1933, **John Dillinger** and his gang pulled off their first bank robbery in DALEVILLE (1,749), east of Anderson. The robbery netted the gang only $3,500. Dillinger went on to become America's "Public Enemy No. 1." He was shot down by G-Men in Chicago a year later.

PENDLETON (pop. 2,130), south of Anderson on US 36 a mile east of I-69, was the site of the brutal murder of two Indian men, three women and four children in 1824. Four of the five white culprits were apprehended and three of these white men were hanged. The fourth, an 18 year old youth, was pardoned at the last minute by the governor.

ELWOOD (pop. 10,867), in the northwest part of the county on IN 28, is the birthplace of Wendell Lewis Willkie (1892-1944), who ran against Franklin D. Roosevelt for the U.S. presidency in 1940. A Democrat, Willkie switched to the Republican Party in 1940 as he could not accept Roosevelt's New Deal and became the Republican presidential nominee. His nomination speech was delivered from Elwood on August 17, 1940 where 250,000 are said to have gathered in the small town for his acceptance speech. The speech was aired over national radio. He was defeated in the election but garnered 22,000,000 of the popular vote. In 1941-42, he served as Roosevelt's personal representative on visits to England, the Near East, Russia, and China. Between 1942-44, he led the fight to liberalize the Republican Party, mainly attacking isolationism.

Willkie wrote his book, *"One World,"* after his 1941-42 world tour and it went through seven printings and sold more than 750,000 copies. Willkie died of a heart attack on October 8, 1944 and is buried in East Hill Cemetery in Rushville, Indiana, his wife's hometown. He was the fourth child of Herman and Henrietta Willkie; born February 18, 1892. Interestingly, he was named Lewis Wendell but when he joined the army in 1917 it became Wendell Lewis through a clerical error. Since he didn't care for his original name, he adopted Wendell as his first name and Lewis eventually was reduced to the initial "L."

**James J. Davis** (1873-1947), a resident of Elwood, became

This monument in Elwood Park honors native Wendell L. Willkie, 1940 Republican presidential nominee. He was also author of "One World."

director general of the Loyal Order of the Moose in 1907 and was active in the development of the Lodge. He was appointed Secretary of Labor by President Warren G. Harding in 1921 and served in the same post in the administration of Calvin Coolidge. He served until 1930 when he was elected to the United States Senate from Pennsylvania, an office he held until 1945. Davis was born in Wales and arrived in the U.S. at the age of eight.

Elwood was laid out in 1853 and incorporated in 1872. The town was first called Quincy but since the name had already been taken by another Indiana community, the name was changed.

From Anderson it is 35 miles to downtown Indianapolis.

# Chapter 7
# Highway US 31 South

*This route takes the visitor from Mishawaka south and ranging east and west from US 31 to such places as Bremen, Walkerton, Plymouth, Twin Lakes, Culver, Knox, Warsaw, Winona Lake, Mentone, Oswego, Rochester, Winamac, Peru, Grissom AFB, Logansport, Kokomo, Greentown, Tipton, Noblesville, and Westfield. The counties to be visited on this route are Marshall, Starke, Kosciusko, Fulton, Pulaski, Miami, Cass, Howard, Tipton, and Hamilton.*

# During and Following WW II

Governor Henry Schricker led the state through the World War II years. He was replaced in 1945 by Republican F. Gates of Columbia City.

A first occurred in 1948 when Henry Schricker, out of office for four years, was elected governor and assumed office in 1949.

The governors to follow include George Craig, a Brazil Republican, in 1953; Republican Harold W. Handley of LaPorte in 1957; Matthew E. Welsh, a Democrat from Vincennes in 1961; Democrat Roger D. Branigin of Lafayette in 1965; Edgar D. Whitcomb, a Republican, in 1969; Dr. Otis "Doc" Bowen, a Bremen Republican, in 1973 and again in 1973. In 1981, Republican Robert Orr became governor and he was reelected in 1985.

# Chapter 7
# Highway US 31 South

US 31 crosses the Michigan state line just west of South Bend. For the purposes of this guide South Bend is included in Chapter 5 that follows the general route of I-80 and I-90 east and west.

From the intersection of US 33 and US 31 it is two miles to MISHAWAKA (pop. 41,500).

From the same intersection it is 16 miles south to the intersection of US 31 and US 6. East eight miles on US 6 is BREMEN (pop. 3,487) in the northeast corner of Marshall County. The **Bremen Stand Pipe**, an American Water Landmark, was built in its unique design in 1892. It stands 110 feet tall. The home of **Dr. Otis R. Bowen**, former Speaker of the Indiana House of Representatives, governor, and Secretary of Health and Human Services, is located just east of Bremen.

West of the US 31 and US 6 intersection five miles is WALKERTON (pop. 2,006).

The STUNTZ-INDIAN MUSEUM, 20451 N County Line, Tyler Road, has a collection of arrowheads and antiques donated by Indians in the area. The museum was started by Ervin Stuntz, who died in 1993 at the age of 93. An Indian burial ground is at the rear of the property. The museum is open from 10:00 a.m. to 5:00 p.m. Monday through Friday with extended hours during the Christmas season.

Traveling further south on US 31 in Marshall County it is seven miles to the intersection of US 31 and US 30. The county seat of Marshall County is PLYMOUTH (pop. 7,693). The county, named for **U.S. Supreme Court Justice John Marshall**, was established April 1, 1836.

MARSHALL COUNTY HISTORICAL SOCIETY MUSEUM opened in October 1993 on North Michigan Street. Its exhibits and displays focus on county and area history. For more information, call 1-800-626-5353.

There are several structures in Plymouth listed on the National Register of Historical Places (NRHP). These include the **Marshall County Courthouse** (1872), 117 West Jefferson Street; **Plymouth Fire Station** (1875), 220 North Center Street; and the **East LaPorte Street Footbridge** (1898), spanning the Yellow River. Elsewhere in the county the **Dietrich-Brown House (Governor Bowen House)** (1900), 304 North Center Street in Bremen, nine miles east of US 31 on US 6, and **Woodbank (Rasmussen Cottage)** (1894), 2738 East Shore Lane on Lake Maxinkuckee in the Culver area southwest of

The Marshall County Historical Society Museum is located in downtown Plymouth.

Plymouth are also listed on the NRHP.

The statue of **Chief Menominee** was erected in 1909 near Twin Lakes south of Plymouth. The memorial is located off 12th Street on Peach Street south. Chief Menominee played a role in the infamous **Trail of Death** episode in America's history. It was near this area in September 1838, 859 Potawatomi Indians were removed from northern Indiana to Osawatomi, Kansas, a 640-mile trek.

Approximately 14 miles west of Plymouth, via IN 17 and IN 8, is KNOX (pop. 3,519), county seat of Starke County, created

This statue of Chief Menominee of the Potawatomi Indians was erected near Twin Lakes south of Plymouth. Chief Menominee played an important role in the removal of Indians in this area to Osawatomi, Kansas, in September 1838, creating the infamous Trail of Death.

February 7, 1835 and named for **John Stark** an army officer who served during the French and Indian War and Revolutionary War. As in the case of many handwritten records of that time, an "e" was added to the name for the county designation.

The community of Knox was named for another army officer and friend of George Washington. The first settlers arrived in 1835 and Knox was designated the county seat in 1850. The county grew slowly and the population in the 1870 census was placed at only 244.

STARKE COUNTY MUSEUM, 401 South Main Street and Schricker Drive, is operated by the Starke County Historical Society. It features memorabilia relating to the county. The museum is open from 12:00 noon to 4:00 p.m. weekdays. Admission is free.

The county courthouse, 1897, is listed on the NRHP.

Twenty-four miles east of the intersection of US 31 and US 30, on US 30, is WARSAW (pop. 11,400), county seat of Kosciusko County, established June 1, 1837 and named in honor of **Thaddeus Kosciuszko**, a young Polish nobleman who served as an aide to General George Washington during the Revolutionary War. Warsaw was settled c. 1836 and incorporated in 1854.

A visitor examines one of many exhibits in the Kosciusko County Jail Museum in Warsaw.

224

Excitement ran high in Warsaw Friday, April 13, 1934 when the notorious **John Dillinger** robbed the Warsaw police station of two pistols and three bullet proof vests. Dillinger and another gang member, **Homer Van Meter**, both armed with machine guns, captured **Police Officer Jud Pittenger** at 1 a.m. two blocks from the police station and after clubbing him several times forced him to take them to police headquarters. Pittenger managed to escape from his captors as they were ransacking the office. Dillinger and Van Meter gave chase briefly and then fled in a dark sedan. The robbers were not apprehended.

Warsaw's jail, built in 1870, serves as home of the Kosciusko County Museum and Genealogy Library.

One of the most noted criminal trials held in Kosciusko County Circuit Court took place in May, 1921. Four men were tried for the murder of Culver, Indiana, **Fire Chief Jacob Seine** while making their escape after robbing the State Exchange Bank in Culver. The trial had been moved from Marshall County, where the crime occurred, to Kosciusko County for legal reasons. The noted attorney of the early 1900s, **Clarence Darrow** defended the four that included **Joseph Burns, Art Silbert, Joe Beyers**, and **Peter Fox**. Darrow was able to save them from the electric chair by they were sentenced to life imprisonment in the Indiana State Prison on May 20th. Joseph Burns was one of the ten escapees from the Indiana State Prison in September, 1933. Burns, with a $100,000 reward for his capture, was the last of the ten Michigan City escapees to be captured. He was involved in several criminal activities with Dillinger after his escape and was captured in an apartment on Chicago's south side about five months after Dillinger's death. Burns was paroled from Indiana State Prison August 22, 1943 and pardoned by the governor October 20, 1944.

    **Merritt R. Longbrake** of Kosciusko County became one of the FBI's "most wanted" for a series of bank robberies in Indiana and Ohio. He began his criminal career inauspiciously in 1931 when he was arrested and convicted of grand larcency (stealing hogs) that earned him a sentence to the Indiana State

Evangelist Billy Sunday lived in this home in Winona Lake.

226

Prison. After serving time briefly he was paroled and then went on his crime spree. By the time he was captured in Omaha, Nebraska, in 1935, he was on the FBI's most wanted list.

JAIL MUSEUM, 121 North Indiana Street, was formerly the old jail built in 1870 and used through 1982. It has been adapted to house the **Kosciusko County Museum and Genealogy Library**. The building is listed on the NRHP. The museum is open from 10:00 a.m. to 4:00 p.m. Thursday, Friday, and Saturday, and from 1:00 to 4:00 p.m. Sunday and all other times by special appointment, (219) 269-1078. A donation is requested.

The Old Iron Bridge, 3.5 miles west of Warsaw, is owned by the Kosciusko County Historical Society. Built in 1897 on the Tippecanoe River, this bridge separated the Indian reservations of Chief Mota and Chief Checosee. There is ample parking.

The Courthouse and Justice Building, 100 West Center Street, are open for tours. The county courthouse, built on three floors, was constructed in 1884; the justice building was dedicated in 1982. Tours lasting about an hour begin at 9:00 a.m. and end at 3:00 p.m. Admission is free.

Just east of Warsaw is WINONA LAKE (pop. 2,827) once the home of the famed evangelist **Billy Sunday** (1863-1935). A native Iowan, Sunday played professional baseball in Chicago, Pittsburgh and Philadelphia from 1883 to 1890 and was employed by the YMCA in Chicago from 1891 to 1895. In 1896, he became an evangelist and drew large crowds to his revival meetings. A flamboyant speaker, Sunday is said to have preached to over 100 million persons and converted over a million in his campaigns. He was ordained in 1903 in the Presbyterian Church.

BILLY SUNDAY HOME, 12th Street and Sunday Lane, is open for viewing only; there are no tour guides available. It takes about 20 minutes to walk through the home. The house was donated by **Mrs. Helen A. Sunday** as a historical site. Call for an appointment, (219) 372-5232. Admission is free; donations are accepted.

From Warsaw it is 13 miles via IN 25 to MENTONE (pop. 973), hometown of **Lawrence Dale "Larry" Bell**, famous aviation pioneer.

Larry Bell, the youngest son of **Isaac** and **Harriet Sarber Bell**, was born in Mentone on April 5, 1894 and lived with his family here until 1907 when they moved to California. In 1912, Larry joined his older brother, Grover, a noted stunt pilot of the day. Grover was killed in an air crash in 1913 and Larry briefly quit aviation. The call to aviation was too strong and he joined the Glenn L. Martin Company. By the time he was 20 years old he was a shop foreman. Within a few years he was promoted to vice president and general manager of the company. He left Martin in 1928 to work for Consolidated Aircraft. By 1935, he

227

The Bell Aircraft Museum in Mentone honors the aviation pioneer Lawrence "Larry" Bell.

formed his own company, Bell Aircraft Corporation, and in its first 20 years recorded 20 firsts in aviation. For these accomplishments he was honored with the Daniel Guggenheim Medal, the Collier Trophy, a presidential citation, the French Legion of Honor, honorary degrees and many others.

Here are his 20 "firsts" in aviation: the twin-engine fighter (Airacuda); first aircraft to mount 37 mm cannon and flexible gun turrets (Airacuda); first modern multi-place fighter, establishing a new type for the Army Air Corps (Airacuda); first American fighter airplane designed around its armament (P-39 Airacobra); first use of a tricycle landing gear on modern military aircraft (P-39); first satisfactory .50 caliber machine gun shock dampener which became standard on both Army and Navy airplanes; first modern all-wood military fighter (XP-77); first helicopter with automatic stabilizing control; first jet-propelled fighter in the United States (P-59); first commercial helicopter; first supersonic airplane (X-1); first commercial helicopter with 200 hp engine and skid landing gear; first airplane able to vary degree of wing sweepback during flight (X-5); first radio-guided bomb (Tarzan); first helicopter designed specifically for anti-submarine warfare (HSL-1); first airplane able to fly at speeds two and a half times the speed of sound and at altitudes of 90,000 feet (X-1A); first turbine-powered helicopter (XH-13F); first jet-propelled vertical take-off and landing airplane (VTOL); first automatic carrier landing system; and first convertiplane incorporating tilting-rotor system (XV-3). At the time of his death in 1956, Bell was dean of American aviation, having served in the industry 44 years.

LAWRENCE D. BELL MUSEUM, Oak St. off IN 25, provides the history of aviation pioneer Lawrence Bell, builder of the supersonic aircraft, the XI, and developer of the first commercial helicopter. The museum is open from 1:00 to 5:00 p.m. Sunday and Monday through Saturday by appointment, (219) 353-7551 from June 1 through September. An admission is charged.

The Pound Store Museum in Oswego occupies a building dating back to 1838.

North six miles on IN 15 is LEESBURG (pop. 629) and from here turn east on the county road to OSWEGO on the banks of the Tippecanoe River. Oswego was originally part of Indian Chief Musquabuck's village.

POUND STORE MUSEUM is housed in the oldest commercial building in the county. It features a number of unusual collections. Open only by appointment, call (219) 267-8434. A donation is suggested.

Back in Warsaw the **Warsaw Cut Glass Company** (1911), 505 South Detroit Street and the **Warsaw Courthouse and Jail Historic District** (1881-1930), bounded by Center, North Lake, Main, and Indiana Streets, are listed on the NRHP.

ARGOS (pop. 1,393) is on US 31 seven miles south of Plymouth. It is home of the ARGOS MOTORCYCLE MUSEUM. More information may be obtained in Argos.

West of Argos, via IN 10, is CULVER (pop. 1,783), home of the **Culver Academies**, a private secondary school for boys and girls. Founded by **Henry Harrison Culver**, The "Culver Academy," for boys, opened September 24, 1894 with 45 cadets. One of the best known Culver Military Academy traditions is the **Black Horse Troop** founded three years after the academy

The Chapel at Culver Academies. Henry H. Culver founded the private secondary school in the late 19th century.

The Fulton County Museum and Round Barn are located four miles north of Rochester.

opened. The Black Horse Troop has a long tradition of participating in presidential inaugural parades and in 1913 served as guard of honor for the incoming vice president, Thomas Marshall. To the Culver Military Academy was added in 1970 the Culver Academy for Girls, later to become the Culver Girls Academy.

It is 21 miles south on US 31 from Plymouth to ROCHESTER (5,050), county seat of Fulton County, named in honor of inventor **Robert Fulton**, famous for his steamboat. The county, the Round Barn Capital of the World, was created February 7, 1835. Rochester was founded by **Alexander Chamberlain** in 1835 and organized as a town in 1853. A descendant, **John Chamberlain**, has been acclaimed as one of the outstanding sculptors in the world.

The noted poet **Joaquin Miller** lived in Fulton County from 1848 to 1852. The poet was born Cincinnatus Heine Miller in Liberty, Indiana. He became famous as a frontier poet with the publication of his book "*Songs of the Sierras,*" in 1871.

Rochester served as a winter headquarters for **Cole Brothers Circus** from 1935-40. The wild animal trainer **Clyde Beatty** and high wire performers **The Great Gretonas (Willi and Clara Lamberti, Franz Heinzmann, Eugen Lechler and Otto Gretona)** lived here during that period. A circus family, the Zoppes, who performed for the Cole Brothers Circus and Ringling Brothers, Barnum & Bailey Circus, still live in

Rochester (in 1993) and take their several acts to circuses and fairs around the country. **Jorgen Christiansen**, circus horse trainer and Circus Hall of Famer, trained the first Liberty Act (horses trained to perform without being tied to anything "at liberty") for Barnum & Bailey in 1924. He performed with the circus touring Russia during the 1917 Revolution and wrote a book about his experiences during this tour.

"The Pacing Farmer" **Oliver Powell** was a Rochester native. He raised and trained pacing horses for more than a half century and had horses that set four world records for the breed. **Colonel Isaac Washington Brown** (1848-1914), traveled across the country giving speeches to save the birds, sponsored by wealthy philanthropist, Helen Gould. He is buried in the IOOF cemetery in Rochester.

Actor **Elmo Lincoln**, another native, played the first Tarzan on the screen in 1918. Lincoln was born Otto Elmo Linkenfeldt in Rochester in 1889, descendant of one of the earliest settlers. Still another native, Paul Spotts Emrick, invented the forming of block letters by marching bands in 1907, first to do illuminated night formations, gyrating letter formations, fanfare trumpets and massed lyrabells during his half century as director of the Purdue University band. Other locals to gain fame in the music world were **The Kings Jesters**, the trio comprised of **John Ravencroft**, **George Howard**, and **Francis Bastow**. They were popular in the 1920s and performed with the Paul Whiteman Orchestra in the same decade. The trio performed for more than four decades.

**Dr. Otis Brown**, born in Fulton County, served as the governor, 1972-80, and as Secretary of Health in President Reagan's 1985-88 cabinet. **Floyd J. "Jack" Mattice**, the attorney who defended Japanese war criminals during the 1945 Tokyo trials, died here in 1970. Interestingly, Mattice was the first in America to broadcast a sports event over the radio in 1903. After World War II, he worked for the FBI. **Congressman Henry A. Barnhart** (1908-18) started the Rochester Telephone Company in 1895.

The Potawatomi Trail of Death began in the Plymouth area on September 4, 1838. The next day the 859 Indians marched through Rochester. The first of 39 members of the tribe died six miles south of Rochester at Mud Creek during the two month ordeal that ended on a reservation on the Osage River in Kansas on November 4, 1838. A historical marker has been set at this site on IN 25. When Chief Menominee refused to acknowledge the 1832 treaties, **Governor David Wallace** sent **Colonel Abel C. Pepper** to remove the tribe from the state.

THE FULTON COUNTY MUSEUM & ROUND BARN, on US 31 four miles north of Rochester, relates the history of the county in 17 displays. The Round Barn Museum, in connection, has farm machinery and tool displays. The barn was originally built in 1924. The museums are open from 9:00 a.m. to 5:00 p.m. Monday through Saturday, May through October. Admission is free.

There are three other Fulton County Historical Society museums that make up a Living History Village—the **Rochester Depot** and **Pioneer Woman's Log Cabin**, adjacent to the Fulton County Historical Society museum and **Round Barn Museum**—depicting farm life during the 1900-1925 period. Several other buildings will be added to the Living History Village over time. The **Leiters Ford Depot**, northwest of Rochester on the Tippecanoe River, is another Society museum. It is open June through August by appointment only. For more information, call (219) 223-4436. The Fulton County Historical Society is (in 1993) restoring the 1832 William Polke house which will become part of the Living History Village. Polke was wounded in the Battle of Tippecanoe and was a delegate to the 1816 Indiana Constitutional Convention. He was Rochester's first settler, arriving in 1830 as a surveyor for the Michigan Road. He was also involved in the conducting of the Trail of Death episode in 1838.

There are six structures in Fulton County listed on the NRHP. Two of these, the **Lyman Brackett House** (1886), 328 West 9th Street, and the **John W. Smith House** (1892), 730 Pontiac Street, are in Rochester. The **Leedy Round Barn** (now Round Barn Museum) and **Haimbaugh Round Barn**, north of Rochester on IN 25. The other two are in the Akron area and include the **Prill School** (1876), and **Utter-Gerig Round Barn** (1915). There are also more than 10 round barns in the county worth viewing. Remember to seek the landowners' permission to view these barns if you enter private property.

Just southeast of Rochester is Lake Manitou and it was here in 1837 the Manitou Monster was sighted. For those interested in these kinds of mysteries, a visit is suggested to Lake Manitou and some of the inhabitants who can relate the legend.

Twenty two miles west of Rochester, via IN 14, is WINAMAC (pop. 2,370), county seat of Pulaski County. The county was established May 6, 1839. Winamac was settled in 1837 and incorporated in 1868.

PULASKI COUNTY HISTORICAL MUSEUM, behind the library and county building off Riverside Drive facing the Tippecanoe river bank, focuses on county and local history. The museum is open from 1:00 to 4:00 p.m. Friday April through December. It is closed January, February and March.

The **Dr. George W. Thompson House** (1897), 407 North Market Street, is listed on the NRHP.

From Rochester it is 30 miles south to PERU (pop. 12,843), county seat of Miami County. The county, named for the **Miami**

(Above) Composer and lyricist Cole Porter was born in this house at 102 East Third Street in Peru. (Below) The Peru Circus Center features circus memorabilia.

**Indians**, was established March 1, 1834. The Wabash & Erie Canal ran through the county.

Perhaps one of Peru's most famous personalities was **Cole Porter**, the internationally famous American composer and lyricist. Among some of his most well-known songs are *"Night and Day," "Kiss Me, Kate," "Begin the Beguine," "What Is This Thing Called Love?"* and *"In the Still of the Night."* His birthplace at 102 E. Third Street is identified by a marker.

Peru has been a winter headquarter for circuses for decades. **The Wallace Circus and American Circus Corporation Winter Headquarters,** 1892-1929, 2.5 miles southwest of Peru just off IN 124, is listed on the NRHP.

PERU CIRCUS CENTER, Broadway and 7th Street, contains costumes, photographs, model circus wagons, and other memorabilia. A nationally acclaimed amateur circus festival begins the third Wednesday of July. The Center is open 9:00 a.m. to 5:00 p.m. weekdays. An admission charge is made during Circus City Festival, donation at other times.

MIAMI COUNTY MUSEUM, 51 N. Broadway, focuses on county history through a variety of exhibits and displays. It is open from 10:00 a.m. to 5:00 p.m. Tuesday through Saturday and from 1:00 to 4:00 p.m. Sunday. Admission is free.

PUTERBAUGH MUSEUM, Senger Building north of the county courthouse, is open during the same hours. Admission is free. The Brownell Block/Senger Dry Goods Company Building, 1884, is listed on the NRHP.

The Miami County Museum is housed in this former department store in downtown Peru.

235

On October 20, 1933, shortly after his escape from the Lima, Ohio, jail, aided by escaped convicts from the Indiana State Prison in Michigan City, bank robber **John Dillinger** and his gang robbed the Peru police arsenal of several firearms and a large supply of ammunition. Dillinger had been arrested and was being held in the Ohio jail on charges of bank robbery in the state on August 14, 1933.

Several early day automobiles were built in Peru: the Bryan, 1918-1923, by Byran Steam Motors; the Great Western, 1908-1916, by Great Western Automobile Company; the Izzer, 1911, by Model Gas Engine Company which also built the Model (the name given the car), 1906-1909 , and the Star, 1908.

Three miles southwest of Peru on IN 124 is the **Godfroy Cemetery**. The cemetery, listed on the NRHP, is the burial place of **Francis Godfroy**, last Miami Indian war chief. His trading post was across the road.

Other NRHP listings include the **James Omar Cole House** (1883), 27 East 3rd Street, and the **Brownell Block/Senger Dry Goods Company Building** (1884), Broadway and Fifth Streets, in Peru, and the **Paw Paw Creek Bridge No. 52** (1874), at Chili north of Peru on IN 19.

Grissom Air Force Base, located seven miles south of Peru on US 31, was home of the 305th Air Refueling Wing. Formerly the Bunker Hill Naval Air Station, it was named for **Virgil "Gus" Grissom**, the Indiana astronaut killed in an accident on the launch pad. The air base has been scheduled to be deactivated in the 1990s. An Air Park at the entrance to the air base has been

Just outside the main gate of Grissom AFB is the Heritage Museum in Air Park.

Among several aircraft on display in Heritage Park at the entrance to Grissom AFB are the B-47 Stratojet (above) and the F-107 (below). Several World War II vintage aircraft are displayed here.

designated a Heritage Museum with displays of World War II and other aircraft.

West of Peru on US 24 approximately 16 miles is LOGANSPORT (pop. 17,400), county seat of Cass County. The county, named in honor of **General Lewis Cass** who was instrumental in signing of Indian treaties, was established April 13, 1829. Logansport, named for an Ohio Shawnee chief who was

237

killed during the War of 1812 fighting for the Americans, was incorporated in 1838. The Wabash & Erie Canal reached Logansport in 1838 and rail service arrived in 1855.

After the first railroad arrived, Logansport built railroads leading out of the city in nine different directions. Its transportation facilities were equal to or greater than any other city in the state except Indianapolis. By 1921, the city had grown into a large rail center with 228 trains daily. Almost 3,000 men were employed by the railroads. Five hundred workers lost their jobs and others were transferred to Fort Wayne and Columbus where the railroads relocated as a result of a violent workers' strike in late 1921.

Support pilings for the Wabash & Erie Canal may still be seen on the south bank of the Eel River between the Third and Sixth Street bridges.

In Old Towne Park, near Logansport, are two graves of the only U.S. soldiers killed in battle in Cass County. These were two mounted Kentucky riflemen under General James Wilkinson's command killed in a 1791 battle with the Miami Indians. Inquire locally for directions.

The ReVere Motor Car Corporation built the ReVere automobile, 1917-1926, here as was the Bendix, 1907-1910, by The Bendix Company.

CASS COUNTY HISTORICAL SOCIETY MUSEUM, 1004

The Cass County Historical Society Museum is housed in Logansport's Jerolaman-Long House dating back to 1853.

East Market (US 24E), is housed in the Jerolaman-Long House dating back to 1853. It is listed on the NRHP. The museum features Indiana artifacts, paintings, lustreware, fine furniture, a Civil War library and other items of local and area interest. A re-erected pioneer cabin and barn adjoin the museum. The museum is open Tuesday through Saturday and the first Sunday afternoon of the month. Admission is free.

IRON HORSE RAILROAD MUSEUM, Fourth and Melbourne just south of Market Street, provides a history of railroading in this area. The museum is open from 8:00 a.m. to 12:00 noon and from 1:00 to 5:00 p.m. weekdays. Admission is free, contributions are welcome.

Of special interest is the **Logansport Carousel** comprised of 44 wooden animals hand carved by Gustav Dentzel and his artisans more than 100 years ago. It is the only original "ring catch" carousel in the United States. In Riverside Park on the Eel River, the carousel is open from Memorial Day to Labor Day. There is a charge to ride the carousel. It is listed on the NRHP.

Other structures listed on the NRHP in Logansport include the **Thompson Barnett House** (1854), on IN 25; **Ferguson House** (c. 1895), 803 East Broadway; **Kendrick-Baldwin House** (c. 1860), 706 East Market Street; and **Pollard-Nelson House** (1845, 1910), Seventh and Market Streets.

Back on US 31 west of Peru it is 19 miles south to KOKOMO (pop. 46,500), county seat of Howard County. The county, named in honor of **Tilghman Ashurst Howard**, Indiana district attorney and representative, was created May 1, 1844. The city, named for **Miami Chief Kokomo**, was settled in 1840 and laid out in 1844.

The University of Indiana has a campus here.

Probably no name in Kokomo's history stands taller than that of scientist and inventor **Elwood Haynes** who lived in the city for 33 years. This remarkable Indianan, a native of Portland, built the first gasoline driven automobile in 1893-94 with the trial run performed July 4, 1894 down Pumpkinvine Pike in Kokomo. Speed for that run was six or seven miles per hour. This site is identified with a large historic marker.

Haynes conceived the idea of a "horseless carriage" and prepared drawings for its construction in 1891. He completed the plans for the construction of his "horseless carriage" in 1892 when he and his family moved to Kokomo. In November 1893, he purchased a one-horse marine upright two-cycle gasoline engine and a short time later hired **Elmer** and **Edgar Apperson** to build his "horseless carriage" from the plans he had developed at their Riverside Machine Shop in Kokomo. He paid the Apperson brothers forty cents an hour for their work. The original car was placed in the Smithsonian Institution in 1910, a gift from Haynes.

239

The remarkable Elwood Haynes and his invention, the first suceesful gasoline driven automobile.

The **Haynes-Apperson Automobile Company** was organized on May 24, 1898 although the partnership built their first car, the Haynes-Apperson, a year earlier. This partnership was dissolved in 1902 and each started his own automobile company. The Apperson, 1902-1926, was built by Apperson Brothers Automobile Company from 1902 to 1926 with the company named changed in 1924 to the Apperson Automobile Company. The Haynes, 1904-1925, was first built by Haynes-Apperson from 1902-1905 and the Haynes Automobile Company the balance of the production.

The automobile industry was thus launched in Indiana and since that time over 250 different makes of cars have been built in the state.

Haynes received a number of patents in metallurgy. Perhaps his most significant invention in this area was stainless steel and Stellite, an alloy still used today. When he was only 15 years old he invented an apparatus for making gas and succeeded in melting brass, cast-iron and high carbon steel, using a furnace and blower he made himself. When he became manager of the Portland Natural Gas and Oil Company in 1886 he invented a small vapor thermostat to regulate heat in homes. In 1890, he discovered how to dry gas by refrigeration to prevent pipeline freezing. This not only evaporated the water but also reduced lower-boiling constituents to gasoline. He introduced aluminum in automobile engines in 1895 and nickel steel into the automobile in 1896. In 1903, he invented and built a rotary gas valve engine.

Haynes ran unsuccessfully for the United States Senate on the Prohibition Party ticket in 1916. He was a member of the Indiana Board of Education and Indiana State Library Board from 1921 until his death on April 13, 1925. He graduated from Worcester (MS) Polytechnic Institute and did post-graduate studies at John Hopkins University. He received an Honorary Doctor of Laws Degree from Indiana University and was presented the John Scott Medal, the highest award given to a scientist in the U.S., in 1922. Haynes was honored during World War II when the 269th Liberty ship built by Permanente Metals Corporation was launched as the *S. S. Elwood Haynes* on January 26, 1944.

When the Haynes family moved to Kokomo they first lived in a small cottage at Washington and Mulberry. A bronze plaque marks the site of the home.

ELWOOD HAYNES MUSEUM, 1915 South Webster Street, is housed in the home acquired by the auto pioneer in 1915. Listed on the NRHP, it was donated to the City of Kokomo by Bernice Haynes Hillis and family in 1965. Featured in the museum are artifacts commemorating the famous inventor's life and accomplishments as well as Kokomo industrial displays

The Elwood Haynes Museum is housed in this former Kokomo residence owned by the auto pioneer.

241

The Howard County Museum is housed in the elegant former Sieberling Mansion in Kokomo.

highlighting developments of the past and present. Of special interest are the four antique cars displayed, including a 1905 Haynes Model L and a 1923 Haynes Roadster. The museum is open from 1:00 to 4:00 p.m. Tuesday through Saturday and 1:00 to 5:00 p.m. Sunday. Admission is free.

HOWARD COUNTY HISTORICAL MUSEUM/ SEIBERLING MANSION, 1200 West Sycamore Road, combines the Historical Society's holdings relative to the county history and the elegant Monroe Seiberling mansion restored to its turn-of-the-century grandeur. Seiberling, founder of Diamond Plate Glass Company and the Kokomo Strawboard Works, completed the house in 1891 for $50,000. Listed on the NRHP, the mansion's Art Nouveau stained glass windows enhance its gracious elegance. Seiberling left Kokomo in 1895 and one of the subsequent owners was George Kingston, inventor of the Kingston carburetor. Indiana University at Kokomo acquired the property in 1946 and it was turned over to the Howard County Historical Society in 1972. The museum and mansion are open from 1:00 to 4:00 p.m. Tuesday through Sunday, February through December. It is closed in January. Admission is free.

Ten miles east of Kokomo on IN 22 is GREENTOWN (pop. 2,265), home of the GREENTOWN GLASS MUSEUM, 112 North Merdian Street. The exhibits highlight the variety and distinctive look that has made Greentown Glass popular with collectors. The glass was first produced in 1894 by the Indiana Tumbler and Goblet Company, located in Greentown. The small factory flourished until destroyed by fire in 1903. The most remarkable styles, "chocolate" glass and "golden agate," were creations of Jacob Rosenthal, a gifted chemist who worked in the factory for three years before it was destroyed by fire. The museum is open from 10:00 a.m. to 12:00 noon and from 1:00 to 4:00 p.m. Tuesday through Friday and from 1:00 to 4:00 p.m. weekends from Memorial Day through October 31. It is open from 1:00 to 4:00 p.m. weekends during November and December and March and April. Admission is free.

Other structures in Howard County listed on the NRHP include the **Kokomo City Building** (1893), 221 West Walnut Street; **Lerner Building** (c. 1904), 107-111 East Sycamore Street, both in Kokomo; the **Henry W. Smith House** (1859), five miles west of Kokomo; the **Frederick Youngman House** (1876), southeast of Kokomo at 200 East Road; and the **Hy-Red Gasoline Station** (1930), 203 East Main Street, Greentown.

Driving south from Kokomo it is 20 miles to TIPTON (pop. 4,762), county seat of Tipton County. Tipton is five miles east of US 31 on IN 28. The county, named in honor of Indiana militia **General and Senator John Tipton**, was established May 1, 1844. The town was founded as Canton October 16, 1844. The name of the town was changed to Tipton, in honor of General Tipton, in 1848 and incorporated in 1853.

Among some of the notables from Tipton are **Glen Cooper Hinshaw**, an artist; **John G. Brady**, governor of Alaska; **Cal Stewart**, an actor; **Rossni and Marjorie Waugh**, musicians; and **Ed Castor**, literacy advocate.

The **Tipton County Courthouse** (1894), on the public square, and **Tipton County Jail and Sheriff's Home** (1895),

203 South West Street, are listed on the NRHP.

Returning on US 31 and continuing south it is six miles east on IN 32 to NOBLESVILLE (pop. 12,851), county seat of Hamilton County, named in honor of **Alexander Hamilton**, established April 7, 1823.

There are several structures in Hamilton County listed on the NRHP. Four are in Noblesville or in the vicinity and include the **William Conner House** (1823), south of Noblesville at 30 Connor Lane; **Hamilton County Courthouse Square, Jail** (1876), and Courthouse (1879), downtown; **Dr. Samuel Harrell House** (1898), 399 North 10th Street; and **Judge Earl S. Stone House** (1849), 107 South 8th Street. The **Davenport-Bradfield House** (1875), 106 East 2nd Street in Sheridan in the northwest corner of the county and the **Roads Hotel** (1893), 150 East Main Street in Atlanta north on IN 19 on the Tipton/Hamilton county line are also listed. The other two listings include the **John Kinzer House** (1828, 1840), east of Carmel on IN 234, and the **Micah Newby House** (c. 1880), 1149 West 116th Street, Carmel.

West of Noblesville seven miles via IN 32 is WESTFIELD (pop. 1,837) at the junction of US 31. The town was laid out in 1834. Most of the early settlers belonged to the Society of Friends, and from the beginning it was known as a Quaker town.

Westfield's most notbable claim to historical uniqueness was its role in aiding escaped slaves on their way from the south to freedom in Canada. **Frederick Douglass**, the black abolitionist and noted orator, was one of the refugees who came through Westfield, housed at the home of Ephraim Stout. A large majority of people were not sympathetic to the operators of the underground railroad thus the Quakers were split on the issue of aiding fugitive slaves.

From Westfield, US 31 runs through Indianapolis and then south almost parallel with I-65 (see Chapter 4).

# Chapter 8
# East on I-74

*This route takes the visitor to Covington and Veedersburg in Fountain County, Newport and Dana in Vermillion County, Attica and Williamsport in Warren County, Crawfordsville and Darlington in Montgomery County, Danville in Hendricks County, Shelbyville in Shelby County, Rushville in Rush County, Greensburg and Westport in Decatur County, Versailles and Batesville in Ripley County, Brookville in Franklin County, Lawrenceville and Aurora in Dearborn County, Rising City in Ohio County, and Vevay and Patriot in Switzerland County.*

# The Indiana Counties

## Chapter 8
# East on I-74

It is 75 miles from the Illinois state line to Indianapolis and 78 miles from Indianapolis to the Ohio state line via I-74. Running almost parallel with west I-74 is US 136 and from Indianapolis east I-74 and US 421 run together for about 40 miles when US 421 turns southeast at Greensburg. From this point to the Ohio state line IN 46 runs parallel with the interstate.

The first community entering Indiana from Illinois is COVINGTON (pop. 2,883), county seat of Fountain County, established April 1, 1826. The county was named in honor of **Major James Fontaine** (note difference in spelling). Covington, on US 136 about two miles north of the interstate, was laid out the same year.

**Lew Wallace**, the noted author, military leader and diplomat, was prosecuting attorney for a period for Fountain County. He lived in a house at 8th and Crockett Streets until 1853 when he moved to Crawfordsville. It was here he wrote *"The Fair God."* **Daniel Voorhees**, "the Tall Sycamore of the Wabash," succeeded Wallace as prosecuting attorney. He later moved to Terre Haute and was elected to the U.S. Senate.

Daniel Voorhees was appointed U.S. attorney by President James Buchanan in 1857. He defended John E. Cook, John Brown's lieutenant at the attack on Harper's Ferry and though he failed to get his client acquitted he gained national attention. It is claimed he was the first to perfect the defense of temporary insanity. In 1860, Voorhees was elected to the U.S. Congress and he served three terms before he was defeated. After sitting out a year he ran again and won two more terms in the House of Representatives. In 1877, he was named U.S. Senator to succeed Oliver P. Morton, the state's Civil War governor, who had died. He remained in the Senate until 1896. He pushed for the building of the Library of Congress.

The gravesite of **Esther Test Wallace** (1807-1834), the first wife of Governor David Wallace and the mother of Lew Wallace, author of *"Ben Hur,"* is identified with a historial marker in the Covington Cemetery. "She influenced the lives of two important Hoosiers," reads part of the inscription.

Structures listed on the National Register of Historic Places

Lew Wallace's mother, Esther Test Wallace, is buried in the Covington Cemetery. She died in her late twenties.

(NRHP) in Covington include the **William C.B. Sewell House**, dating back to 1867, 602 East Washington Street, and the **Carnegie Library**, opened in 1914, 622 South Fifth Street.

**Edward A. Hannegan** (1807-1859), who lived in Covington, served as a U.S. representative and senator from Indiana. His home here was located at the corner of Fifth and Jefferson Streets. President Polk appointed him minister to Prussia in 1849. A flamboyant, impulsive man, Hannegan dazzled the Prussian court until he was recalled upon the request of Frederick Wilhelm IV for

248

publicly kissing the hand of the Queen. He returned to Covington in 1851 and entered the race for presidential nomination after being defeated in state elections. With his nomination almost a certainty, he returned to Covington to rest but mortally wounded his brother-in-law in a quarrel. This squashed any dreams of a presidential nomination and he went to St. Louis to practice law. He died from an overdose of morphine.

The **Savage Murals**, covering 25,000 square feet, in the *Fountain County Courthouse reflects the growth of a people* through struggles with nature, battles and hardships; as well as the successes and joys that came with civilizing the Wabash Valley. Noted artist Eugene Savage directed local artists in the painting of the murals in his boyhood hometown. Savage contributed two panels which are located at the entrance of the 1937 courthouse. The courthouse is open from 8:00 a.m. to 4:00 p.m. weekdays.

**Cade Hollow Covered Bridge**, dating back to 1854, is located between Veedersburg and Covington on US 136.

Seventeen miles south of the intersection of I-74 and IN 63, via IN 63, is NEWPORT (pop. 704), county seat of Vermillion County, established on February 1, 1824. The county was named for the Vermillion Rivers.

South of Newport via IN 71 is DANA (pop. 803), birthplace of Pulitzer Prize winning World War II correspondent **Ernie Pyle**. Pyle was born on a nearby farm on August 3, 1900, however, his birthplace home has been moved to the **Ernie Pyle State Historic Site** on IN 71 in downtown Dana. This site pays tribute to the man, who, more than any other, helped bring World War II home to the millions of Americans who remained behind as their sons, brothers, and husbands went overseas to war. He was killed by sniper fire on Ie Shima in the Pacific on April 18, 1945.

ERNIE PYLE STATE HISTORIC SITE, in Dana, is housed in his birthplace home and is typical of the farm houses in the rural midwest in the late 19th century. The first floor contains two rooms of period furniture, a museum room where many of Pyle's personal belongings, letters, photographs, columns, and other items are displayed, and a room where a life-like talking mannequin recites some of his newspaper columns. A theater room has been set up in the basement to show films pertaining to the columnist to groups of visitors. The Site is open from 9:00 a.m. to 5:00 p.m. Tuesday through Saturday and 1:00 to 5:00 p.m. Sunday, March through December. It is closed on Monday. Admission is free. Donations appreciated.

Newspaperman Ernie Pyle, who gained fame for his front line reports back home during World War II, was born in this house.

On US 36, a mile and a half east of Dana, is **Ernie Pyle Park** with a replica of the Army engineers tribute to the newspaperman on Ie Shima. A covered bridge has been moved to this roadside park. There is a memorial on the island in the Pacific where he was killed.

The **Salem Methodist Episcopal Church** (1878), north of Clinton on IN 63, is listed on the NRHP.

*Back on I-74.*

ATTICA (pop. 3,841) is located seven miles east and 11 miles north on US 41.

South of Attica, along US 41 is a historical sign marking the site of the boyhood home of **Daniel W. Voorhees,** "the Tall Sycamore of the Wabash."

The **Shawnee Covered Bridge** crosses Big Shawnee Creek three miles south of Attica on US 41.

The **Marshall M. Milford House** (c. 1845-55), 414 West Main Street, Attica, is listed on the NRHP. There are two historic districts on the register here and include the **Brady Street Historic District** (c. 1840-1930), roughly bounded by S. Perry, E. Jackson, S. Council, and E. Pike Streets, and the **Old East**

Williamsport Falls is Indiana's highest free-fall waterfall.

**Historic District** (c. 1865-1930) that includes the 400 block of E. Washington and the 400-500 blocks of E. Monroe Street.

West of Attica five miles is WILLIAMSPORT (pop. 950), county seat of Warren County established March 1, 1827. The county is named for **Dr. Joseph Warren**, killed in the Battle of Bunker Hill during the Revolutionary War.

**J. Frank Hanly** came to Warren County as a youth and began his career here, eventually serving as governor of Indiana from 1905-1909.

**Colonel Vern L. Burg** of Warren County was a pioneer of the U.S. Army Air Corps and was the first enlisted man to fly a plane for the Army.

**Horace Greeley** and **Colonel James R. Bryant**, a prominent Civil War figure, were founding members of the Grand Harmonial Institute established in the county in 1853.

WARREN COUNTY HISTORICAL SOCIETY MUSEUM in Williamsport focuses on county history. The museum is open from 2:00 to 4:00 p.m. Tuesday through Saturday. For information call (317) 762-2821.

The **Kent House and Hitchens House** (1854), 500 Main and 303 Lincoln Streets, Williamsport, and the **Andrew Brier House** (c. 1855), Old Highway 41 in Carbondale, are listed on the NRHP.

The **William Harrison Trail** is marked on the route of William Henry Harrison and his troops as it wound through the county enroute to the Battle of Tippecanoe. There are 10 sites on the trail in Warren County.

**Williamsport Falls**, at nearly 100 feet, is Indiana's highest free-falling waterfall. It is near downtown.

The **Potholes**, on 150N-50E northwest of Williamsport, is somewhat of a mystery. The potholes, seen from a parking area just before reaching the bridge, are in varying sizes and depths and were thought to be work of Indians or were created when an early-day mill is thought to have been erected in here. However they were created they are unusual and worth a view to those interested in mysteries.

**College Rock**, on CR 600E near Independence, is a glacial boulder that weighs somewhere between 150 and 200 tons above ground. Its name came from the school located across from the boulder which operated in the late 1800s. It is believed the boulder was brought here by a glacier from Canada.

**Zachariah Cicott**, the French fur trader and Indian scout for William Henry Harrison and his Army troops, took part in the Battle of Tippecanoe. The stone on his grave in Independence Cemetery on Independence and Pine Village Road was used by Indians to grind corn. He founded the town of INDEPENDENCE (unincorporated) located north of Williamsport along the Wabash River.

North of Williamsport on a county road east off of US 41 is unincorporated Rainsville, dating back to 1833, virtually demolished by a tornado in 1974.

Returning to US 136 just north of I-74 it is eight miles east of Covington on US 136, just south of I-74, is VEEDERSBURG (pop. 2,261).

The **Clinton F. Hesler Farm** (1887-1939), County Road south between 200 East and 300 East in the Veedersburg area, is listed on the NRHP.

Continuing east 22 miles, on US 231 two miles south of I-74, is CRAWFORDSVILLE (pop. 13,584), county seat of Montgomery County, established March 1, 1823. The county was named in honor of **General Richard Montgomery**, killed in the assault on Quebec. Crawfordsville was settled in 1822. The town was named

Lew Wallace was one of Crawfordsville's most famous residents. He was known as an author, soldier, and diplomat. (Photograph by Indiana Historical Society Library, Negative No. C5830).

for Secretary of the Treasury **William H. Crawford** by Major Ambrose Whitlock, Receiver of Public Lands.

Crawfordsville is home of Wabash College, for men, opened in 1832 and chartered in 1834 as Wabash Manual Labor College and Teachers Seminary. It was renamed in 1851.

One of the community's most famous residents was **Lew Wallace**, author of the best seller *"Ben Hur"* published in 1880. The multi-talented man was born in **Brookville**, in the eastern part of the state, on April 10, 1827. After reading law with his

253

Lew Wallace in his later years spent much of his time at his Crawfordsville study and in the garden area. (Photograph by Indiana Historical Society, Negative No. C5428).

father, who had served as the governor of Indiana, Wallace joined the Army and served in the Mexican War. He was serving as the adjutant general of the Indiana militia at the outbreak of the Civil War and was quick to begin the mobilization of troops for the Union cause. He attained the rank of major general for gallantry at Fort Donelson.

He was stationed in Baltimore in 1864 when he helped save Washington from being captured by Confederate General Jubal Early by halting the drive long enough for Grant to send in reinforcements. Wallace served as a member of the court that tried the conspirators in the assassination of President Lincoln.

After returning to his law practice , he was appointed governor for the Territory of New Mexico (1878-81) followed by an appointment as minister to Turkey (1881-85). He returned to Crawfordsville and died here in 1905. He is buried in Oak Hill

Lew Wallace died in 1906 and is buried in Crawfordsville's Oak Hill Cemetery. His grave is marked with this monument.

Cemetery.

Among his other novels are *"The Fair God"* (1873), a story of the conquest of Mexico, and *"The Prince of India"* (1893). Wallace designed and built his Study on a 4.5 acre site near his home between 1895 and 1898.

THE LEW WALLACE STUDY, Pike Street and Wallace Avenue, houses a collection of artifacts belonging to the famous soldier, statesman, and author, and his descendants. Included are Civil War uniforms and souvenirs, as well as costumes and

255

Henry S. Lane, congressman, governor, and Civil War senator, owned this large mansion in the background. He was a strong supporter of President Abraham Lincoln and the Union.

mementos from the two films of "Ben Hur." The study is listed as a National Historic Landmark as well as on the NRHP. It is open from 1:00 to 5:00 p.m. daily, except Mondays and holidays, from April 1 to October 31. An admission is charged.

Another noted resident of Crawfordsville was **Henry S. Lane**, the first Republican elected governor of Indiana. Influential in creating the Republican Party, Lane was elected governor in 1860 but served only three days before being elected to the U.S. Senate. He had already served in both houses of the state legislature and as a U.S. Congressman. Lane supported Lincoln in his presidency and was appointed chairman of the president's second inauguration. He served as honorary pallbearer for the slain president.

THE LANE PLACE, South 212 Water Street, was the home of Henry S. Lane and his wife, Joanna. He bought the four acre site with a three-room brick cottage in 1844. The Lanes added four rooms and central halls and decorated their mansion with furnishings from Cincinnati, New Orleans, New York, and Europe. The mansion is listed on the NRHP. It is open from 1:00 to 5:00 p.m. daily, except Mondays and holidays, from April 1 through October 31. Extended hours are scheduled during the months of June, July and August. An admission is charged.

THE OLD JAIL MUSEUM, 225 North Washington Street, features the only known operational rotary cells, referred to as "the squirrel cage," in the world. There were 17 known rotary jails built in the late 19th century. The patent for the rotary cell jails was issued to **William H. Brown** and **Benjamin F. Haugh**, both of Indianapolis, in July, 1881. The Crawfordsville jail was built in 1882 and housed the sheriff's quarters and a three-story cell area. The cellblock was constructed to turn on a system of shafts and gears so prisoners could be controlled through a single exit. The building was used as a jail until June 1973. It is listed on the NRHP. It is open from 1:00 to 4:30 p.m. Tuesday through Sunday, April and May and September and October and from 10:00 a.m. to 4:30 p.m. Tuesday through Saturday and 1:00 to 4:30 p.m. Sunday June, July and August. Bus tours, admission per person, donations for individuals.

Among other noted persons with Crawfordsville roots are **Maurice Thompson**, author of such books as *"Alice of Old Vincennes"* and *"Hoosier Mosiacs"* and **Meridith Nicholson**, playwright and author of *"The Barker," "Love is Like That,"* and *"The Tom Show,"* all popular plays in the past. **Frances Rickett**, author of *"The Prowler," "Tread Softly,"* and *"A Certain Slant of*

257

Crawfordsville's Old Jail Museum features the only known operational rotary cells or "squirrel cages."

*Light*," is a native daughter. **Maurine Watkins**, author of the play "*Chicago*," and **Catherine Clugston**, playwright, received their early training here. **Richard Banta**, author of "*The Ohio*," and **Will H. Hays Jr.**, author of "*Dragon Watch*," live here. It was home of Misses **Mary Hannah** and **Caroline Krout**, writers of national prominence.

**Amalia Kussner Coudert** (1863-1932), one of the world's foremost painters of miniature portraits, was born in Crawfordsville. Among her clients were the Prince of Wales, who later became King Edward VII of England in 1901, and Czar Nicholas II of Russia.

Seven nationally-noted cartoonists–**Dave Gerard**, **Bandel Linn**, **Bill Holman**, **Allen Saunders**, **Frank Beaven**, **Tom Henderson**, and **Paul McCarthy**–credit their training to *The Caveman*, Wabash College's humor magazine.

The **Wabash Merry Bowmen**, an archery club, was founded by **Maurice Thompson** in 1874. He published his book "*The Witchery of Archery*" in 1887 and this, with an article written for *Scribner's Magazine*, set off the archery craze in America. The **National Archery Association** was formed in 1879 with its headquarters in Crawfordsville and Thompson as the founding president.

258

There are several buildings in Crawfordsville, in addition to those already identified, on the NRHP. These include the **Colonel Isaac C. Elston House**, (1882), 400 East Pike Street; **McClelland-Layne House**, (1869), 602 Cherry Street; **St. John's Episcopal Church**, (1837), 212 South Green Street; Otto **Schlemmer Building**, (1854), 129-131 North Green Street; and Yount's **Woolen Mill and Boarding House**, (1851, 1864), 3729 Old Indiana 32 West.

Ten miles northeast of Crawfordsville, via IN 47, is DARLINGTON (pop. 811). A toll-house, built in 1867, was moved to its present location on Main Street in 1880. Toll roads here were abolished in 1889.

**Winnie Ruth Judd**, a native of Darlington, was convicted of murdering two girls in Phoenix, Arizona, dismembering their bodies, cramming the pieces into two trunks and a suitcase and shipping them to Los Angeles, California in 1931.

The **Darlington Covered Bridge**, built in 1868, is on County Road 500N and 500E over Sugar Creek. It is listed on the NRHP.

Eleven miles north of Crawfordsville, on US 231, is LINDEN (pop. 700). The **Linden Depot** (1905), 202 North James Street, is listed on the NRHP.

Nine miles south of Crawfordsville, on US 231, and six miles east on IN 234 is LADOGA (pop. 1,151). Southwest of Ladoga on County Road 350E is **Ashby House** (1883), listed on the NRHP.

It is 34 miles from the junction of US 231 and I-74 to Indianapolis.

At the Lizton exit on I-74, is IN 39 and 13 miles south this highway leads to DANVILLE (pop. 6,500), county seat of Hendricks County, established on April 1, 1824. Hendricks County was named for Indiana governor and U.S. Senator **William Hendricks**. Danville was settled in 1824 and incorporated in 1835, named in honor of **Dan Wick**. It is approximately 15 miles from Indianapolis.

Danville was once the home of **Canterbury/Central Normal College** which graduated a large number of Indiana teachers.

There are two buildings in Danville listed on the NRHP. One is the **Hendricks County Jail and Sheriff's Residence**, (1867), 170 South Washington Street, and the other is the **Wilson-Courtney House**, (1850), 10 Cartersburg Road.

(See Chapter 2 for Indianapolis highlights and historical sites and attractions.)

I-74 continues at the southeast corner of Indianapolis and

leaves Indiana two miles east of the New Trenton Exit.

SHELBYVILLE (pop. 14,400), county seat of Shelby County, is 28 miles from Indianapolis on IN 9, two miles south of I-74. Shelby County was established April 1, 1822 and was named in honor of **Isaac Shelby**, twice governor of Kentucky and a noted soldier of the Indiana wars. Shelbyville was platted in 1822 and incorporated January 21, 1850.

In 1843, **Judge William J. Peasley**, a local railroad enthusiast, constructed his own "railroad," a horse drawn vehicle that ran on a mile and a quarter of wooden track from town to a picnic area on Lewis Creek. It was soon abandoned.

Two Shelbyville citizens gained national recognition. **Thomas A. Hendricks**, who served as governor (1873-77) and held other elective offices, became Vice President of the United States in 1884, serving under President Grover Cleveland. He died after serving only nine months in office. The other was **Charles Major**, a novelist, who is best known for his book *"When Knighthood Was In Flower."*

The Meteor automobile, 1914-1930, was built by Meteor Motor Car Company in Shelbyville and Piqua, Ohio. The Clark Motor Car Company built the Clark, 1910-1912, here.

The GROVER MUSEUM, 52 West Broadway, is across the street from the Library. It features a 3/4-scale walk through town, depicting what the average town in Shelby County would have

Shelbyville's Grover Museum is located across from the city's library.

looked like at the turn of the century. The museum is open from 1:00 to 4:00 p.m. Friday, Saturday, and Sunday. For additional information, call (317) 392-4634.

In the Shelby County fairgrounds is the boyhood cabin of Thomas A. Hendricks. This site is always open the first weekend in October during the Blue River Valley Pioneer Fair that features local craftsmen demonstrating crafts from pioneer times.

The **John Hamilton House** (1853), 132 West Washington Street, is listed on the NRHP. Two historic districts, also on the NRHP, include the **Shelbyville Commercial Historic District** (1822-1930), bounded by Broadway, Tompkins, Mechanic, and Noble Streets, and the **West Side Historic District** (1853-1939), bounded by W. Pennsylvania, N. Harrison, N. and S. Tompkins, W. Hendricks, Montgomery, and N. Conrey Streets.

Elsewhere in Shelby County, the **Junction Railroad Depot**, built in 1868, is in MORRISTOWN (pop. 989), north of Shelbyville on US 52, is listed on the NRHP. The **Cooper-Alley House** (1864), located south of WALDRON (pop. 800), southeast of Shelbyville, is also listed on the NRHP.

Two miles east of Shelbyville and 17 miles east on IN 44 is RUSHVILLE (pop. 6,113), county seat of Rush County, established on April 1, 1822. The county and town were named for **Dr. Benjamin Rush**, one of the signers of the Declaration of Independence. Rushville was settled in 1821.

**Wendell L. Willkie**, a native of Elwood, married Edith Wilk in Rushville at the Wilk homestead, January 14, 1918. He ran unsuccessfully for the U. S. presidency in 1940 against Franklin D. Roosevelt, who was seeking a third term. Willkie died in 1944 and is buried in Rushville's East Hill Cemetery.

There are a number of structures in Rush County listed on the NRHP. Six of these are in Rushville or the Rushville area—**Dr. John Arnold Farm** (1820-1920), County Road 450 East; **Durbin Hotel** (1855), 137 West Second Street; **Melodeon Hall** (1872), 210 North Morgan Street; **Rush County Courthouse** (1896), 210 North Morgan Street; **Hall-Crull Octagonal House** (c. 1855); and **Archibald M. Kennedy House** (c. 1864), on IN 200. The **Walnut Ridge Friends Meetinghouse** (1866), west of Carthage, is also listed on the register.

Six covered bridges are listed and include the **Norris Ford Covered Bridge** (1916), IN 150; **Ferree Covered Bridge** (1873), on Base Road; **Forsythe Covered Bridge** (1888), on IN 650; **Moscow Covered Bridge** (1886), on IN 875 and 625; **Offutt**

261

**Covered Bridge** (1884), on IN 550; and **Smith Covered Bridge** (1877), on IN 300.

From Shelbyville it is 21 miles southeast on I-74 and two miles south on US 421 to GREENSBURG (pop. 9,254), county seat of Decatur County, established March 4, 1822. The county was named in honor of naval hero **Stephen Decatur**. Greensburg was founded in 1821 and incorporated in 1837.

Greensburg is the hometown of **Wilbur Shaw**, former champion in the Indianapolis "500" race and prominent in the development of the famed speedway.

The tree on Courthouse Tower is known worldwide. In the early 1870s the residents of Greensburg notice a small bit of greenery growing on the northwest corner of the courthouse tower. It finally became a tree and then more trees sprouted to create five trees in all. Afraid that the trees might cause damage to the tower roof, a steeplejack was hired in 1888 to remove three of them. The tallest tree reached a height of 15 feet. The trees on this corner of the tower died but another started to grow on the southeast corner

The Museum of Decatur County Historical Society is housed in this 1830's residence in Greensburg.

262

The famous tree in the courthouse tower in Greensburg has drawn thousands of the curious.

of the tower. No one has been able to explain how the seeds of the first trees found their way to the tower, 110 feet above the courthouse yard.

The Tree City Festival and Greensburg Power of the Past Antique Farm Show is held the third weekend in August every year.

MUSEUM OF THE DECATUR COUNTY HISTORICAL SOCIETY, 222 Franklin, focuses on county history. It is located in what has become known as the Shannon-Lathrop Home, dating back to 1830. The museum is open from 2:00 to 4:00 p.m. Thursday and Friday.

The **Decatur County Courthouse** (1860), on Courthouse Square; the **Knights of Pythias Building and Theater** (1899), 215 North Broadway; and the **Bromwell Wire Works** (1903), 1st and Ireland Streets, are all listed on the NRHP.

The **Westport Covered Bridge** (1880), east of WESTPORT (pop. 1,450), is also listed on the NRHP. Westport is 14 miles south of Greensburg on IN 3.

It is approximately 17 miles east on I-74 to BATESVILLE (pop. 4,152), in the northwest corner of Ripley County. **Teunis Amack** was the first settler in what was to become Batesville. In 1835, he bought 120 acres of government land and sold this acreage to the Callahan Trust Company which laid out 45 lots that comprised the original town. The town was named for **Joshua Bates**, the Callahan Trust engineer and surveyor.

The county seat of Ripley County, established April 10, 1818, is VERSAILLES (pop. 1,560). The county is named for **Eleazar Wheelock Ripley,** a general in the War of 1812. Versailles is 24 miles south of Greensburg via US 421. From Batesville it is 22 miles via IN 229 to IN 48 then west three miles to US 421.

A gang of burglars harassed the citizenry of Versailles in 1897 until a detective was able to infiltrate the gang. When a robbery was planned, the detective notified the police and five would-be robbers were captured and jailed in Versailles. A mob of 400 persons descended on the jail, and took the quintet to a nearby tree and hanged them. The burglaries came to a quick end.

RIPLEY COUNTY HISTORICAL SOCIETY, at the corner of Main and Water Streets, has three buildings on their site including a museum housed in the old G.A.R. Hall, an Archives Building housing the genealogy department and the Smith-Engel log cabin moved from Laughery Township. The museum and archives are open from 2:30 to 4:30 p.m. weekends from June to Labor Day.

General Pleasant A. Hackleman of Brookville was killed in the Civil War. (Photograph by Bass Photo Co. Collection, Indiana Historial Society Library, Negative No. 50811F).

The **Fernando G. Taylor House** (c. 1860), on the northeast corner of Main and Tyson Streets, is listed on the NRHP.

In NAPOLEON, 11 miles north of Versailles on US 421, there are two residences listed on the NRHP–the **Central House** (c. 1856), on IN 229, and the **Elias Conwell House** (c. 1822), on Wilson Street and US 421.

Back on I-74 and at Batesville it is 21 miles north to BROOKVILLE (pop. 2,980), county seat of Franklin County, named in honor of **Benjamin Franklin**, established February 1, 1811. Brookville was platted in 1808 and incorporated in 1814. From the Greensburg Exit on I-74, Brookville can be reached driving 12 miles north on IN 229, then east eight miles on US 52.

During the early days, Brookville served as the cultural and political center of Indiana. During the period of 1825 to 1840, every governor called Brookville his home. The importance of the community waned when the State Land Office (1820-1825) was transferred to Indianapolis. Prosperity returned in 1834 when construction began on the 76-mile **Whitewater Canal** from Cambridge City to Lawrenceburg. The canal was replaced in 1865 when the towpath became property of the **White Water Valley Railroad Company**.

The floods of 1913 destroyed many buildings in the town and caused roads and railroads to bypass it.

Author, soldier, diplomat, **Lew Wallace** was born in Brookville in 1827 and lived here several years. His birthplace is marked.

Indiana artists T. C. Steele and **J. Ottis Adams** arrived in Brookville in 1898 and built their studio they called "The Hermitage" at 650 East Eighth Street . It was home for an art colony for several years where Steele, Adams, **William Forsythe** and **Otto Starke** painted.

Two members of the same family, the Nobles, resided in Brookville. **James Noble** was the first Indiana Senator from this area; **Noah Noble,** was one of the first governors. The Noble site is marked.

**General Pleasant A. Hackleman**, from Brookville, was the only Indiana general killed in the Civil War.

The home of **James Brown Ray**, built in 1821-22, still stands at 18th and Franklin. Ray served as governor of Indiana from 1825 to 1831. The Palladian window and transom fan-light was considered too aristocratic by early Hoosiers.

Old Brookville Church and Cemetery were built in 1820 by the Methodists. Four Revolutionary veterans are buried in the cemetery.

The **Little Cedar Grove Baptist Church**, three miles south of Brookville on US 52, is said to be the oldest church in Indiana still standing on its original foundations. The church dates back to 1812 and is listed on the NRHP.

Construction of the **Franklin County Seminary**, 412 Fifth Street, began the fall of 1828 and was completed in January, 1830 at a total cost of $1810.04. Students paid a tuition which went to pay the teacher. The first teacher was **Reverend Isaac Ogden**, a Presbyterian minister. Early records indicate the teacher was paid $54 for a 12 week term. One of the students here was **John S. Tarkington**, father of author **Booth Tarkington**. John

266

Tarkington was the Methodist minister serving Brookville. When Indiana provided for free schools in 1852 the tuition seminaries went out of existence. The seminary property was transferred to public school officials in 1863 and was used as a public school until 1873. The Franklin County Historical Society acquired the property in 1968 and established a museum here in the renovated historical building. It is listed on the NRHP.

The other sites listed on the NRHP include the **Brookville Historic District** (1808-1913), bounded by East and West Forks of Whitewater River and IN 101; **Joseph Shafer Farm,** dating back to 1883, northeast of Brookville on Flinn Road; and **Whitewater Canal Historic District** (1823-1853), from Laurel Feeder Dam to Brookville, Metamora.

In OLDENBURG (pop. 770) the **Oldenburg Historic District** (1837-1931), bounded by Sycamore, Church land woods, Indiana and Water Streets and Gehring Farm, is listed on the NRHP. Oldenburg is two miles north of I-74 at the Oldenburg/Batesville Exit.

From this exit it is 15 miles east on I-74 to LAWRENCEVILLE, in northern Dearborn County.

The county seat of Dearborn County is LAWRENCEBURG (pop. 4,403), laid out in 1802 and incorporated in 1846. The town was founded in 1801 by **Captain Samuel C. Vance**, a soldier under General Washington and an aide to General Anthony Wayne. He named the town in honor of his wife, whose maiden name was Lawrence. The county, formed March 7, 1803, was named in honor of **General Henry Dearborn**, at the time Secretary of War.

Lawrenceburg was not always the county seat. It was moved to WILMINGTON a few miles south in 1835 where it remained for 10 years. In 1845 the county seat was moved back to Lawrenceburg where it has remained since.

**James Buchanan Eads**, considered one of the most successful 19th century engineers in the country, was born in Lawrenceburg. Eads was responsible for building eight partially armored gunboats in less than 100 days used to capture New Madrid and Island No. 10 by Union forces on April 7, 1862. Eads bridge across the Mississippi River at St. Louis, Missouri, was designed and built under the supervision of the Indianan, 1867-74. It was the world's first steel truss bridge and the first in the U.S. to have piers built within pneumatic caissons. The 6,220 foot bridge, still in use, was dedicated July 4, 1874.

**President-Elect Abraham Lincoln** stopped in Lawrenceburg in February, 1861, and spoke briefly here on his way to Washington.

On July 19, 1863, **General John Morgan** and his 2,500 Confederates swept through the state and crossed Dearborn County.

Lawrenceburg has been devastated several times by floods. The floods of 1882-1883 were very destructive with eight manufacturing plants, two businesses, 40 homes, three stables, and many other buildings completely destroyed in the '83 flood. This was followed in 1884 by one of the greatest floods in the history of the Ohio Valley with water covering High Street for two weeks.

Twenty buildings and stables were destroyed by a fire that swept the town in July, 1866. The local fire department was not organized until 1882.

Flooding continued in the 20th century. A 68-foot levee was built in 1907 but this levee broke in January, 1913, causing another flooding of the community. In March, 1913, a second flood left mass destruction as water stood in the town for a week. In all of the flooding only one drowning was recorded. In January, 1937, the town suffered the devastation of the worst flood of all. The levee was built stronger and higher and when flood waters poured over the area in 1945 the town was spared. In March, 1964, another flood struck causing a major loss in property and drove residents from their homes along the river but the city property remained safe behind the levee and its flood gates.

In 1909, the James automobile was manufactured here by the J & M Motor Car Company.

There are several buildings and sites in Lawrenceburg listed on the NRHP. Included are the **Dearborn County Courthouse** (1871), High and Mary Streets; **Hamline Chapel** (1847), High and Vine Streets; **Jennison Guard Site**, 0.75 miles northeast of town; and the **Downtown Lawrenceburg Historic District** (1802-1940), bounded by Conrail Tracks, Charlotte, Tate, Williams, and Elm Streets.

South of Lawrenceburg on US 50 is AURORA (pop. 3,816). The town was laid out in 1819.

**Elmer Davis** (1890-1958), popular newspaperman and radio commentator in the 1920s and 1930s, was born in Aurora. A Rhodes scholar, Davis served as director of the Office of War Information (1942-45) where he was often criticized for his delay in releasing foreign news. He was also an author and wrote several novels, short stories, and two volumes of essays—*"Show Wind"* (1927) and *"Not to Mention the War"* (1940).

HILLFOREST (1853-55), 213 Fifth Street overlooking the Ohio River, Aurora, was the home of industrialist and financier **Thomas Gaff** and his family between 1855 and 1891. The design of the home has been attributed to Isaiah Rogers, a noted architect of that period. It is listed on the NRHP and a designated National Historic Landmark (NHL). Thomas Gaff was not only a successful businessman but a civic leader as well. He was founder of the Aurora school system and served on the City Council. One of the many holdings of Thomas and his brother James was the Crescent Brewing Company, one of the largest breweries in the country in the late 19th century. The 12-room restored and furnished mansion is open for tours from 1:00 to 5:00 p.m. (EDT) Tuesday through Sunday, April 1 through December 23 and December 26 to the 30th. An admission is charged.

**Veraestau** (1810), one mile south of Aurora on IN 56, and two bridges, the **Laughery Creek Bridge** (1878), south of Aurora and west on IN 56, and **George Street Bridge** (County Bridge No. 159) (1887), George, Main, and Importing Streets, and **Aurora Public Library** (1913) are also listed on the NRHP.

Nine miles south of Aurora, via IN 56, is RISING CITY (pop. 2,478), county seat of Ohio County, established March 1, 1844. The county is named for the Ohio River and the state. Rising City, whose name came from the expression, "oh look at the rising sun" across the Ohio River to the Kentucky Hills, was platted in 1814.

Rising City has survived two major fires, in 1866 and 1885; three major tornadoes, 1921, 1948, and 1972; and three major floods, 1894, 1913, and 1937.

Among the first settlers was **Samuel Fulton**, an uncle of **Robert Fulton**, inventor of the steam engine.

The most noted person from Rising City was **J. W. "Row" Whitlock**, who built and raced speedboats. His "Hoosier Boy" was raced throughout the midwest and was never beaten in competition. Whitlock, who owned a furniture company, also built ferry boats, passenger boats, cruisers, a swamp buggy, and smaller pleasure boats. He invented the automatic harp which was later sold to Wurlitzer and owned a radio patent later sold to Crosley.

OHIO COUNTY HISTORICAL SOCIETY MUSEUM, in Rising City, features exhibits and artifacts that focus on county history. Also on display is Whitlock's "Hoosier Boy," the automatic harp, a pin ball machine he developed, and several pieces of furniture manufactured in his factory. It is open weekend afternoons from June through October. An admission is charged.

Traveling south on IN 156 about 30 miles along the Ohio River one comes to VEVAY (pop. 1,343), county seat of Switzerland County, established October 1, 1814. The county is named for the country of Switzerland. Vevay was settled by Swiss-French c. 1802 and was laid out in 1813.

**Edward Eggleston**, author of *"The Hoosier Schoolmaster,"* *"Roxy,"* and *"The Circuit Rider,"* and other novels and history books, was born here on December 10, 1837. His brother, George, also became an author of some note.

Other famous sons from Switzerland County include **Elwood Mead**, the engineer who headed the U.S. Bureau of Reclamation during the construction of Boulder Dam, and after whom Lake Mead is named; **Will H. Stevens**, noted artist and art instructor at Tulane University; **Dr. John Shaw Billings**, physician and librarian, who supervised construction of Johns Hopkins University Hospital, and later organized and supervised the building of the New York Public Library; and **Augustus R. Hatton**, specialist in political science and the city charter form of government.

There are about 30 Amish families who live in the county.

SWITZERLAND COUNTY HISTORICAL MUSEUM, corner of Main and Market Streets, is housed in an 1860 Presbyterian Church. Among its several exhibits and displays is the oldest piano in Indiana, period clothing, crib of Edward Eggleston, and Ohio River lore, including river boat models. It is open from 12:30 to 4:30 p.m. Wednesday through Sunday. An admission is charged.

The SWITZERLAND COUNTY PUBLIC LIBRARY, 210 Ferry Street, Vevay, also houses special collections on local history and genealogy, and Indiana history. It is open from 10:00 a.m. to 7:00 p.m. Monday and Friday; 12:00 noon to 7:00 p.m. Tuesday through Thursday; 9:00 a.m. to 5:00 p.m. Saturdays. It is closed on Sundays. Admission is free.

Favorite places on the walking tour in Vevay include the birthplace of Edward Eggleston; U.P. Schenck house, built in 1844, home of the Swiss flatboat magnate; and She-Coon Saloon, dating back to 1816, once visited by Daniel Boone.

Eighteen miles east of Vevay, via IN 156, is unincorporated PATRIOT, birthplace of **Dr. Elwood Mead**, chief engineer of the Hoover Dam project on the Colorado River at the Arizona-Nevada state line. Construction began in 1931, and the dam was completed in 1936. It is one of the largest dams in the world.

There are four structures in Switzerland County listed on the NRHP. These include the **Edward Eggleston and George Cary House** (c. 1830), 306 West Main Street; **Old Hoosier Theatre** (1837), Cheapside and Ferry Streets, both in Vevay; the **Merit-Tandy Farmstead** (1845), northeast of Patriot on IN 156; and the **Thomas T. Wright House** (1838), southwest of Vevay on IN 56.

Back on I-74 it is 13 miles from Lawrenceville to the Ohio state line.

William Jones played an influential role in young Abraham Lincoln's life during his boyhood years in Indiana. Operating a store in Jonesboro near the Lincoln cabin in Spencer County, Jones employed the future president as his helper. Young Abe worked for Jones until the family moved to Illinois in 1830. Lincoln visited Jones and his family and stayed overnight with them in 1844 while campaigning for Henry Clay's presidential candidacy. William Jones was serving as a lieutenant colonel in an Indiana regiment during the Civil War when he was killed in the Battle of Atlanta on July 22, 1864.

INDIANA'S
FIRST RAILROAD

An experimental two mile road was completed to this point on July 4, 1834. A horse-drawn car carried Hoosiers on a railroad for the first time.

An experimental two mile road was completed in Shelbyville July 4, 1834 to become Indiana's first railroad. The rail car was powered by horses. This historical marker in the east part of town marks the "end of line."

# Chapter 9
# IN 37 to Bloomington

*This route takes the visitor south from Indianapolis to Bloomington in Monroe County; Nashville in Brown County; Spencer in Owen County; Bedford, Buddha and Mitchell in Lawrence County; Shoals in Martin County; and Paoli, French Lick and West Baden in Orange County.*

## COUNTIES/COUNTY SEATS

Adams, Decatur
Allen, Ft. Wayne
Bartholomew, Columbus
Benton, Fowler
Blackford, Hartford City
Boone, Lebanon
Brown, Nashville
Carroll, Delphi
Cass, Logansport
Clark, Jeffersonville
Clay, Brazil
Clinton, Frankfort
Crawford, English
Daviess, Washington
Dearborn, Lawrenceburg
Decatur, Greensburg
DeKalb, Auburn
Delaware, Muncie
Dubois, Jasper
Elkhart, Goshen
Fayette, Connersville
Floyd, New Albany
Fountain, Covington
Franklin, Brookville
Fulton, Rochester
Gibson, Princeton
Grant, Marion
Greene, Bloomfield
Hamilton, Noblesville
Hancock, Greenfield
Harrison, Corydon
Hendricks, Danville
Henry, New Castle
Howard, Kokomo
Huntington, Huntington
Jackson, Brownstown
Jasper, Rensselaer
Jay, Portland
Jefferson, Madison
Jennings, Vernon
Johnson, Franklin
Knox, Vincennes
Kosciusko, Warsaw
LaGrange, LaGrange
Lake, Crown Point

LaPorte, LaPorte
Lawrence, Bedford
Madison, Anderson
Marion, Indianapolis
Marshall, Plymouth
Martin, Shoals
Miami, Peru
Monroe, Bloomington
Montgomery, Crawfordsville
Morgan, Martinsville
Newton, Kentland
Noble, Albion
Ohio, Rising Sun
Orange, Paoli
Owen, Spencer
Parke, Rockville
Perry, Cannelton
Pike, Petersburg
Porter, Valparaiso
Posey, Mt. Vernon
Pulaski, Winamac
Putnam, Greencastle
Randolph, Winchester
Ripley, Versailles
Rush, Rushville
St. Joseph, South Bend
Scott, Scottsburg
Shelby, Shelbyville
Spencer, Rockport
Starke, Knox
Steuben, Angola
Sullivan, Sullivan
Switzerland, Vevay
Tippecanoe, Lafayette
Tipton, Tipton
Union, Liberty
Vanderburgh, Evansville
Vermillion, Newport
Vigo, Terre Haute
Wabash, Wabash
Warren, Williamsport
Warrick, Boonville
Washington, Salem
Wayne, Richmond
Wells, Bluffton
White, Monticello
Whitley, Columbia City

## Chapter 9
# IN 37 to Bloomington

Starting off I-465 just south of Indianapolis IN 37 provides an interesting drive south to Bloomington and then on to I-64 west of Corydon in the southernmost part of the state.

On this route it is 50 miles to BLOOMINGTON (pop. 53,100), home of Indiana University and county seat of Monroe County. The county, named for **President James Monroe**, was established April 10, 1818. Bloomington was settled about 1816 and selected as a site for a seminary by President Monroe. One of the conditions imposed on the Territory of Indiana for statehood was that two townships in the proposed state should be reserved for seminaries to provide education for the area. The town was laid out in 1818 and made seat of the newly created county.

A militia was formed by **Colonel John Storm** in 1819 to protect settlers from Indians.

In 1820 the state selected Bloomington for site of Indiana University, then called Indiana State Seminary. It was designated Indiana College in 1828 and became Indiana University in 1838. The school officially opened in May, 1824, with 10 male students.

**Alfred Charles Kinsey**, professor of zoology at the university, published "*Sexual Behavior in the Human Male*" as the first of several reports from his noted research project in 1948.

Indiana limestone, known to geologists as Salem limestone, has dominated the national material as a premier building stone for well over a century. The earliest known Indiana limestone quarry was opened in 1827 by **Richard Gilbert** with early applications of the stone including building footers, lintels, and foundations for bridges. Indiana limestone is a freestone, which means that it exhibits no preferential direction of splitting and can, therefore, be cut and carved in an almost limitless variety of shapes and sizes. The New York Empire State Building is made from limestone quarried in this area. Over 70 buildings in Washington, D.C., are also built from local limestone.

Many of the earliest settlers were Quakers and Covenanters who had migrated from the South because of their strong opposition to slavery. They established several Underground Railroad stations east of Bloomington that operated from 1830 to 1861.

Ten companies of militia were raised under **Colonel James**

**Mulkey** in Monroe County in the early part of the Civil War. There was some resistance to the draft during 1862 and 1863 but locals flocked to the Union cause after John Morgan's raid through Indiana in July, 1863. During World War I, Monroe Countians joined Battery F and left with the Rainbow Division to fight in Europe.

Disasters struck in Bloomington as it did elsewhere throughout the country during the early days. After the second major fire on the campus of Indiana University in 1883, the school was moved to its present location east of town in 1888 because of the need for more space. An influenza epidemic swept the city in 1918 and 1919.

April 29, 1885, the American Express Company's car on the Monon Railroad was robbed 10 miles south of Bloomington, two miles north of the Harrodsburg station. Three men, believed to be the robbers, boarded the train when it stopped to take on water. A lone bandit entered the express car catching employees Peter Webber and George Davis off guard. Davis was pistol whipped so severely he never recovered fully from the beating. Webber was wounded and identified a suspect. Chesley Chambers, a Monroe County citizen, was finally arrested for the crime and went to trial. The first trial ended with a hung jury. Chambers was found guilty when retried and sentenced to serve two years in the state penitentiary. Three years after the robbery, James Nason was shot while stealing horses in Kansas. As he lay dying, he confessed to planning and perpetrating the Monon train robbery.

**Dave Van Buskirk**, a Bloomington native, was the tallest Union soldier in the Civil War. His height was estimated from 6 feet 10 inches to 8 feet tall and his weight was estimated from 300 to 350 pounds.

Songwriter **Hoagy Carmichael** was born in Bloomington and wrote the legendary song, *"Stardust,"* in a Bloomington restaurant. He is buried in Rose Hill Cemetery on the city's west side.

**Henry Gentry** began his circus, which became one of the five most respected in the country, in Bloomington from a Dog and Pony Show.

The award-winning movie *"Breaking Away,"* was filmed in Bloomington and is based on the Little 500 bicycle race held each spring at Indiana University.

In 1910, Bloomington was the population center of the U.S. The city also boasts the only Tibetan Memorial, The Chorten, in the country.

276

The Monroe County Historical Society Museum occupies the former Carnegie Library in Bloomington.

MONROE COUNTY HISTORICAL SOCIETY MUSEUM, 202 East Sixth Street, provides exhibits and memorabilia relating to the county's long history. It is housed in the old Carnegie Library built in 1918 and now listed on the National Register of Historic Places (NRHP). The Monroe County Genealogy Library is located in the museum's lower level. The museum is open from 10:00 a.m. to 5:00 p.m. Tuesday through Friday; from 10:00 a.m. to 5:00 p.m. Saturday; and from 1:00 to 4:00 p.m. Sunday. It is closed on Mondays. The genealogy library is open from 1:00 to 4:00 p.m. Tuesday through Friday. Admission is free.

STONE'S SCOUT MUSEUM, 2290 West Bloomfield Road, retraces the history and heritage of international Boy Scouts and Girl Scouts. The exhibit is the collection of 60-year Scouter Thornton Stone. Open daily by appointment. Admission is free.

Five walking tours through historic districts of the city are laid out with maps and photographs. Check with the Chamber of Commerce for pamphlets.

Tour of the limestone buildings and The Old Crescent on Indiana University campus is set out in a pamphlet created by the university. The Old Crescent (1884-1908), is listed on the NRHP.

There are several museums and collections on campus worthy

of note. The INDIANA UNIVERSITY ART MUSEUM in the Fine Arts Plaza ranks among the nation's best university museums. It is open during the summer from 10:00 a.m. to 5:00 p.m. Wednesday through Friday and 12:00 noon to 5:00 p.m. weekends. Admission is free. The schedules change from time to time.

The ELIZABETH SAGE COSTUME COLLECTION in Wylie Hall features historic dress dating back to 1820. It is open for research by appointment. (There was no public gallery in 1993 and no notice of such in the future). For information, call the assistant curator, Pat Roath, (812) 855-4627.

The HOAGY CARMICHAEL ROOM in Morrison Hall is dedicated to Bloomington's famed musician and songwriter. It is open from 3:00 to 5:00 p.m. Tuesday and Friday or by appointment (812) 855-8632. Admission is free.

Other offerings include the museum in the GLENN A. BLACK LABORATORY OF ARCHAEOLOGY at 423 N. Fress Street and 9th Street. This museum is devoted to Great Lakes/Ohio Valley archaeology and American Indians past. Its hours are from 8:00 a.m. to 5:00 p.m. weekdays and through Mathers Museum on weekends. Admission is free.

WILLIAM HAMMOND MATHERS MUSEUM at 416 N. Indiana Avenue features changing exhibits focusing on anthropology, history and folklore. Call (812) 855-MUSE for exhibit information. It is closed on Mondays. Admission is free.

The Cyclotron Facility on Milo B. Sampson Lane, off 46 Bypass, houses the largest variable energy light-ion cyclotron in the world. It is used by scientists throughout the world to explore the mysteries of the atomic nucleus. Call (812)855-9365 for their tour schedule. The Lilly Library in the Fine Arts Plaza is an internationally known rare book library with more than 350,000 books, six million manuscripts, and 100,000 musical scores and compositions. It is open from 8:00 a.m. to 8:00 p.m. Monday through Thursday, from 8:00 a.m. to 5:00 p.m. Friday, from 9:00 a.m. to 12:00 noon and from 2:00 to 5:00 p.m. Saturday, and from 2:00 to 5:00 p.m. Sunday. Admission is free.

There are several buildings listed on the NRHP in Bloomington and elsewhere in the county. These include the **Elias Abel House** (c. 1850), 317 North Fairview Street; **Blair-Dunning House** (c. 1835), 698 West Third Street; **Bloomington City Hall** (1915), 122 South Walnut Street; **Cantol Wax Company Building** (1905), 211 North Washington Street; **Cochran-Helton-Lindley House** (1850), 405 North Rogers Street; **Illinois Cen-**

278

Songwriter Hoagy Carmichael was born in Bloomington and introduced his famous song, "Star Dust," in a local restaurant. He is buried in Bloomington's Red Oak Cemetery. (Photograph by Bass Photo Co. Collection, Indiana Historical Society Library, Fol. 429).

tral Railroad Freight Depot (1902), 301 North Morton Street; Monroe County Courthouse (1908), Courthouse Square; Morgan House (1890), 532 North Walnut Street; J. L. Nichols House and Studio (1900), 820 North College Avenue; Princess Theatre (1892, 1913, 1923), 206 North Walnut Street; Seminary Square Park, College Avenue and East Second Street; Wicks Building (1915), 116 West Sixth Street; and Andrew Wylie House (1835), 307 East Second Street, all in Bloomington.

Elsewhere in the county those structures on the NRHP include the Epsilon II Archaeological Site; Kappa V Archaeological Site; Honey Creek School (1921), northeast of Bloomington on Low Gap Road; Joseph Mitchell House (1835), 7008 Ketcham Road in the Smithville area; St. John's Lutheran Church (1831), on Old Dutch Church Road in the Elletsville area; and Daniel Stout House (1828), northeast of Bloomington off IN 46 on Maple Grove Road.

The Courthouse Square Historic District (1847-1936), Bloomington, is bounded by 7th, Walnut, and 4th Streets and College Avenue.

The Visitors Center is located at 2855 North Walnut in Bloomington.

Blacks or Afro-Americans were often lynched or beaten if they had any undo contact with whites for several decades. Many times they were lynched or shot even after being found not guilty by the

The 1834 Andrew Wylie House is one of several historic structures found in Bloomington.

courts. Some times whites who affiliated in any way paid a price for "mixing the races." An example of this occurred in Bloomington on April 26, 1903, when 38 white men, objecting to blacks boarding with whites, broke into the boarding house owned by Rebecca and Ida Stephens and whipped the landlords and their black roomer, Joe Shively.

Twenty one miles east of Bloomington, via IN 46, is NASH-VILLE (pop. 707), county seat of Brown County. The county, named in honor of **Major General Jacob Brown**, a hero of the War of 1812, was established February 4, 1836 with the tiny settlement of Nashville selected as the county seat. The town was incorporated in 1872.

A colony of noted artists were drawn to Brown County, led by **T. C. Steele** who built a home near Belmont and **Adolph Schulz** arrived in Nashville. Several others, among them **Will Vawter, V. J. Cariani, Marie Goth, C. Curry Bohm**, and **Dale Bessire**, settled in Nashville and as a result the BROWN COUNTY ART GALLERY opened in 1926 drawing thousands of tourists annually.

Theodore Clement Steele (1847-1926) was a noted Indiana artist and member of the Hoosier Group of American regional impressionist painters, inspired by the picturesque scenes he encountered in Brown County. In 1907, Steele and his second wife, Selma Neubacher Steele, purchased 211 acres in Brown County

The home of noted artist T. C. Steele between Nashville and Bloomington is a state historic site today.

281

and constructed the home they named "The House of the Singing Winds." They built a large studio for the artist's works and landscaped the surrounding hillsides to enhance the beauty of the property. Mrs. Steele created several acres of gardens around the home. The Steeles spent the winters of 1907-1921 in Indianapolis always returning to Brown County in the spring. They established a home in Bloomington in 1922 when Steele became artist in residence at Indiana University. Selma Steele died in 1945, bequeathing the T. C. Steele estate to the State of Indiana as a tribute to her husband.

T. C. STEELE STATE HISTORIC SITE is located between Nashville and Bloomington just off IN 46. (Turn south at the motel in Belmont, and drive 1 1/2 miles to the front entrance.) Located on the site are the Steele Home, large studio, several hiking trails, the partly restored gardens, and the Dewar log cabin. The site is listed on the NRHP. Guided tours are offered through the home and studio, where an average of 80 original paintings are displayed. Visitors are invited to wander the gardens and grounds at their leisure. The site is open from 9:00 a.m. to 5:00 p.m.Tuesday through Saturday and from 1:00 to 5:00 p.m. Sunday. It is closed Monday and most holidays. From January 1 to March 15, only

This is one of several buildings in the Brown County Historical Museum in Nashville.

prearranged tours are available. For information call (812) 988-2785. Admission is free, but donations are encouraged.

BROWN COUNTY HISTORICAL MUSEUM, Old School Lane, features a collection of buildings and artifacts focusing on local history. Among the buildings are the 1898 country doctor's office, the two-story log jail built in 1879, a pioneer cabin dating back to 1844, a log cabin and loom room, and a replica of an 1826 blacksmith shop. The museum is open from 1:00 to 5:00 p.m. weekends and holidays from May through October. Donations are requested.

MUSEUM OF THE AMERICAN FRONTIER AND TRADING POST, 82 East Gould, provides a wide range of frontier memorabilia. Also provided are documentary film showings depicting life on the American frontier. The museum is open from 10:00 a.m. to 5:00 p.m. daily April through October and from 11:00 a.m. to 5:00 p.m. weekends November through March. An admission is charged.

THE JOHN DILLINGER HISTORICAL WAX MUSEUM, 90 West Washington Street, was established in 1975 by Barton N. Hahn, a Special Agent for the FBI, and Joe M. Pinkston, a Pinkerton detective and co-author of *"Dillinger: A Short and*

The John Dillinger Historical Wax Museum in Nashville recounts the days of Indianan John Dillinger and other gangsters active during the 1930s.

283

*Violent Life.*" Hundreds of photographs and newspaper articles and over 25 wax figures recount the John Dillinger story and other gangsters of that period. The museum is open from 10:00 a.m to 6:00 p.m. daily March through December and from 1:00 to 5:00 p.m. daily December through February (weather permitting). An admission is charged.

Five sites in Brown County are listed on the NRHP. These include **Axsom Branch Archaeological Site**, 3000-1500 BC; **Refuge No. 7 Archaeological Site**, 3000-1500 BC; **F. P. Taggart Store** (1875), Main and Van Buren Streets, Nashville; **T. C. Steele House and Studio** (1907), southwest of Nashville off IN 46; and **Thomas A. Hendricks House and Stone Head Road Marker, House** (1891), **Marker** (1851), IN 135 and Bellville Road, Stone Head.

The **Brown County Courthouse Historic District** (1873-1937), includes the courthouse, old log jail, and the Historical Society Museum Building.

From Bloomington it is 16 miles northwest on IN 46 to SPENCER, county seat of Owen County (see Chapter 4 for listing).

Returning to Bloomington it is 26 miles southwest on IN 45 and IN 54 to BLOOMFIELD (pop. 2,705), county seat of Greene County. The county, named for **General Nathaniel Greene** of the Revolutionary War, was established January 5, 1821. The town was laid out in 1824.

The **Osborn Site**, southwest of Bloomfield, is listed on the NRHP.

Driving south on IN 37 it is 28 miles to BEDFORD (pop. 14,100), county seat of Lawrence County. The county, named for War of 1812 naval war hero **Captain James Lawrence**, who issued the orders "Don't give up the ship," was established January 7, 1818.

Lawrence County is the home of the Indiana limestone industry. First use of the stone was promoted by a Dr. Foote, who is buried off US 50 east of Bedford. His tomb was carved from solid bedrock.

The Postal Auto & Engine Company of Bedford built the Postal automobile, 1907-1908.

The LAWRENCE COUNTY HISTORICAL MUSEUM is located in the basement of the county courthouse in Bedford. It focuses on county history and also offers a small genealogy room providing the personal side of the county's history. It is open from 9:00 a.m. to 12:00 noon and from 1:00 to 4:00 p.m. weekdays.

The Lawrence County Historical Museum is located in the lower level of the courthouse in Bedford. Shown is one of the exhibits.

Admission is free, donations are accepted.

There are four sites in the county listed on the NRHP. These include the **Bono Archaeological Site; Mitchell Opera House** (1906), Seventh and Brooks Streets, Mitchell; **C. S. Norton Mansion** (1897), 1415 15th Street, Bedford; and **Williams Bridge** (1884), southwest of Williams on CR 11.

Southwest of Bedford, via US 50, it is 29 miles to SHOALS (pop. 967), county seat of Martin County created January 17, 1820. The county was named for **John P. Martin**. The town was founded in 1816 as Memphis and briefly became the county seat in 1844. It became the permanent county seat in 1869.

North of Bedford on IN 24 is OOLITIC (pop. 1,424) that boasts a statue of Joe Palooka, a comic strip character.

Ten miles south of Bedford just off IN 37 is MITCHELL (pop. 4,641), founded in 1853 and incorporated in 1858.

**Virgil I. "Gus" Grissom**, one of the seven original astronauts and the second American to travel in space, was Mitchell's most famous citizen. He flew the project Mercury sub-orbital mission, Liberty Bell 7, July 21, 1961, that almost had a disasterous ending when the hatch flew open prematurely during the landing. Minutes after his rescue at sea by the Navy the capsule sunk. As command pilot on the first Gemini flight March 23, 1965, Grissom

285

This memorial to Mitchell's astronaut Virgil "Gus" Grissom is on the site of an elementary school he once attended. Bricks from the school were used in part of the enclosure.

became the first person to venture out into space twice. The popular astronaut, selected as the command pilot of the first Apollo mission, and two fellow astronauts were killed January 27, 1967, in an explosion during the preparation of the first Apollo flight, the first of 11 missions in the moon landing program. For his contributions to the space program, he was presented the Congressional Space Medal of Honor posthumously. The Mitchell astronaut is buried in Arlington National Cemetery. The Virgil I. Grissom Memorial, at Sixth and College Avenue, is a reminder of a modern frontiersman—a pioneer in the Space Age.

"Gus" Grisson, born April 3, 1926, attended schools in Mitchell graduating from high school in 1944. He joined the Army Air Corps August, 1944, and was discharged in November, 1945, with the rank of corporal. In 1946 he entered Purdue University where he earned a degree in mechanical engineering. Upon graduation he entered the Air Force and received his pilot's wings in 1951 and was assigned as an F-86 fighter pilot. He volunteered for duty in Korea and flew the wing position on 100 missions in less than six months to be awarded the Distinguished Flying Cross and Air Medal with cluster. He requested to fly another 25 combat missions but the request was denied and he was returned stateside. The young jet pilot was assigned to flight instructors school in Selma, Alabama, and upon graduation was assigned to Bryan, Texas, as a jet flight instructor. In the summer of 1955, Grissom enrolled in the Air Force Institute of Technology at Wright Patterson Air Force Base, Ohio, where he studied aeronautical engineering. In 1956 he was assigned to Test Pilot School at Edwards Air Force Base, California, where he specialized in advance-design fighter planes. Following graduation the Mitchell native returned to Wright Patterson AFB as a test pilot and by the time he was accepted into the astronaut program, he had become one of the nation's top test pilots. He held the rank of lieutenant colonel.

An outside memorial, in the shape of a spacecraft, was erected on a site next to the Mitchell Municipal Building. The memorial was built on the site of Riley Elementary School attended by Grissom from grades one through six. Bricks from the old school were used for part of the enclosure around the memorial. Inside the municipal building are a few exhibits focusing on the astronaut's life.

THE GRISSOM MEMORIAL BUILDING is located in Spring Mill State Park, three miles from downtown Mitchell via IN 60. It houses "The Molly Brown" Gemini space capsule, Grissom's space suit, and numerous other exihibits relating to the space program and Gus Grissom's life specifically. The Memorial is open daily from 8:00 a.m. to 4:00 p.m. daily. There is an admission into Spring Mill State Park.

A restored village of the early 1800s and a pioneer cemetery are

287

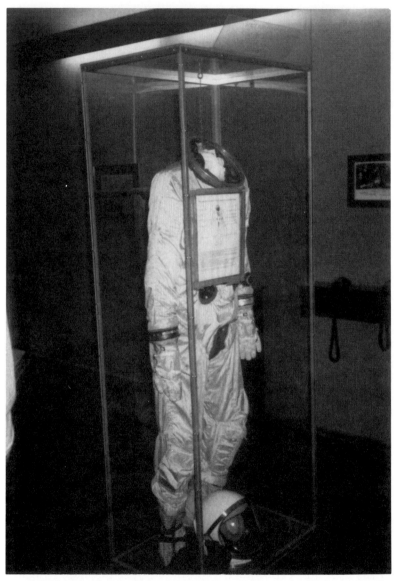

A space suit worn by astronaut Gus Grissom is displayed in the Grissom Memorial Building in Spring Mill State Park just outside of Mitchell. Several exhibits relating to America's space program are displayed here.

located in Spring Mill State Park also.

The Mitchell Municipal Building was built on the site of the Southern Indiana Normal College founded in 1880. The school did not have admission requirements and was unusual in other ways. It was destroyed by fire in 1900 and never rebuilt.

The infamous bank and train robber **Sam Bass** was born near BUDDHA (pop. 80) in Lawrence County south of Bedford July 21, 1851. After trying several occupations, Bass became a bandit while in the Dakota Territory where he and several others robbed seven stagecoaches. He and his gang gained national notoriety when they robbed a train at Big Spring, Nebraska, in 1877 and got away with $60,000. The following year, Bass and his gang robbed four trains in Texas. He was shot and killed in Round Rock, Texas, July 21, 1878, during an attempted bank holdup.

From Mitchell it is 10 miles south via IN 37 to PAOLI (pop. 3,637), county seat of Orange County. The county, named for Orange County, North Carolina and **Prince William IV of Orange**, was created December 26, 1816. The town was settled in 1807 and incorporated in 1869.

ORANGE COUNTY MUSEUM, on the west side of Courthouse Square, provides a glimpse into local history. It is open from 1:00 to 3:00 p.m. Wednesday and 9:00 a.m. to 12:00 noon Saturday from May through September. Admission is free, donations are accepted.

The LINDLEY HOUSE in Paoli is open by appointment. It dates back to the late 1860s and is listed on the NRHP. The home was acquired by the Orange County Historical Society in 1974 and has been restored to reflect the period 1850-1869 when it was used as a farm home.

There are three structures in Paoli listed on the NRHP and these include the **Thomas Elwood Lindley House** (c. 1869), Willow Creek Road; **Orange County Courthouse** (1847), Public Square; and **Thomas Newby Braxtan House** (1893), 210 North Gospel Street. Elsewhere in the county the **West Baden Springs Hotel** (1902), west of IN 56, West Baden, is also listed.

Nine miles west on US 150 and two miles south of PROSPECT is FRENCH LICK (pop. 2,265), founded in 1811 and named for an animal lick within the borders of the settlement and the fact a trading post had been operated by the French here earlier.

**Dr. William A. Bowles**, a French Lick businessman, was the military leader of the anti-Union Knights of the Golden Circle during the Civil War. He was one of the leaders of the organization

289

convicted of fomenting rebellion and sentenced to death by a military commission in 1864. The Milligan, ex parte, case as it was heard before the U.S. Supreme Court in 1866 reversed the sentence and those held by the military authorities were released.

Adjacent to French Lick is WEST BADEN SPRINGS, birthplace of professional basketball star **Larry Bird**. Born December 7, 1956, the Boston Celtic wizard won nearly every award and championship the game had to offer: Three-time All-American; NCAA Consensus College Player of the Year; NBA Rookie of the Year; three time NBA Most Valuable Player; 12-time NBA All-Star and All-Star MVP Award and Olympic Gold Medalist. He went to Indiana State University and was an honorable mention selection to The Associated Press All-American team as a sophomore. The next year he was named AP first team All-American. In his senior year, 1978-79, the Indiana State Sycamores trounced Wichita State 109-84 with Bird scoring 49 and ISU became ranked as the number one team in the country. They finished the season 33-1. losing the NCAA championship to Michigan State led by Ervin "Magic" Johnson, 75-64. Bird joined the Boston Celtics upon graduation and was a leader on the 1981, 1984 and 1986 NBA championship Celtic teams. He retired from basketball in 1993.

On IN 37 south of Paoli it is 27 miles to I-64. This route goes through ENGLISH, county seat of Crawford County.

It is 45 miles southeast, via US 150, from Paoli to the Louisville area.

# Chapter 10
# West on I-65 to Illinois

*This route and its side trips go through some of the most historic parts of the state. From Corydon, the first state capitol; to Abraham Lincoln's boyhood home in Spencer County; then to New Harmony, where two of the most significant community experiments occurred; and ending at Vincennes, brimming with early day history, there is much to see all along this route.*

Great Seal of Indiana

Chapter 10

# West on I-64 to Illinois

I-64 runs across southern Indiana from the Louisville area to the Illinois state line.

CORYDON (pop. 2,724), just off I-64 on IN 135, is the county seat of Harrison County and served as the first state capitol from 1816 to 1825. The county, named in honor of **William Henry Harrison**, was established December 1, 1808; the town was founded the same year. It served as the territorial capital from 1813 to 1816, moved from Vincennes. When the territorial capital moved here the territorial officers shared the quarters with Harrison County officials in the Courthouse on the Hill. The first state general assembly met in Corydon in the new capitol building on November 4, 1816.

The 43-members of the Constitutional Convention met in Corydon in June, 1816, to draft Indiana's state constitution. According to the story, the territorial capitol was too small and too hot and the delegates met under a huge elm tree nearby where they completed their work. The tree, known now as the Constitution Elm, died in the 1920s but the trunk has been preserved and is a state memorial.

The only battle of the Civil War fought in Indiana occurred on July 9, 1863, just south of Corydon when **General John Hunt Morgan** and his Confederate raiders attacked the town. Corydon was defended by the 6th Regiment, a force of about 400, of the Harrison Home Guard commanded by **Colonel Lewis Jordan**. Morgan and his force of some 2,000 men crossed over the Ohio River into Indiana, landing not far from Mauckport the afternoon of July 8th. They camped that night at Frakes Mill, about seven miles north of the river.

Home Guards, alerted to the impending attack, barricaded the road about a mile south of Corydon. The next morning Morgan and his men marched toward the town arriving at the defensive positions of the Home Guard about 11 a.m. They brought up their artillery and began shelling the town over the barricades and within 30 minutes, those who did not retreat surrendered. About 300 of Jordan's men were captured. They all were paroled when Morgan and his troops entered the town. Morgan made his headquarters in the original Kintner House, at

293

the northwest corner of Capitol Avenue and Beaver Street. The structure burned shortly after the Civil War.

Morgan's raiders immediately began to sack the town. They plundered stores and collected ransom money not to burn the local mills. They did not stay long and later in the afternoon rode north out of town, taking some 500 horses in exchange for their worn Kentucky thoroughbreds. They rode on to Salem where they commandeered the town on July 11th. Their raid in Indiana lasted a week.

After leaving Indiana, the raids continued in Ohio for 13 days before Morgan and the last few hundred of his troops surrendered near New Lisbon, Ohio, on July 26th. Morgan's Raid began in eastern Tennessee on June 11th and moved across Kentucky until July 8th. This action, covering over 1,000 miles, was the longest cavalry raid of the Civil War.

**William Henry Harrison**, governor of the Indiana Territory and ninth president of the United States, owned the land where Corydon stands.

Vigilantes swooped down on the Harrison County Jail on June 12, 1880 and took men accused of burglary and lynched them on the West Bridge. The original jail was a log structure built in 1809 and until 1823 the whipping post in front of the jail was used for public punishment. The present building was erected in 1969.

**James Best**, an actor who is best known for his role as Roscoe P. Coltrain in the TV series, *"Dukes of Hazard,"* is from Corydon. Another actor, **Ken Kerchval**, who played the part of Cliff Barnes on TV's *"Dallas"*, was part owner of one of the local popcorn companies at one time.

There are several historic sites in Corydon.

Foremost of the town's landmarks is the CORYDON CAPITOL STATE HISTORIC SITE, 200 East Walnut Street, constructed in 1816. The first General Assembly met on November 4th with 29 representatives, 10 senators and the lieutenant governor. The governor was **Jonathan Jennings**. Corydon remained as the state capital until 1825 when it was moved to Indianapolis. The site is open from 9:00 a.m. to 5:00 p.m. Tuesday through Saturday and from 1:00 to 5:00 p.m. Sunday. It is closed on Monday. Admission is free.

BATTLE OF CORYDON CIVIL WAR SITE is located on IN 135 just south of town. It is listed on the National Register of Historic Places (NRHP). The tombstone or memorial at the site

294

The Corydon capitol building dates back to 1816.

lists the Confederate dead on one side and the Union dead on the other. It is only one of four such tombstones in the United States. The site is open from 8:00 a.m. to dusk daily from April 1 to September 30. Guided tours are available by appointment, (812) 738-2137.

POSEY HOUSE MUSEUM, 225 Oak Street, was the home of **Colonel Thomas Posey** built in 1817 whose father, Thomas, was Indiana's last territorial governor. Colonel Posey, who never married, raised 14 orphan children here. He occupied the house, then twice its present size, until his death in 1863. Colonel Posey

This tombstone on the Corydon Civil War site lists the names of three privates killed and notes that eight others were killed and 40 wounded when Morgan's men attacked Corydon.

was prominent in Corydon's early history as merchant, banker and State Adjutant General. The museum hours are 12:00 noon to 5:00 p.m. Tuesday through Sunday, May through October and 12:00 noon to 5:00 p.m. Tuesday through Friday, November through April. It is open at other times by appointment. Donations are appreciated.

GOVERNOR HENDRICKS' HOUSE, Walnut Street, was built in 1817 and served as the home of **William Hendricks**, Indiana's second governor (1822-25). This two story, Federal-style brick house was purchased by Judge William A. Porter in 1841 and remained in his family until the state acquired it and opened it to the public in 1975.

Dating back to 1817, the former residence of Colonel Thomas Posey serves as a museum in Corydon.

SQUIRE BOONE CAVERNS AND VILLAGE, IN 135 South; the caverns were discovered by Squire Boone and his brother, Daniel, on a hunting trip in 1790. The caverns are open for tours every 20 minutes daily from Memorial Day weekend through August 20, and weekends through Labor Day. The rest of the year tours leave at 10:00 a.m., 12:00 noon, 2:00 p.m., and 4:00 p.m. (Louisville time). They are closed Thanksgiving, Christmas, and New Years and weekends during January and February. Squire Village includes Boone's Mill and log cabin houses where crafts people display the making of soap, candles, wood and leather products, and homemade candies. Also here is an Indian relic museum. The village is open daily from Memorial Day to August 20 and weekends through Labor Day. An admission is charged.

CORYDON SCENIC RAILROAD, Walnut and Water Streets, offers a 16 mile round-trip starting from Corydon. A train schedule and fare information is available at the station or Chamber of Commerce.

HARRISON-CRAWFORD STATE FOREST is located on 7240 Old Forest Road, Corydon.

The WYANDOTTE CAVE, west of Corydon off I-64, is the third oldest commercial cave in the United States. Over six miles of the huge caverns are accessible via six different guided tours. Call (812) 738-2782 for tour schedules and information.

The following structures in Corydon are listed on the NRHP— **Kintner House Hotel** (1873), 201 South Capital Avenue, and **Kintner-McGrain House (Cedar Glade)** (c. 1808), 740 North Capital Avenue. Also on the NRHP is the **Corydon Historic District** (1808-1865). Elsewhere in the county the **Kintner-Withers House (Cedar Farm)** (1837), south of Laconia on Kintner Bottom Road, and **Swan's Landing Archaeological Site**.

Swan's Landing Archaeological Site was a ferry boat landing where boats crossed from southern Indiana to Meade County, Kentucky, during the mid-1800s. Several Indian tribes once traveled through this area along the Ohio River. Various Indian artifacts have been found up and down the river as well as around Swan's Landing.

Nineteen miles west of the Corydon exit on I-64 and nine miles north on IN 337 is ENGLISH (pop. 633), county seat of Crawford County. Crawford County, named for **Colonel William Crawford**, a Revolutionary War soldier and Indian fighter who was burned at the stake, was established March 1, 1818.

Eight miles east of English, via IN 64, is MARENGO (pop, 892) and the MARENGO CAVE, registered as a National Natural Landmark. It is open the year-round. From Memorial Day through Labor day the hours are 9:00 a.m. to 6:00 p.m., spring and fall weekdays from 9:30 a.m. to 5:30 p.m. and 9 a.m. to 6 p.m. weekends, and the rest of the year from 9:00 a.m. to 5:00 p.m. It is closed Thanksgiving Day and Christmas. Guided tours leave every 30 minutes for both the Dripstone Trail and Crystal Palace sections. An admission is charged.

In the southern tip of Crawford County, along the Ohio River, is unincorporated ALTON, home of the CRAWFORD COUNTY INDIAN MUSEUM. The displays here point up the richness of the Indian heritage and lore of the county. For more information about this unique museum, call (812) 739-4564.

The **Potts Creek Rockshelter Archaeological Site** in the county is listed on the NRHP.

Continuing another seven miles on I-64, 23 miles south on IN 32 and six miles on IN 237 is CANNELTON (pop. 2,373), county seat of Perry County. The county, named in honor of naval hero **Oliver Hazard Perry,** was established November 1, 1814; the town was laid out in 1835.

These structures in Cannelton are listed on the NRHP– **Cannelton Cotton Mills** (1851), bounded by Front, 4th, Washington, and Adams Streets; **Cannelton Historic District** (1837-1936), bounded by Richardson, Taylor, First, and Madison Streets; and **St. Luke's Episcopal Church** (1845), Third and Washington Streets. The **Old Perry County Courthouse** (1818), Town Square, Rome; **Rickenbaugh House** (1874), southwest of St. Croix in Hoosier National Forest; **Nester House** (1863, c. 1870), 300 Water Street, Troy; and **Rockhouse Cliffs Rock Shelters**, are also listed on the NRHP.

Back on I-64 it is 22 miles west to the IN 162 exit and three miles north is FERDINAND (pop. 2,318), hometown of **Albert F. Sondermann** who developed the self-computing gas pump in 1917.

Continuing west six miles on I-64 to the US 231 exit it is 14 miles north on IN 5 to JASPER (pop. 10,030), county seat of Dubois County. The county, named in honor of **Toussaint Dubois,** a French immigrant, was established February 1, 1818; Jasper was platted in 1830 and incorporated in 1866.

Jasper is the permanent host of the Indiana Baseball Hall of Fame. It is located on the campus of Vincennes University, Jasper Center, on IN 162.

There are three structures in Jasper listed on the NRHP. These include the **Gramelspacher-Gutzweiler House** (1849), 11th and Main Streets; **John Opel House (Green Tree Hotel)** (c. 1850); and **St. Joseph Catholic Church** (1868-1888, 1904), 1215 North Newton Street. Elsewhere in the county, **Convent Immaculate Conception Historic District** (1883-1924), 802 East 10th Street, Ferdinand, three miles off I-64 on IN 162; **Huntingburg Town Hall and Fire Engine House** (1861), 311 Geiger Street, Huntingburg, eight miles north of I-64 on IN 56; **Evangelische Lutherische Emanuels Kirke** (1901), CR 445E, one mile south of IN 56, Dubois; and **Shiloh Meeting House and Cemetery** (1849), southeast of Ireland on 150 Road North, are all listed on the NRHP.

Seven miles south of Jasper on IN 45 is HUNTINGBURG (pop. 4,794), founded in 1837.

Huntingburg's League Stadium in the city park was a filming site for the 1992 movie, *"A League of Their Own."*

**Old Town Hall,** on Geiger Street, is listed on the NRHP.

299

Construction was completed in 1886.

From I-64 it is 24 miles south on US 231 and IN 62 to ROCKPORT (pop. 2,590), county seat of Spencer County. The county, named in honor of **Captain Spear Spencer,** was established February 1, 1818; Rockport saw the first settlers arrive in 1808.

It was in Spencer County that young **Abraham Lincoln** spent most of his youth, from 1816 to 1830. He was born in Hardin County (now LaRue County), Kentucky, February 12, 1809, and his father, Thomas, moved the family to 160 acres of land in the Indiana wilderness of Spencer County. His mother, **Nancy Hanks,** died in 1818. A short time later Thomas married a widow, **Sarah Bush Johnston,** who Abraham came to love as his mother.

A town was named for Abraham Lincoln's family but **Lincoln City** was not laid out until 1872.

LINCOLN BOYHOOD NATIONAL MEMORIAL represents the southern Indiana farm where Abraham Lincoln grew from

Life on a pioneer southern Indiana farm is demonstrated on the Lincoln Living Farm at the Lincoln Boyhood National Memorial.

The grave of Nancy Hanks Lincoln (above) and the Lincoln cabin site (below) are found at the Lincoln Boyhood National Memorial in Spencer County.

youth to manhood. It is located in Lincoln City, take US 231 south from I-64, and IN 162 two miles east from Gentryville. The 200-acre wooded park includes walking trails, picnic areas, a living farm, and visitor center with memorial halls, museum, film, and book sales. Nancy Hanks Lincoln (Abraham's mother) is buried on a wooded knoll just north of the visitor center. The visitor center is open daily from 8:00 a.m. to 5:00 p.m. (Central Time) except Thanksgiving, Christmas, and New Year's Day. The Lincoln Living Historical Farm is an operating farmstead representative of the one Abraham Lincoln's father built in the Indiana wilderness. Using authentic methods and materials, "costumed pioneers" demonstrate daily farming and domestic chores. The farm is open seven days a week, late April through most of September. The visitor center and living farm are wheelchair accessible. An admission is charged excluding educational groups, disabled individuals, children under 17, and senior citizens over 61. Informational inquiries can be directed to: Lincoln Boyhood National Memorial, Lincoln City, Indiana, 47552 or telephone (812) 937-4541.

LINCOLN PIONEER VILLAGE AND MUSEUM, adjacent to Rockport, City Park, stands as a memorial to the life and times of Lincoln, his neighbors and friends during his years in Spencer County. There are a number of cabins and artifacts in the village and museum. Among the cabins is the Jones Store located at Jonesboro (now Gentryville). Abraham Lincoln clerked in this store for 25 cents per day. The mansion owned by James Gentry, a Lincoln neighbor, is furnished with articles from the Gentry family. Lincoln worked on the Gentry farm. Azel Dorsey's, one of Abraham's school teachers, home is displayed. The first court of law in the county was held in this house. Another building in the village is the Old Pigeon Baptist Church, a replica of the structure which Thomas Lincoln and his son helped build. All members of the Lincoln family were members except Abraham. These are only a few of the offerings in this tribute to the Lincoln family. The Village is open from 9:00 a.m. to 5:00 p.m. Tuesday through Sunday, May through October. An admission is charged.

A few miles down the road from Abraham Lincoln's boyhood home is GENTRYVILLE (unincorporated) and just east is the **Jones House State Historic Site**.

**William Jones**, born in Vincennes in 1803, and came to Spencer County to farm in the 1820s and he and his family also operated a store and the post office. As they prospered, they built

302

The 1830's home of William Jones is preserved at the Jones House State Historic Site near Gentryville.

the present house next to their store in 1836. Jones employed Abraham Lincoln as a helper in his store until Lincoln left for Illinois in 1830. In 1844 Lincoln visted Jones while campaigning for Henry Clay's presidential candidacy and spent the night in the family home. The little village became Jonesboro and it was here that William and Rachel Jones raised five boys. Two others were killed in a gun powder explosion that became the subject of ghost stories which later circulated in the neighborhood. In 1838 to 1841 Jones served as a Whig representative in the state legislature. In the 1850s the Jones family moved their business and residence one-half mile east to Gentryville which had surpassed Jonesboro in importance. A successful businessman, farmer, and politician, William Jones was commissioned a lieutenant colonel in the 53rd Regiment of the Indiana Volunteers during the Civil War and was later promoted to the rank of colonel. He was killed in the Battle of Atlanta on July 22, 1864.

JONES HOUSE STATE HISTORIC SITE preserves the 1834 (or 1836) home of the Jones family. It was donated to the State of Indiana in 1990 by William and Gayle Cook who had restored the home upon acquiring it in 1976. The home is open from 9:00 a.m. to 5:00 p.m. Wednesday through Saturday and from 1:00 to 5:00 p.m. Sunday. It is closed on Monday and Tuesday and from January 1 to March 15. An admission is charged.

The two structures listed on the NRHP in Rockport are the **Brown-Kercheval House** (1880), 315 South 2nd Street, and **Mathias Sharp House** (1867), 319 South 2nd Street. Four structures in the northern part of the county are listed on the NRHP–**Deutsch Evangelische St. Paul's Kirche** (1880), Santa Fe Road, south of Santa Claus; **Colonel William Jones House** (1834), Troy-Vincennes Road, west of Gentryville; **Lincoln Boyhood National Memorial**, IN 162, Lincoln City; and **St. Boniface Church** (1865), IN 545, Fulda.

Northeast of Lincoln City on US 460 and IN 62 is ST. MEINRAD (pop. 600), home of **St. Meinrad College** founded in 1854.

*Back at Lincoln City.*

Just north of the US 231 interchange on I-64 is **Dr. Ted's Musical Marvels Museum**. A variety of music and instruments on display include some 20 street organs, nickelodeons, orchestrions, and a Wurlitzer carousel organ.

Seventeen miles west of the IN 55 and US 231 and Indiana exit on I-64, is IN 61 exit. Ten miles south on IN 61 is BOONVILLE (pop. 6,300), county seat of Warrick County. The county, named in honor of **Captain Jacob Warrick**, who fought in the War of 1812, was established April 1, 1813; Boonville was platted in 1818.

**Wilford Bacon Hoggatt** of Boonville served as governor of Alaska.

The WARRICK COUNTY MUSEUM is located on the second floor of the Warrick County Court House Annex, South 1st Street between Locust and Walnut. The exhibits and displays focus on county history. The museum is open from 11:00 a.m. to 2:00 p.m. Monday through Thursday and from 1:00 to 4:00 p.m. weekends. For additional information, call (812) 897-0835.

**Boonville Public Square Historic District** (1855-1934), bounded by First, Sycamore, Fourth, and Walnut Streets, and **Old Warrick County Jail** (1877), 124 East Main Street, are listed on the NRHP. **Old Newburgh Presbyterian Church** (1851), North State and West Main Streets; **Original Newburgh Historic District** (1841-1925), bounded by IN 662, Water, Monroe, Main, and Middle Streets; and **Roberts-Morton House** (1834), 1.5 miles east of Newburgh on IN 662, are listed on the

304

NRHP. Also listed is the **Yankeetown Archaeological Site**.

From Boonville it is a short 15 miles west via IN 62 to EVANSVILLE (pop. 128,800), on the Ohio River, county seat of Vanderburgh County. The county, named for an Indiana judge, **Henry Vanderburgh**, was established February 1, 1818; the city, named in honor of legislator **Robert M. Evans**, was settled in 1817, incorporated as a town in 1819, and as a city in 1847. It is 13 miles south of I-64 at the US 41 exit.

During the 1840s, many German immigrants found their way here from New York as they sought work. The German heritage remains strong.

Before the Civil War, Evansville was on the Underground Railroad which helped blacks escaping slavery. During the Civil War the town served as a major supply depot. During World War II, Evansville became a defense building center and Navy LSTs and P-47 Thunderbolt fighter planes were built here. They made ammunition as well as other war goods and supplies.

Flooding of the Ohio River in 1883, 1884 and in 1937 were major natural disasters that confronted the city.

The coach and 14 members of the University of Evansville basketball team were killed in 1977 when their chartered jet crashed on takeoff from Evansville. The **University of Evansville** was founded in 1854.

Among the noted sports figures from Evansville are **Don Mattingly** and **Andy Benes**, professional baseball players, and football star **Bob Griese** with the Miami Dolphins.

Other well-known personalities include **Red Skelton**, comedian and actor; **Ron Glass**, actor who appeared as a regular in the *"Barney Miller"* TV series; and **David Eisler**, broadway actor and singer. **Halston**, the fashion designer, also has roots in Evansville.

Several early day automobiles were built in Evansville. Among these were Evansville, 1907-1909, and the Simplicity, 1906-1911, by Evansville Automobile Company; the Single-Center, 1906-1908, by the Single-Center Buggy Company; the Traveler, 1906-1913, by Traveler Motor Car Company; and the Windsor, 1906, by the Windsor Automobile Company.

ANGEL MOUNDS STATE HISTORIC SITE, 8215 Pollack Avenue, eight miles southeast of Evansville, is the site of a large prehistoric Indian town that existed on the banks of the Ohio River from approximately 1300 to 1500 A.D. Occupied by Middle Mississippian Indians, the site's Central Mound is one of the

This modern structure houses the Evansville Museum of Arts and Science.

largest prehistoric structures in the Eastern United States. The interpretive center houses a number of exhibits on Indian culture. Angel Mounds have been designated a National Historic Landmark and are listed on the NRHP. The site is open from 9:00 a.m. to 5:00 p.m. Wednesday through Saturday and from 1:00 to 5:00 p.m. Tuesday and Sunday.

EVANSVILLE MUSEUM OF ARTS AND SCIENCE, 411 S.E. Riverside Drive, features art, science, and history collections. Also included are "Rivertown U.S.A.," a re-creation of a 19th century village; a large permanent art collection; a complete steam railroad exhibit; science galleries and planetarium. Changing thematic displays keep the museum an ever appealing attraction. The museum is open from 10:00 a.m. to 5:00 p.m. Tuesday through Saturday and from 12:00 noon to 5:00 p.m. Sunday year-round. Admission is free.

OLD COURTHOUSE CENTER, 4th and Vine Streets, was completed in 1891 and is one of the Midwest's outstanding examples of Beaux-Arts architecture. Particularly notable are the statuary groups and bas-relief limestone carvings encrusting the interior. The old courthouse is listed on the NRHP. It is open from 8:00 a.m. to 5:00 p.m. weekdays and from 1:00 to 5:00 p.m. weekends. Guided tours are by appointment only. For information, call (812) 423-3361.

REITZ HOME MUSEUM, 224 S.E. First Street, is in the

306

French Second Empire mansion built by lumberman **John
Augustus Reitz** in 1871. The mansion is furnished in authentic
period furniture, much of it original. Francis Joseph Reitz, the
oldest son, redecorated the home in a grand Victorian manner in
1898 with gilded chandeliers, ornate fireplaces, stained glass,
parquet floors, and decorative ceilings. The last of John Reitz'

A museum now occupies the 1871 residence of Evansville
lumberman John Reitz. The mansion is furnished in period furniture, much of it original.

children died in 1931 and the mansion was left to the Daughters of Isabella, a Catholic organization. Bishop Grimmelsman, the first Catholic Bishop of the Evansville diocese, lived in the home for 28 years. It was donated to The Reitz Home Preservation Society in 1974. The mansion has been placed on the NRHP. It is open from 1:00 to 4:00 p.m. Wednesday through Sunday, February through mid-December. An admission is charged.

There are 87 individual structures listed in the county. In Evansville these include the **Alhambra Theatorium** (1913), 50 Adams Avenue; **William Bedford Sr.**, **House** (1874), 838 Washington Avenue; **Bernardin-Johnson House** (1916), 17 Johnson Place; **Bitterman Building** (1923), 202-204 Main Street; **John W.** Boehne House (1913); 1119 Lincoln Avenue; **William Carpenter House** (1849), 405 Carpenter Street; **Evansville College** (1916-1940), 1800 Lincoln Avenue; **Evansville Municipal Market** (1918), 813 Pennsylvania Street; **Evansville Post Office** (1879), 100 block of Northwest Second Street; **Former Vanderburgh County Sheriff's Residence** (1891), Fourth Street between Vine and Court Streets; **Garvin Park** (1915), North Main Street and Morgan Avenue; **Greyhound Bus Terminal** (1939), 102 Northwest Third Street; **Michael D. Helfrich House** (1920), 700 Helfrich Lane; **Hooker-Ensle-Pierce House** (1839), 6531 Oak Hill Road; **Hose House No. 10** (1888), 119 East Columbia Street; **Hose House No. 12** (1908), 1409 First Avenue; **Edgar A. Iglehart House** (1932), 5500 Lincoln Avenue; **Koester-Patberg House** (1874), 504 Herndon Drive; **Liberty Baptist Church** (1886), 701 Oak Street; **Peter Augustus Maier House** (1873), 707 South Sixth Street; **McCurdy Building (Sears, Roebuck and Company Building)** (1920, 1937, 1943), 101 Northwest Fourth Street; **Mead Johnson River-Trail-Truck Terminal and Warehouse** (1931), 1830 West Ohio Street; **Old Bitterman Building** (c. 1885), 200 Main Street; **Ridgeway Building** (1895), 313-315 Main Street; **Michael Schaeffer House** (1894), 118 East Chandler Avenue; **Robert Smith Mortuary** (1930), 118-120 Walnut Street; **Soldiers and Sailors Memorial Coliseum** (1917), 350 Court Street; and **Willard Library** (1888), 21 First Avenue.

The **McJohnston Chapel and Cemetery** (1880), Kansas Road and Erskine Lane, McCutchanville, is also listed on the NRHP.

In the Downtown Evansville Multiple Resource Area, 1817-

Evansville's Old Courthouse Center provides an example of Beaux-Arts architecture. Construction was completed in 1891.

1943, the following are included on the NRHP–**Albion Flats** (1910), 701 Court Street; **American Trust and Savings Bank** (1914), 524-530 Main Street; **Auto Hotel Building** (1929), 111-115 SE Third; **Hillary Bacon Store** (1921), 527 Main Street; **Barrett's Britz Building** (c. 1875), 415 Main Street; **Buckingham Apartments** (1911), 314-16 SE First Street; **Building at 223 Main Street** (1910); **Busse House** (1901), SE First Street; **Cadick Apartments** (1917), 118 SE First Street; **Central Library** (1931), 22 SE Fifth Street; **Citizens National Bank** (1916), 329 Main Street; **Conner's Bookstore (Dallas Music)** (c. 1865), 611-13 Main Street; **Court Building** (1909), 123-25 NW Fourth Street; **Daescher Building** (1886), 12-12 1/2, SE Second Street; **Eagles Home** (1912), 221 NW Fifth Street; **Evansville Brewing Company** (1893), 401 NW Fourth Street; **Evansville Journal News** (1910), 7-11 NW Fifth Street; **Fellwock Garage (Glass Specialty Company)** (1908), 315 Court Street; **Firestone Tire and Rubber Store** (c. 1930), 900 Main Street; **Fred Geiger and Sons National Biscuit Co.** (1894), 401 NW Second Street; **Gemcraft-Wittmer Building**

(1892), 609 Main Street; **German Bank** (c. 1883), 301-03 Main Street; **Harding and Miller Music Co.** (1891), 518-20 Main Street; **Huber Motor Sales Building** (1916), 215-219 SE Fourth Street; **Andrew Hutchinson House** (c. 1850), 410 Fulton Avenue; **Indiana Bell Building** (1929), 129-33 NW Fifth Street; **Ingle Terrace** (1910), 609-19 Ingle Street; **Kuebler-Artes Building** (1915), 327 Main Street; **Charles Leich and Co.** (c. 1900), 420 NW Fifth Street; **Lockyear College** (1911), 209 NW Fifth Street; **Masonic Temple** (1913), 301 Chestnut Street; **McCurdy Hotel** (1917), 101-111 SE First Street; **Morris Plan** (1930), 20 NW Fourth Street; **National City Bank** (1913), 227 Main Street; **M.G. Newman Building** (c. 1900), 211-13 SE Fourteenth Street; **O'Donnell Building** (c. 1900), 22 NW Sixth Street; **Old Fellwock Auto Company** (1922), 214 NW Fourth Street; **Old Hose House No. 4** (1860), 623 Ingle Street; **Orr Iron Company** (1912), 1100 Pennsylvania Street; **Parson and Scoville Building** (1908), 915 Main Street; **Pearl Steam Laundry** (c. 1923), 428 Market Street; **L. Puster and Company Furniture Manufactory** (1887), 326 NW Sixth Street; **John H. Roelker House** (c. 1860), 555 Sycamore Street; **Rose Terrace** (1910), NW Seventh Street; **Salem's Baptist Church** (1873), 728 Court Street; **Siegel's Department Store** (c. 1903), 101-05 SE Fourth Street; **Skora Building** (1912), 101-03 NW Second Street; **St. John's Evangelical Protestant Church** (1921), 314 Market Street; **Van Cleave Flats** (c. 1910), 704-08 Court Street; **Victory Theater and Hotel Sonntag** (1921), 600-14 Main Street;. **Wabash Valley Motor Company** (c. 1919), 206-08 SE Eighth Street; **Montgomery Ward Building** (1934), 517 Main Street; **YMCA** (1913), 203 NW Fifth Street; **YWCA** (1924), 118 Vine Street; and **Zion Evangelical Church** (1855), 415 NW Fifth Street.

The historic districts in Evansville listed on the NRHP—**Bayard Park Historic District** (1893-1935), bounded by Gum, Kentucky, Blackford and Garvin Streets; **Culver Historic District** (1890-1929), bounded by Madison Avenue, Riverside Drive, Emmett and Venice Streets; **Independence Historic District** (1857-1920), bounded by Iowa and Illinois Streets, Wabash and St. Joseph Streets; and **Washington Avenue Historic District** (1880-1920), bounded by Madison and Grand Avenues, East Gum and Parrett Streets.

It is only 17 miles via IN 62 from Evansville to MOUNT VERNON (pop. 7,656), on the Ohio River, county seat of Posey

310

County. Posey County, named for **Thomas Posey,** Revolutionary War general and governor of the Indiana Territory from 1813 until statehood, was established November 1, 1814. The first county seat was Blackford but was soon moved to Springfield. Originally called McFaddin's Bluff, the town was settled in 1806. Mount Vernon, named for George Washington's home, was laid out in 1816, and became the county seat in 1825.

Mount Vernon was home to three Civil War generals–**Alvin P. Hovey,** who became governor in 1889; **Thomas Pitcher,** who served as superintendent at West Point; and **William Harrow,** a prominent lawyer.

At the outset of the war, Harrow raised a company of volunteers and began his military career when he was appointed a captain of the Knox County Invincibles, April 24, 1861 by Governor Oliver P. Morton. By August 14, 1862, he had attained the rank of colonel and promoted to brigadier general in the winter of 1863-64. He participated in a number of battles throughout the Viriginia Campaign. At Gettysburg his adjutant was shot down at his side and his own life saved by two Mexican coins and the daguerreotype of his wife. By the end of the war he had been breveted a major general. He died of injuries suffered in a train accident in 1872 while campaigning for a friend.

Pitcher was born in Rockport and entered West Point in 1841. He entered the Army as a second lieutentant and served in the Mexican War, followed by duty on the frontier until the outbreak of the Civil War. He defended Harper's Ferry and served in the Virginia Campaign. At the Battle of Cedar Mountain he was so seriously wounded that he was no longer fit for active duty. He was promoted to major after the battle. He held a number of military assignments and at the end of the war was breveted lieutenant colonel, colonel, and brigadier general "for gallant and meritorious service during the Rebellion." He became superintendent of the Military Academy at West Point.

Hovey was commissioned a first lieutenant during the Mexican War. At the call of President Lincoln for volunteers upon the firing on Fort Sumter, Hovey organized a regiment and was commissioned a colonel. For his gallantry in the Battle of Shiloh, Hovey was promoted to brigadier general. He became a war hero because of his fierce fighting at the Battle of Champion Hill, key to the Vicksburg Campaign. In 1864, he was breveted major general by General Grant to raise 10,000 volunteers for Union service. Late in 1864, Hovey was appointed military commander

311

A Civil War hero, General Alvin Hovey from Mount Vernon was the first native born Indianan to be elected governor of the state. He was elected to the U.S. Congress in 1886 and governor in 1888. (Photograph by Bass Photo Co. Collection, Indiana Historical Society Library, Negative Number 29730).

in Indiana. During this assignment he fought strenuously against the Knights of the Golden Circle whose goal was to disrupt the Union cause. He served as Envoy Extraordinary and Minister Plenipotentiary of Peru. Hovey was elected to Congress in 1886 and in 1888 was elected governor, the first born Indianan to occupy that high office.

The two most significant developments in the growth of the county and the county seat was a plank road built between Mount Vernon and New Harmony in 1851 and the arrival of the railroad in 1871.

Posey County has a significant German population which began arriving in the 1830s and '40s. Agriculture is the primary industry although oil, coal and mineral deposits were discovered in the 1930s.

The buildings and sites in Mount Vernon and vicinity listed on the NRHP include the **Ashworth Archaeological Site;** **William Gonnerman House** (1895); 521 West Second Street; **Posey County Courthouse Square** (1876), 300 Main Street; **I.O.O.F. and Barker Buildings** (1898), 402-406 Main Street; **Mann Site,** in the Mount Vernon vicinity; and **Murphy Archaeological Site,** southwest of Mount Vernon. The Ashworth, Murphy and Mann Sites are Indian sites whose locations are not identified because unqualified persons may attempt to dig up these Indian mounds.

Historic NEW HARMONY (pop. 945), on IN 68, is situated on the banks of the Wabash River, seven miles south of I-64. It was here that one of the most significant religious settlements in America was founded.

**Harmonie,** as it was first called, was laid out in 1814 by the **Harmonie Society**, a group of Lutheran Separatists led by **George Rapp.** The Harmonists, as the group became known, left Wurttemburg, Germany, in 1803 seeking religious freedom

The Atheneum/Visitors Center (above) and a view from the center (below) into historic New Harmony.

and founded a community in Butler County, Pennsylvania. Rapp moved his 800 followers to Posey County after visiting the Indiana Territory in 1812. The **Harmonists** purchased large tracts of land throughout the county and into nearby Illinois. Harmonie quickly became self-sufficient; in addition to their own dwellings and churches, the Harmonists built and operated a lumber mill, cotton factory, and a brewery. Society goods were sold at Harmonists stores in Indiana and Illinois, and in other markets as far away as New Orleans. More than 150 structures were built in the Harmonisit town. Many of their buildings, including two large brick dormitories, survive today.

In 1825 Rapp sold the town of Harmonie and almost 20,000 acres to **Robert Owen** (1771-1858), a Welsh-born industrialist and social reformer from New Lanark, Scotland. Rapp moved his followers to Economy, Pennsylvania. Owen set about to create a cultural and scientific center. While Rapp's Harmonie was based on religious beliefs, Owen sought to introduce social reform and establish a model social community as he had done in his mill town of New Lanark earlier. He was one of the earliest proponents of women's rights, child labor laws, and public education. One of the first free public school systems was established in New Harmony

Many prominent scientists and intellectuals were brought to the community by the eminent geologist **William Maclure**, who joined Owen as a financial partner. Among them were **Thomas Say**, the American naturalist; **Charles-Alexandre Lesueur**, French naturalist; **Mme Marie Duclos Fretageot**, French Pestalozzian educator; **Joseph Neef**, European Pestalozzian educator; **Gerard Troost**, Dutch geologist; and **Frances Wright**, early feminist. Their early contributions to education, geology, natural science, trade schools, and women's suffrage had national impact.

The social experiment lasted only two years and the dissolution of the community was announced in March, 1827. Owen failed to gain the support of the government partly because of his avowed agnosticism. He left New Harmony but four of his sons and a daughter remained to become prominent in politics, science, and education.

**David Dale Owen** (1807-1860) served as a United States Geologist and State Geologist of, successively, Indiana, Kentucky, and Arkansas. He completed surveys of 12 states, mapping mineral resources throughout the region and opening the

314

Robert Dale Owen was the son of Robert Owen, the Welsh-born industrialist who sought social reform and create a model social community. The son, while a member of Congress, sponsored legislation that created the Smithsonian Institution in the District of Columbia. (Photograph by Bass Photo Co. Collection, Indiana Historical Society Library, Negative No. 47282).

way for the industrial development of the Midwest. From 1830 to 1860, New Harmony was an important training and research center for geology in America.

**Robert Dale Owen** (1801-1877)served in the Indiana legislature and later was elected to the U.S. House of Representatives (1843-47) where he sponsored legislation establishing the Smithsonian Institution. David and Robert were involved in the planning, design, and construction of the Institution's first building, which still stands in Washington, D.C. In 1853-58 he served as minister to the Kingdom of the Two Sicilies. In the 1860s and 1870s he was a prominent author of works on spiritualism.

**Richard Owen** (1810-1890) succeeded his brother David as state geologist of Indiana. He distinguished himself as a science professor at Indiana University and served as the first president of Purdue University. A colonel in the Civil War, he supervised a prisoner-of-war camp at Camp Morton in Indianapolis where he was noted for his humane treatment of Confederate prisoners.

**William Owen** (1802-1842) was left in charge of New Harmony when his father left in 1825 to recruit New Harmony adherents before returning to Scotland on family business. William was active in banking and agriculture, and was an editor of the New Harmony newspaper. He also founded the New

Harmony Thespian Society in 1827.

**Jane Dale Owen** (1806-1861) conducted two schools in New Harmony and assisted her brother, David, with his papers on geology. She married Robert Henry Fauntleroy, a surveyor and inventor, and it was in their home that their daughter, Constance, helped to found the Minerva Society, one of the nation's earliest women's literary societies.

HISTORIC NEW HARMONY is open from 9:00 a.m. to 5:00 p.m. daily from April through October. It is open only on weekends November through March, call for schedule of tours. An admission is charged. For information call (812) 682-4482. Historic New Harmony is a unified program of the University of Southern Indiana and the Division of Indiana State Museums and Historic Sites.

Tours of New Harmony and its important historic sites begin at The Atheneum/Visitors' Center, North and Arthur Streets. In addition to the tours, the Center provides information on shopping, lodging, professional summer theatre, dining, and camping facilities.

These structures are listed on the NRHP in New Harmony— **George Bentel House** (c. 1823), Brewery and Granary Streets; **Ludwig Epple House** (c. 1823), 520 Granary Street; **Mattias**

One of the unique sights in New Harmony is this vine covered granary. Interestingly the Owen social experiment here lasted only two years.

316

Examples of life in early New Harmony abound through this historic village.

**Scholle House** (c. 1823), Tavern and Brewery Streets; and **New Harmony Historic District** (1814-1874), Main Street between Granary and Church Streets. The New Harmony Historic District is also designated a National Historic Landmark.

In the northern part of the county, the **Bozeman-Waters National Bank,** (1924), 19 West Main Street, Poseyville, is listed on the NRHP. Elsewhere the **Hovey Lake Archaeological District** is also listed on the NRHP.

Back on I-64 at the US 41 exit (26 miles east of the Illinois state line) it is 15 miles north on US 41 and two miles east on IN 64 to PRINCETON (pop. 8,976), county seat of Gibson County. Gibson County, named for **General John Gibson,** governor of the Indiana Territory, was established April 1, 1813; Princeton, named for **Captain William Prince,** was settled c. 1812 and incorporated in 1818.

The **Gibson County Courthouse** (1886), in Princeton is listed on the NRHP. Also listed are the **Mussel Knoll Archaeological Site** and **Weber Village Archaeological Site**.

The **Haubstadt State Bank** (1904), 101 South Main Street,

Haubstadt, is listed on the NRHP. Haubstadt is a small community in the southern part of the county just west off US 41.

Also listed on the NRHP is the **William M. Cockrum House** (1876), 627 West Oak Street, Oakland City on IN 56/57.

North of Oakland City, via IN 67, is PETERSBURG (pop. 2,987), county seat of Pike County, established February, 1817. The county was named for **Zebulon Montgomery Pike**, discoverer of Pike's Peak in Colorado. Petersburg was laid out in 1817 but was not incorporated until 1924. It was named for **Peter Brenton** who gave the land for the town.

Petersburg is the boyhood home of **Gil Hodges**, star of the Brooklyn Dodgers and manager of the world champion New York Mets.

A devastating tornado struck the community on June 7, 1990 and rebuilding continued in 1992.

Ten miles southeast, via IN 56 and 61 is WINSLOW (pop. 1,017). **The Palace Lodge** (1892), Center and Main Streets, Winslow, is listed on the NRHP.

It is 16 miles from Petersburg on IN 57 to WASHINGTON (pop. 11,100), county seat of Daviess County, named in honor of **Captain Joseph Hamilton Daviess**. It was established February 15, 1817. Washington was settled in 1805 and laid out in 1817. Originally the county seat was called Liverpool for Robert Banks Jenkins, the second earl of Liverpool. Lord Liverpool gained fame as the man who sent Napoleon into exile on St. Helena in 1815. A schoolmaster, Thomas Heyward, suggested the new name was more appropriate than the hated British label.

There are several historic sites in the area including 32 miles of the Wabash and Erie Canal ditch; the now defunct B & O Railroad shops; reputed underground railroad stations; St. Peter's Church, the second oldest Roman Catholic parish west of the Alleghenies, and several Victorian-style homes. The unofficial origin of **Notre Dame University** was in MONTGOMERY (pop. 390), seven miles east of Washington on US 50 and 150.

The only stop for **Dwight D. Eisenhower's funeral train** in Indiana was at Washington on April 1, 1968 for a crew change. Both **Richard M. Nixon** and **Robert F. Kennedy** made campaign appearances here in 1968.

Thirty miles or more of the **Wabash and Erie Canal** operated through the county from 1852 to 1858. The **O & M Railroad** came through the county in 1857. In 1889 the **B & O**

318

**Railroad** shops were opened.

The 1913 Blue Hole flood created extensive damage in the county.

A large number of Amish and Mennonite families settled in the northwest part of the county.

The AMISH VILLAGE provides a view of Amish life through guided tours for groups of 15 or more. These tours are available at 9:00 a.m. and 1:00 p.m. Meals are available at Der Deutsche Gasthof. It is open from 11:00 a.m. to 8:00 p.m. Monday, Tuesday, and Thursday, from 8:00 a.m. to 8:00 p.m. (during the flea market season) Wednesday, from 11:00 a.m. to 9:00 p.m. Friday, and 8:00 a.m. to 9:00 p.m. Saturday. There are charges for the tours. For information on reservations, call (812) 486-3977.

DAVIESS COUNTY MUSEUM, Donaldson Road, South Washington (Lickskillet), focuses on county and local history. It is open from 10:00 a.m. to 4:00 p.m. Monday, Wednesday, and Friday. An admission is charged.

The **Robert C. Graham House** (1912), 101 West Maple Street, Washington, is listed on the NRHP. Elsewhere in the county the **Glendale Ridge Archaeological Site** and the **Prairie Creek Archaeological Site** are listed on the NRHP. Neither of these archaeological sites are open to the public.

Twenty miles west of Washington on US 50 and 150 is VINCENNES, county seat of **Knox County**, established June

The Daviess County Museum is housed in this former school building.

20, 1790 and extended from the Ohio River to Canada and from present-day Ohio to Peoria, Illinois. The county is named for the first **Secretary of War Henry Knox**. Vincennes is the oldest town in Indiana, founded as a town in 1732. Almost certainly French fur traders were here much earlier. From I-64, Vincennes is 41 miles north via US 41.

The earliest people here were Indian mound builders hundreds of years ago. While a great mystery surrounds this period of Indiana history, the Son of Tabac Prehistoric Indian Mound, 2401 Wabash Avenue, is the largest in the state. The Piankeshaw Indians called the area home.

The settlement of fur trappers and traders was fortified by **Francois-Marie Bissot, Sieur de Vincennes**, in 1732. Vincennes led an expedition against the Mississippi Chickasaws, was captured near present-day Tupelo, Mississippi, and burned at the stake on Palm Sunday, 1736. To honor Sieur de Vincennes the fort on the Wabash was renamed **Post St. Vincennes**. The French held the territory until 1762 when they saw defeat at the hand of the British in the French and Indian War and ceded vast interior lands to Spain. Three months later, in 1763, the British received these same lands at the Treaty of Paris.

Vincennes was occupied by the British in 1763 and during the American Revolution it became one of the major objects of the expedition of militia led by **George Rogers Clark**. Clark captured **Fort Sackville**, as it was called by the British, in the summer of 1778. His force was unable to hold it and Captain Leonard Helm, left in command, was forced to surrender to **British Lieutenant Governor Henry Hamilton** on December 17, 1778. With the heroic aid of **Francis Vigo, Francois Bosseron**, and **Father Pierre Gibault**, Clark finally recaptured the garrison February 25, 1779 to open the Northwest Territory.

At this point it is necessary to briefly look at the background of the young military commander George Rogers Clark. Born in Virginia on November 19, 1752, he moved to the Kentucky region in 1772 and by 1775 he had organized the Kentucky militia and served as commander of its defenses. Standing 6 feet 2 inches tall, with auburn-reddish hair, he was only 25 years of age when he was able to convince the Virginia governor and legislature to let him take the war into British-controlled territory north of the Ohio River. He was commissioned a lieutenant colonel and authorized to raise a force of 350 men. His secret

320

George
Rogers
Clark

(Photo-
graph by
B a s s
Photo Co.
Collection,
Indiana
Historical
Society Li-
b r a r y ,
Negative
No. 39190)

orders were to operate against the British posts at Kaskaskia and Cahokia in the Illinois country and Vincennes on the Wabash River, with the ultimate objective, the capture of Detroit. On July 4, 1778, he captured Kaskakia without firing a shot. His men took Cahokia on July 6th without resistance.

While Clark captured Vincennes twice, he was never able to capture Fort Detroit but successfully countered British moves in the region during the remainder of the Revolutionary War. His services against the British and their Indian allies were rewarded by the rank of brigadier general in the Virginia State Line and he was made an Indian commissioner. He died at Locust Grove, near Louisville, Kentucky, in 1818.

George Rogers Clark's accomplishments were commemorated in the establishment of the GEORGE ROGERS CLARK NATIONAL HISTORICAL PARK, 401 South Second Street,

This memorial in Vincennes honors George Rogers Clark.

which includes the Clark Memorial dedicated June 14, 1936 by **President Franklin D. Roosevelt**. In the interior of the memorial are exhibited seven large murals depicting Clark's important role in the region west of the Appalachians. A larger-than-life statute of George Rogers Clark stands in the center of the memorial. A statue of Francis Vigo is on the park grounds. Vigo, a fur trader and merchant, had gone to Vincennes to aid Captain Helm, the American commander of Fort Sackville. He was taken prisoner by the British when they recaptured the garrison but was quickly released because he was a Spanish citizen and Spain was neutral at the time. Vigo rushed back to Kaskaskia and provided Clark with information that helped in the American retaking the fort. George Rogers Clark National Historical Park is listed on the NRHP.

The territory was ceded to the United States by Virginia in 1784 and became public domain. From 1800 to 1813, Vincennes was the capital of the Indiana Territory. Several meetings and

Three forts, all named for Secretary of War Henry Knox, were built in the Vincennes area to protect settlers. This is the outline of the second Fort Knox.

negotiations between 1800 and 1811 took place here between Territorial Governor William H. Harrison and the famous **Shawnee Chief Tecumseh** and his brother, the **Prophet**. Vincennes was succeeded as the territorial capital in 1813 when it was moved to **Corydon**.

There were three forts built and garrisoned by the U.S. Army in the Vincennes area to protect settlers. All three were named **Fort Knox** for **Henry Knox**, the first Secretary of War. The first Fort Knox (1787-1803) was in Vincennes and a plaque at the corner of First and Buntin Streets marks its location. The second Fort Knox (1803-1813) was built three miles north of Vincennes on Fort Knox Road. It was from this fort that William Henry Harrison's expedition left for the confrontation with the Indians that emerged into the **Battle of Tippecanoe**, November 7, 1811. **Captain Zachary Taylor**, who like Harrison later became President, was one of the Fort Knox commanding officers in 1811. The site of the second Fort Knox is listed on the NRHP. The outline of this old fort site is marked for self-guided tours daily. Admission is free. The third Fort Knox (1813-1816) was built on the site of old Fort Sackville.

The first newspaper published in Indiana was Elihu Stout's *Indiana Gazette*, appearing July 4, 1804. The name of the paper was changed in 1807 to *The Western Sun*.

The first Protestants to organize in Indiana were the Presbyterians when they met in Colonel John Small's barn in 1806. The Baptists organized the **Maria Creek Chapel** in May, 1809, and the Methodist "Circuit" was established in southern Indiana in 1810.

Vincennes was the boyhood home of **Red Skelton**, comedian, stage and film actor. The one-room house in which **Maurice Thompson**, author of *"Alice of Old Vincennes,"* was born in 1844 has been moved from Fairfield, Indiana, to the **Harrison Historical Park**.

Vincennes was also the home of two Indiana governors — **"Blue Jeans" Williams**, the 14th, and **Matthew E. Welsh**, the 41st.

The Log Cabin Visitor Center is in Harrison Historical Park on Harrison Street next to the Vincennes University campus. It is open daily June through August and weekends April and May and September and October. The Vincennes Area Chamber of Commerce is located at 27 North Third Street where information is also available or call 1-800-886-6443.

WILLIAM HENRY HARRISON MANSION (GROUSELAND), 3 West Scott Street opposite the Indiana

William Henry Harrison called his home in Vincennes "Grouseland." The home was completed in 1804.

The Indiana Territorial capitol in Vincennes was acquired in 1811.

Territorial Capitol, was the residence of the first governor of the Indiana Territory and the first brick building constructed in Indiana. The mansion was built in 1803-04 in a grove of walnut trees, near the Wabash River. There are more than 20 rooms and 10 fireplaces in the mansion that is furnished with 1812 period pieces and earlier. Among the many visitors to Grouseland was **Aaron Burr** who visited Harrison to try to win his support for Burr's scheme to carve out an empire west of the Mississippi River. Shawnee chief Tecumseh met Harrison in a walnut grove on the grounds in 1810 to discuss the Indians' concerns about the white incursion into their lands. Harrison was elected the ninth President of the United States but died in office, 30-days after his inauguration, April 4, 1841, and was buried at North Bend, Ohio. The mansion is listed on the NRHP. Grouseland is open 9:00 a.m. to 5:00 p.m. daily except Thanksgiving, Christmas and New Years for 10 months out of the year. It is also open from 11:00 a.m. to 4:00 p.m. daily during January and February. An admission is charged.

325

A replica of Elihu Stout's 1807 newspaper office where he published Indiana's first newspaper, The Indiana Gazette.

INDIANA TERRITORY CAPITOL STATE HISTORIC SITE, Harrison and First Streets, consists of the **Territory Capitol**, the **Western Sun Print Shop**, the **Maurice Thompson Birthplace**, and the **Old State Bank**. The capitol was acquired through action by the Territory Assembly on November 21, 1811. For the first four years of its existence the Indiana Territory was governed by Harrison and three appointed judges. By 1804, population had increased enough to permit citizens of the Territory to elect representatives to a Territory Assembly but because it met infrequently it had no permanent home. The two-story frame building is held together by wooden pegs. The territorial capitol is listed on the NRHP.

The small frame building, located next to the Capitol of the Indiana Territory, is a replica of the office of *The Western Sun*. **Elihu Stout** who published the *Indiana Gazette* in 1804 renamed his new paper in 1807. The *Gazette* printing plant was destroyed by fire in 1806.

The OLD STATE BANK HISTORIC SITE, 114 North Second Street, serves as an art gallery today. The Vincennes branch of the Bank of Indiana was established in 1834 and was moved to this spot in 1838 and operated until 1877. The first bank in

The Vincennes branch of the Bank of Indiana was established in 1837. Today the building serves as an art gallery.

Vincennes was established in 1814 but failed in 1822. The building is listed on the NRHP. The art gallery presents permanent and changing exhibits of the Northwest Territory Art Guild and local artists. The gallery is open from 1:00 to 4:00 p.m. Wednesday through Sunday, March through October. It is closed on holidays. Admission is free.

Across the street is the **Ellis Mansion.** This stately home owned by Abner Turner Ellis,a borough president, probate judge, and state senator, was built by John Moore in 1838. Ellis promoted the charter of the Ohio & Mississippi Railroad, later part of the B&O Railroad, and was its first president. Abraham Lincoln visited in this home during Henry Clay's campaign in 1844.

OLD FRENCH HOUSE, 509 North First Street, was built c. 1806 by **Michel Brouillet,** a fur trader and scout. It is the only surviving example of a French colonial style home in Indiana. It was built in the French poteaux-sur-sole, or "posts on sill" style, consisting of hewn, upright posts fitted into horizontal sills. Spaces between the sills were filled with a mixture of mud and straw called bousillage. A museum adjacent to the house contains exhibits of the Indian and French periods. It is open 1:00 to 4:00 p.m. daily May through September. An admission is charged.

The Old French House in Vincennes is an example of a French colonial style home in Indiana.

OLD CATHEDRAL COMPLEX, 205 Church Street, contains the Basilica of St. Francis Xavier, Old French Cemetery, and the Brute Library. It is listed on the NRHP. The Old Cathedral of St. Francis Xavier was completed in 1841; construction began in 1826, the third church on the present site. The first church, a crude log building, was built around 1749, and the second was built in 1786 by Father Pierre Gibault. A statue of Father Gibault stands in front of the cathedral. Saint Gabriel's College was built in the courtyard in 1837 and operated by The Eucharist's Fathers. Also here is the St. Rose Chapel, built in 1847 to serve seminary students and later orphans and school children.

In 1834, St. Francis Xavier Church was elevated to a cathedral with **Simon Brute de Remur** as the first bishop of the Diocese of Vincennes. Brute was born in France in 1779 and ordained in 1808. Four years after his appointment as bishop, he sent for his collection of 5,000 books. He died on June 16, 1839, nine months after his books had arrived. A crypt, containing the remains of four bishops who served in Vincennes, is located below the sanctuary of the church.

The **Brute Library**, housed in a modern library adjacent to

328

This small building housed Saint Gabriel's College in the courtyard of the Old Cathedral Complex.

the Old Cathedral, contains the 5,000 rare books owned by the bishop to make up a collection of more than 12,000 documents, books, artworks, some dating back to the 1400s. It is open from 11:00 a.m. to 4:00 p.m. Tuesday through Sunday, June 1 through September 1. Admission is free.

The **Old French Cemetery** is on the church grounds and the remains of over 2,000 early citizens of Old Vincennes are buried here. William Clark, Judge of the Indiana Territory, was buried here in 1802. Many of the Frenchmen buried here served with George Rogers Clark's army. The grave of **Father Jean Francois Rivet**, who played a leading role in the religious and educational life of Vincennes, is located in the center of the cemetery which closed for new burials in 1846. Father Rivet was the first headmaster of the newly created Jefferson Academy in 1801. He died on February 13, 1804.

INDIANA MILITARY MUSEUM, INC., on Bruceville Road, has a well-rounded display of military vehicles, artillery, uniforms, insignia, equipment, and related artifacts dating from the Civil War to the Persian Gulf. Among the exhibits, the General Officers collection is claimed to be one of the best outside of West Point. Letters, documents, flags, insignia and uniforms of more than 20 generals and admirals from World War II through the Persian Gulf are in the collection. Among these are such figures as Generals Dwight D. Eisenhower, George S. Patton, Jr., Omar

N. Bradley, Ira C. Eaker, James A. Van Fleet, Mark Clark, William C. Westmoreland, and Admiral William F. "Bull" Halsey. Large weapons, tanks, and other vehicles are included in the outdoor static displays. The outdoor displays are open from 8:00 a.m. to 5:00 p.m., the indoor exhibits are open from 12:00 noon to 5:00 p.m. daily during the summer. During the winter months the weekday hours vary, weekends the museum is open from 12:00 noon to 5:00 p.m. An admission is charged.

U.S.S. VINCENNES MEMORIAL is located at the foot of the Lincoln Memorial Bridge. The museum is located in the City Hall, 201 Vigo Street. It contains memorabilia from the four ships that have sailed under the name *U.S.S. Vincennes.* The first of these ships was a 24-gun sloop of war commissioned August 27, 1826 and decommissioned August 28, 1865; the second, the heavy cruiser CA 44 was commissioned February 27, 1937 and sunk in battle August 9, 1942; the third, the light cruiser CL 64 was commissioned January 22, 1944 and decommissioned September 10, 1946; and the fourth, the Aegis cruiser CG 49 was commissioned July 6, 1985. The museum is open by appointment only from 8:00 a.m. to 12:00 noon and from 1:00 to 4:00 p.m. weekdays. It is closed on holidays. Admission is free.

The **Spirit of Vincennes Rendezvous** is an annual event commemorating George Rogers Clark's capture of Fort Sackville in 1779. The event is held the Saturday and Sunday of Memorial Day weekend. The rendezvous includes battle reenactments, arts, crafts, entertainment and food from the 18th and 19th centuries.

The Dixie-Flyer, 1916-1923, was an automobile manufactured by the Kentucky Wagon Manufacturing Company in Vincennes and Louisville, Kentucky.

The **Vincennes Historic District** (1733-1809), listed on the NRHP, can be seen on a 45-minute walking tour. For visitor information and parking, it is recommended that the tour begin at the George Rogers Clark Historical Park, 401 S. 2nd Street. Thirteen different styles of architecture are featured on the tour; however, these homes are not open to the public.

The other property listed on the NRHP is the **Ebner-Free House** (1887), 120 Locust Street. The **Kixmiller's Store** (1866, 1878), Carlise and Indianapolis Streets, Freelandville, in the northern part of the county, and the **Pyramid Mound Archaeological Site** are also listed on the NRHP.

# Index

173, 174, 191, 208, 214, 236, 238, 240, 260, 268, 305

B&O Railroad, 318
Back Creek Friends Church, 201
*"Back Home Again in Indiana"*, 57
Baer, Paul, 179
Bakalar, 1st Lt. John Edmond, 77
Bakalar Air Force Base, 77
Baker, Dr. Moses, 69
Balbec, 206
Ball State University, 206
Ball State University Museum of Art, 206
Ballard, Wendell, 74
Banta, Richard (author "The State of Ohio"), 258
Barbour, Ross and Don, 80
Barker, John H., 146
Barker Mansion, 146
Barnard, William O., 111
Barnhart, Congressman Henry A., 232
Barnum & Bailey Circus, 231, 232
Bartholomew, Gen. Joseph, 75
Bartholomew County, 75, 81
Bartholomew County Historical Museum, 80, *81*
Basilica of St. Francis Xavier, 328
Bass, Sam, 289
Bass, Sion, 178
Bass Lake State Beach Park, 24
Bates, Joshua, 264
Batesville, 264
Battle of Corydon Civil War Site, 294, *296*
Battle of the Dunes, 142
Battle of Tippecanoe, 14, 16, 61, *62*, 64, 70, 233, 323
Battle of the Thames 64
Battle of Trail Creek, 145
Battleground, 69
*"Bear Story, The"*, 20, 36
Beard, Charles A., 112
Beardsley, Albert R., 158
Beardsley, Dr. Havilak, 155
Beatty, Clyde, 231

Bedford, 284, *285*, 289
Beecher, Henry Ward, 28
Beechwood (The Isaac Kinsey House), 106
Bell, Greg, 127
Bell, Lawrence "Larry" Dale, 227, *228*, 229
Bell Aircraft Corp., 228
Bell Aircraft Museum, *228*, 229
Bell's Ford Bridge, 87
Belmont, 281
*"Ben Hur"*, 20
Benedict, William Lemuel, 114
Benes, Andy, 305
*"Benjamin Blake"*, 57
Bennett, Thomas W. 104
Benson, Kent, 111
Berne, 194-196, *195*
Best, James, 294
Bethel College, 154
Beveridge, Albert J., 20
Beverly Shores, South Shore Railroad Station, 142
Beyson, D. A., 18
Big Four Bridge, 92
Billie Creek Village, *129*, 131
Billings, Dr. John Shaw, 270
Billy Sunday Home, 227
Bird, Larry, 290
Birds Eye View Museum, 164
Black, Charles H., 30
Black Horse Troop, 231
Blackford, 311
Blackford, Judge Isaac Newton, 203
Blackford County, 202
Blackford Historical Museum, 203
Blondell, Eddie, 80
Blondell, Joan, 80
Bloomfield, 12, 15, 84
Bloomington 275, 276, *279, 280, 281*, 282, 284
Bluffton, 196, *197*
Bobbs, Dr. John S., 29
Bohm, C. Curry, 281
Bondi, Buelah, 141
Bonnell, Zetti, 105

332

Bonneyville Mill, 161
Boone, Daniel, 73
Boone County, 73, 74
Boonville, 304, 305
Booth, Newton, 91
Borman, Frank, 21, 22
Bosseron, Francois, 320
Bowen, Dr. Otis R., 221
Bowen-Merrill booksellers, 29
Bowers, Claude, 126
Bowles, Dr. William A., 17, 185, 289
Bowman, Charles, 141
Bowmar Incorporated, 181
Boyd, Col. John P., 62
Brady, John G., 243
Branigan, Roger D., 74
Brazil, 120, 122
Bremen, 221
Bremen Stand Pipe, 221
Brenton, Peter, 318
Bridgeton Covered Bridge, *130*
Brier, Andrew, House, 73
Bristol, 161, 164, *165*
Brolley, Tom, 82
Broncho John, 141
Brook, 61
Brookville, 153, *265*, 266, 267
Brotherhood of Locomotive Firemen, 123
Brouillet, Michael, 327
Brown, Henry Baker, 141
Brown, Dr. Herbert C., 70
Brown, Col. Isaac Washington, 232
Brown, Maj. Gen. Jacob, 281
Brown, Mark N., 21, 22
Brown, Mordicai "Three Fingered", 127
Brown, Dr. Otis P., 20, 232
Brown, William H., 257
Brown County, 281, 282
Brown County Art Gallery, 281
Brown County Historical Museum, *282*, 283
Brown County State Park, 24
Brownstown, 85, 87

Brownsville, 102
Brute Library, 328
Bryan, William Jennings, 53, 99
Bryant, James R., 251
Buckley Homestead, 55, *56*
Buddha, 289
Bundy, Gen. Omar, 110
Burg, Col. Vern L., 251
Burns, Randall, 142
Burnside, Ambrose E., 102, 104
Burr, Aaron, 325
Buskirk, Dave Van, 276
Butler, Earl, 20
Butler, Ovid, 83
Butler University, 27, 29, 43, 83
Butlersville, 83

Cabin in the Wildflower Woods (Gene Stratton Porter's cottage), 23, 166, *167*
Cade Hollow Covered Bridge, 249
Callahan, Will, 80
Calumet College, 139
Calumet Region, 139
Cambridge City, 106, *108*, 112
Camp Allen, 178
Camp Atterbury, 76, 78, *79*, 80
Camp Colfax, 142
Camp Jackson, 142
Camp Morton, 28
Camp Scott, 179
Camp Tippecanoe, 68
Camp Wayne, 101
Cannelton, 16, 298
Canterbury/Central Normal College, 116, 259
Capehart, Homer, 181
*"Caravan to Xanadu"*, 5
Carey, Max "Scoop", 127
Cariani, V. J., 281
Carlisle, 134
Carmichael, Hoagy, 20, 99, 276, *279*
Carnation Milk Co., 115
Carroll, Charles, 72
Carroll County, 72
Carroll County Historical Mu-

333

Condert, Auralia Kussner, 258
Conn, C. G., 155
Conner, William, 42, *44*
Conner Prairie, 42, *44*
Connersville, 106, 173
Conover, Teresa Maxwell, 105
Constitution Elm, 293
Constitutional Convention
Coolidge, Pres. Calvin, 140
Cooper, Kent, 80
Copeland, Harry, 199
Copshaholm Carriage House, 150
Copshaholm House Museum, 149,
  150, 151
Coquillard, Alexis, 151
Corbus, Limber Jim, 193
Cord, Errett Loban, 173
Corydon, 11, 14, 17, 23, 92, 275,
  293, 294, *295-297*, 298, 323
Corydon Capitol State Historic
  Site, 23, 294
Corydon Scenic Railroad, 297
Costigan, Francis, 90
Council Oak, 11
Covered Bridge Festival, 129, 132
Covered Bridges in Parke County,
  131
Covington, 15, 247
Covington Cemetery, *248*
Craig, George, 121
Crane, Larry, 83
Crawford, William H., 253, 298
Crawford County, 290, 298
Crawford County Indian Museum,
  298
Crawfordsville 22, 68, *252-255*,
  257-259
Crisman, 142
Croghan, Col. George, 66
Cromwell, Oliver, 121
*"Cross of Gold"* (Speech), 99
*Crossroads of America*, 123
Crothers, Sherman Benjamin
  "Scatman", 126
Crow, George, 74
Crowley, James, 152
Crown Hill Cemetery, 48, 117, 118

Crown Point, 22, 53, 55, 137
Cruft, Charles, 126
Cryer, Gretchen Kiger, 115
Cubberly, Ellwood Patterson, 188
Culbertson, William, 95
Culbertson Mansion, 23, 95
Culver, 226, 230
Culver, Henry Harrison, 230
Culver Academies, 230, 231
Cummins, Clessie, 76, 115
Cummins Engine Company, 76
Cyclotron Facility, 278

Daleville, 212, 217
Dana, 23, 249
Daniels, Joseph J., 133
*"Danites, The"*, 104
Danville, 116, 259
Daringer, Clifford, 82
Daringer, Rolla, 82
Darlington, 259
Darrow, Clarence, 226
Daviess, Capt. John Hamilton,
  318
Daviess County, 318
Daviess County Museum, 319
Davis, Elmer, 268, 269
Davis, George F., 139
Davis, James J., 217
Davis, Jim (creator of cartoon
  "Garfield), 20, 200
Davis, Johnnie, 121
Deadman's Curve, 69
Deam, Dr. Charles C., 197
Dean, James, 20, 198, 200-202
Dean, Winton and Mildred, 198,
  *199*
Dearborn, Gen. Henry, 267
Dearborn County, 267
Debs, Eugene Victor, 19, 123, *124*
Decatur, 193
Decatur, Stephen, 262
Decatur County, 262
Deep River County Park, 140
DeKalb, Gen. Johann, 173
DeKalb County, 173
Delaware County, 206, 208

336

Fox, Joseph, 147
Francesville, 18
Francis Costigan House, 90
Francisco, 16
Frankfort, 73
Franklin, 74, *75*
Franklin College of Indiana, 74
Franklin County, 265
Franklin County Historical
Society, 267
Franklin County Seminary, 266
Franklin, Benjamin, 265
*"Freckles"*, 20
Freeman, Ab, 84
Freeman, Lewis, 112
Freeman, Capt. Richard S., 84
Freeman Army Airfield, 83, 84, 86
French Lick, 185, 289, 290
Fretageot, Mme Marie Duclos,
314
Friddle, Burl, 74
Friddle, Carlyle, 74
Friedersdorf, Max, 74
Friends Meetinghouse, 117
*"Friendly Persuasion"*, 83
*"From Dawn to Daylight"*, 28
Fudge Mound, 211
Fulton, Robert, 231, 269
Fulton, Samuel, 269
Fulton County, 231, 232, 233
Fulton County Historical Society,
233
Fulton County Museum Round
Barn, *231*, 232, 233
Funk, Frank, 211

Gaar, Julia Meek, 100
Gable, Clark, 179
Gallagher, Anthony "Skeets", 126
Gant, John, 74
Garfield Park Conservatory, 42
Garrett, 174
Garrett Heritage Park Museum,
175
Garrison, William Lloyd, 145
Gary, 19, 22, 53, 137-139
Gary, Judge Elbert H., 138

Garyton, 142
Gatling, Richard, 17, 28
Gayle, Crystal (Brenda Gail
Webb), 191
General Electric Company, 181
General Lewis B. Hershey Hall,
170
General William Grose House,
110
Geneva, 23, 193, 194
Gentryville, 23, 302, 303
George, Eliza E. (Mother George),
178, *180*
George Rogers Clark National
Historic Park, 321, 322
Geronimo, 179
Gibault, Father Pierre, 12, 320
Gibson, John, 12
Gibson, Gen. John, 317
Gibson County, 21, 317
Gilbert, Richard, 275
Gilson, Clinton D. (barn), 55
Gipp, George, 152
*"Girl of the Limberlost"*, 20
Glass, Ron, 305
Glass Museum, 205
Glenn A. Black Laboratory of
Archaeology, 278
Glidden, Bob, 74
Glucometer, 156
Godfroy, Francis, 236
Goff, Thomas, 269
Goodman, Benny, 146
Good Shepherd Church of the
United Brethren, 188
Goodwin, Frances M., 109
Goodwin, Helen M., 110
Gookins, James Farrington, 126
Goshen, 159, 164
Goshen College, 164
Gosport, 120
Goth, Marie, 281
Governor Hendricks' House, 296
Grand Army of the Republic, 28
Grant, Moses and Samuel, 198
Grant County, 14, 198
Grant Memorial Park Cemetery,

338

199
Gray, Harold L., 69
Great Gretonas, 231
Great Sauk Trail, 53
Greeley, Lt. Adolphus W., 72
Greeley, Horace, 251
Greencastle, 118, 119
Greene, Gen. Nathaniel, 284
Greene County, 284
Greenfield, 36, 115
Greensburg, *262, 263*, 264
Greensburg Courthouse Tower, 262
Greentown, 21, 205, 243
Greentown Glass Museum, 243
Gresham, James B., 21
Gresham, Walter Q., 20
Grey, Pearl Zane, 179
Griese, Bob, 305
Griffin, 21
Grissom, Virgil I. "Gus", 22, 236, 285, *286, 288*
Grissom Air Force Base, 236, 237
Grissom Memorial, *287*
Grissom Memorial Building (Spring Mill State Park), 287, *288*
Grose, Maj. Gen. William, 110
Grover Museum, 260
Gruelle, John, 31
Gruenwald House, 215, 216
GTE Telephone Museum, 182
Guerin, Mother Theodore, 122
Gunness, Belle, 142, 143

Hackleman, Gen. Pleasant A., 265, 266
Hadley, Elias, 116
Hadley, Paul, 117
Hagerstown, 106
Hagerstown I.O.O.F. Hall, 107
Hagerstown Museum, 107
Hahn, Barton N., 283
Hailmann, W. N., 144
Halas, George, 139
Hall, Katie, 138
Halleck, Charles, 57

Halstead, Melvin, 55
Halstead, Melvin A. (House), 55
Halston (fashion designer), 305
Hamilton, Alexander, 244
Hamilton, Lt. Gov. Henry, 66, 320
Hamilton, John, 147
Hamilton County, 244
Hammon, Capt. Stratton, 76
Hammond, George, 139
Hammond, 32, 53, 77, 137, 139, 140
Hammond Professionals (Pros or "Hippos"), 139
Hamtramck, Col. John, 176
Hancock, Audrey, 118
Hancock County, 115
Hancock County Historical Society, 115
"Hangman's Crossing", 85
Hanks, Nancy, 300, *301*, 302
Hanley, James F., 57
Hanly, J. Frank, 251
Hannah Lindahl Children's Museum, 154
Hannegan, Edward A., 248
Hanover College, 15, 88
Hardin, Clifford M., 20, 112
Hardin, Col. John, 175
Harmar, Gen. Josiah, 175
Harmon, Tom, 57
Harmonie State Park, 24
Harmonie Society, 313
Harmonists, 314
Harmony Thespian Society, 316
Harrison, Benjamin, 12, 18, 33, *34*, 35, 48
Harrison, William Henry, 11, *13*, 14, 16, 19, 20, 39, 62, 64, *65*, 92, 120, 294, 323
Harrison County, 19, 293
Harrison County Jail, 294
Harrison Historical Park, 324
Harrison Home Guard, 293
Harrison-Crawford State Forest, 297
Harrodsburg Station, 276
Harroun, Ray, 35, 36

339

Harrow, William, 311
Hart, Aaron, 139
Hartford City, 202
Harvey, E. F. Funeral Home, 118
Haskell and Barker Car Company, 146
Hatcher, Mayor Richard, 138
Hatton, Augustus R., 270
Haugh, Benjamin F., 257
Hawley, Dr. Paul, 104
Hay, Charles, 91
Hay, John Milton, 20, 91
Hayden, 82
Haynes, Elwood, 19, 202, 203, 239, *240*, 241
Hays, William Harrison, 133
Hays, Will H. Jr. (author of "Dragon Watch"), 258
*"Hays Code, The"*, 134
Hazelden Compound, 61
Head, Cecil, 74
Heald, Capt. Nathan, 177
Heffren, Horace, 17, 185
Helgelein, A. K., 142, 143
Heller, Herbert L., 110
Helm, Capt. Leonard, 66, 320, 330
Hemmings, Jim, 83
Hendricks, Thomas A., 260, 261
Hendricks, Thomas H., 20, 31
Hendricks, William, 11, 116, 296
Hendricks County, 116, 259
Henley, Harry, 99
Henry, Patrick, 109
Henry County, 109, 111, 115
Henry County Historical Museum, 110
Henryville, 87, *89*
Heritage Museum in Air Park ( Grissom AFB), *236, 237*
Heritage Preservation Center, 38
Heritage Trail, 161
Herron, John, Art Institute, 27, 42
Hershey Museum, 170
Hickam, Horace, 119
Hickam Field (Hawaii), 119
Hickman, James T., 115
Highland, 140

Highland Historical Society Museum, 140
Highland Lawn Cemetery, 127
*"High Fever"*, 80
Hillforest, 269
Hiner, Cincinnatus (Joaquin Miller), 104
Hinshaw, Glen Cooper, 243
Historic Fort Wayne, 181
Historic New Harmony, 316
Historical Museum of Wabash Valley, 128
Historical Society of Porter County/Old Jail Museum, 141
Hoagy Carmichael Room, 278
Hobart, 53, 140
Hobart Historical Society Museum, 140
Hodges, Gil, 318
Hodson, Moses M., 115
Hoeflinger, Charles, 164
Hoffa, James Riddle "Jimmy", 121
Hoggatt, Wilford Bacon, 304
Holcomb, J. I., Observatory and Planetarium, 43
Holliday Collection of Neo-Impressionist Art, 38
Hollis, Frederic, 120
Holmes, Ensign Robert, 175
Holstein, Maj. and Mrs. Charles L., 36
Home of Eugene V. Debs, 123, *125*
Homesite, 94
Homestead Museum, 55
Hook's Historical Drug Store & Pharmacy Museum, 41
*"Hoosiers"*, 74, 112
*"Hoosiers Schoolmaster"*, 20
Hope, 81, *82*
Hopewell Church, *189*
Hopewell Church Cemetery, 188, *190*
Hopewell Farm, 188
Hopkins, Gen. Samuel, 64
Horsey, Stephen, 185
Horton Washing Machine Company, 180

340

345

Noonan, Fred, 69
Norris, George W., 141
North Manchester, 192
North Vernon, 82
North Vernon High School, 83
Northern Indiana Amish Country, 161
Northern Indiana Historical Society, 150
Notre Dame University, 151, 152, 318

O&M Railroad, 318
O'Connor, Pat, 83
O'Malley, Patrolman Patrick J., 137
Oak Hill Cemetery, 255
Oberholtzer, Madge, 32
Ogden, Rev. Isaac, 266
Ohio County, 269
Ohio & Indiana Company, 178
Ohio County Historical Society Museum, 269
Old Brookville Church & Cemetery, 266
Old Cathedral Complex, 328, *329*
Old Clarksville Site, 94
Old Courthouse Center, 306, *309*
Old Crescent (on Indiana University campus), 277
Old French Cemetery, 328, 329
Old French House, 327, *328*
Old Iron Bridge, 227
Old Jail Museum (Crawfordsville), 257, *258*
Old Lighthouse Museum, 146
Old Log Jail & Chapel in the Park Museum, 115
Old Main, 74
Old Order Amish, 159
Old Pigeon Baptist Church, 302
Old Red Warehouse, 68
Old State Bank, 23, 326
Old Town Park (Logansport), 238
*"Old Swimmin' Hole"*, 115
Oldfield, Barney, 35
Oliver, James, 16, 149

Oliver, Joseph Doty, 149
Oliver Chilled Plow Works, 149
Olsen, Ole, 180
*"On the Banks of the Wabash, Far Away"*, 23
181st Tactical Fighter Group, 123
115th Field Artillery, 21
113th Tactical Fighter Squadron, 123
*"One World"* (by Wendell Willkie), 217
Oolitic, 285
Orange County, 289
Orange County Historical Society, 289
Orange County Museum, 289
*Order of American Knights*, 17
Osborne, Mrs. Fanny, 29
Oswego, 229, 230
Ouiatenon, 11, 12, 66, 67
Overbeck Art Pottery Museum, 106
Owen, Col. Abraham, 119
Owen, David Dale, 314
Owen, Jane Dale, 316
Owen, Jesse, 40
Owen, Richard, 3154
Owen, Robert 14, 314, 315
Owen, Robert Dale, 315
Owen, William, 315
Owen County, 119, 120
Owen's Creek, 18

*"Pacific Poems"*, 104
Palmyra, 17
Panic of 1873, 18
Paoli, 289, 290
Parke, Judge Benjamin, 129
Parke County, 128, *130*
Parke County Convention & Visitors Bureau, 129
Parke County Museum, 132
Parker, Benjamin S., 115
Parker, Crawford T., 111
Parr Postoffice, *58*
Parrish Pioneer Farm, *60*
Patricksburg, 120

347

Patriot, 270
Patschke, Cyrus, 35
Patten Cemetery, 142
Patti, Sandi, 215
Payne, Charles T., 202
Payne, Capt. David L., 200
Peasley, Judge William J., 260
Pendleton, 217
Pennville, 205, 206
*"Penrod"*, 31
*"Penrod and Sam"*, 31
Perry, Cynthia Shepard, 126
Perry, Oliver Hazard, 299
Perry, Oran D., 104
Perry County, 298
Pershing, Gen. John J. "Black
  Jack", 39
Peru, 15, 233, *234*, *235*, 236
Peru Circus Center, *234*, 235
Petersburg, 16, 318
Phi Kappa Psi Fraternity Head
  quarters, 43
Phillips, L. D., 146
Piankashaw Indians, 11, 320
Pierce, James "Babe", 120
Pierce, Marion, 112
Pierpont, Harry, 147
Pigeon Roost, 14, 23, 87, *88*
Pike, Zebulon Montgomery, 318
Pike County, 318
Pinkston, Joe M., 283
Pioneer Village Complex, 91
Pioneer Village at the Jasper
  County Fairgrounds, 58
Pitcher, Thomas, 311
Pittenger, Police Officer Jud, 225
Pittsburg, 15
Plainfield, 116, *117*
Plymouth, 221, *222*, 231, 232
Pokagon State Park, 24
Poland Historical Chapel, 122
Poland Presbyterian Church, 121
Pontiac, Ottawa Chief, 12, 66
"Pontiac Uprising", 66, 175
Port Gibson, 16
Portage, 142
Portage Community Historical

Museum, 142
Portage-Burns Waterway, 142
Porter, Charles Darwin, 190, 193
Porter, Cole, 20, 198, 234, 235
Porter, David, 140
Porter, Gene (Geneva Grace)
  Stratton, 20, 23, 188, 189, 193,
  194
Porter, Judge William A., 296
Porter County, 140-142
Portland, 18, 203-205
Portland's Eastern Indiana
  Normal School, 203
Portland Natural Gas & Oil
  Company, 205
Posey, Thomas, 12, 295, 297, 311
Posey County, 21
Posey House Museum, 295
Post St. Vincennes, 320
Pot Holes, 252
Potato Creek State Park, 24
Potawatomi Indians, 11, 190, 223
Potawatomi Indian Chief
  Shipshewana, 161
Pound, Ezra, 80
Pound Store Museum, *229*
Powell, Oliver, 232
Presbyterian Church Building, 61
Preuss, Capt. Paul T., 84
Prince, Capt. William, 317
Prince William IV of Orange, 289
Princeton, 21, 317
Prophet, 14, 61, 63, 64, 70, 177,
  323
Prophet's Rock, 70
Prophet's Town, 62, 64
Prospect, 289
Pucker, 202
Pulaski, Count Casmir, 154
Pulaski, 154, 155
Pulaski County, 233
Pulaski County Historical
  Museum, 233
Pullman Company, 123
Purdue, John, 69
Purdue University, 18, 69, 197
Purviance, Lt. Col. Helen, 186

351

Stuart, Elfridge Amos, 115
Studebaker Brothers, Henry and Clement, 16, 148, 149
Studebaker National Museum, Inc., *204*, 205
Stuhldreher, Harry, 152
Stuntz, Ervin, 221
Stuntz Indian Museum, 221
Sturm, Jerry, 99
Stutz, Harry C., 33
Sullivan,133, 134
Sullivan, Daniel, 133
Sullivan, Iva Etta, 74
Sullivan, Judge Jeremiah, 90
Sullivan, Patrick H., 74
Sullivan, Patrick Henry Museum, 74
Sullivan County, 16
Sullivan Historic Society Mu seum, 134
*"Sultan of Sula"*, 61
Summit Lake State Park, 24
Sumner, Charles, 145
Sunday, Evangelist Billy, 226, 227
Surgical Institute, 29
Swan's Landing Archaeological Site, 298
Swinney, Thomas W. Homestead, 183
Swiss Colonists, 12
Swiss Heritage Village, 196
Switzerland County, 12, 270
Switzerland County Public Library, 270
Syracuse, 164
Syracuse-Turkey Creek Museum, 164

*"Take Me Out to the Ballgame"*, 29
Tarkington, Booth, 20, 31, 266
Tarkington, John S., 266
Taylor, Charles Bernard "Bud", 127
Taylor, Enos, 188
Taylor, Waller,, 11
Taylor, Capt. Zachary, 14, 122, 323

Taylor University, 199
Tecumseh, Shawnee Chief, 14, 61-64, 177, 213, 323, 325
Ten O'Clock Treaty Line, 120
Tenskwatawa, 64
Terhune, Max, 74
Terre Haute, 15, 18, 62, 122, 123, *125*, 126-128, 133
Terre Haute Brewery & Civil War Museum, 128
Terre Haute School of Industrial Science, 122
Territorial Capital, 325, 326
36th Indiana Regiment, 104, 110
Thomas, Lowell, 141
Thompson, Maurice, 257, 258, 324, 326
Thompson, Col. Richard W., 125
Thornhill, Claude, 127
Thorntown, 73
Thorpe, Jim, 40
Tibetan Memorial (The Chorten), 276
"Time Was" Downtown Elkhart Museum, 156
Tippecanoe, 13, 75
Tippecanoe Battlefield, 64, *65*, 70
Tippecanoe County, 69, 71, 96
Tippecanoe County Historical Association, 67, 70, 71
Tippecanoe River, 61
Tippecanoe State Park, 24
Tipton, 243
Tipton, John, 243
Tipton County, 243
30th Indiana Infantry, 179
32nd Tennessee Regiment, 68
Trail of Death, 222, 223, 232, 233
Treaty of Fort Wayne, 62
Treaty of Paradise Springs, Site of Signing, 190
Treaty Marker, 205
Tri-State Normal School, 170
Tri-State University, 170
Troost, Gerard, 314
Trout, Paul H. "Dizzy", 127
Trueblood, Elton, 99

352

Tucker, Forrest, 117
Turkey Run State Park, 24, 133
Turner, J.M.W., Collection, 38
*"Twelve Months at Andersonville Prison"*, 186
28th Indiana Cavalry Regiment, 142
Twin Lakes, 222, 223
Tyndall, Col. Robert H., 32

U.S. Army Finance Corps Museum, 42
U.S. Steel Corporation, 19,137, *138*
*U.S.S. Indiana,* 21
*U.S.S. Indianapolis,* 27
*U.S.S. Vincennes,* 330
U.S.S. Vincennes Memorial, 330
*"Ulysses"*, 80
*"Uncle Toms Cabin"*, 28
Underground Railroad, 16, 68, 142, 206, 305
Union Christian College 134
Union City Body Co., 211
Union City, 211
Union County, 102, 104
Union Literary Institute, 212
United Church of Christ Merom Conference Center, 134
*United States* (Ship), 92
University of Evanston, 305
Usher, John P., 20
Usher, John Palmer, 126

Valparaiso, 22, 140, 141
Valparaiso Male & Female College, 141
Valparaiso University, 140, 141
Van Devanter, Willis, 198
Van Meter, Homer, 181, 225
Van Studdiford, Grace, 192
Vance, Capt. Samuel C., 267
Vanderburgh County, 305
Vanderburgh, Judge Henry, 305
Vandivier, Robert "Fuzzy", 74
Vawter, Will, 281
Veedersburg, 252

Veraestan, 269
Vermillion County, 249
Vernon Historic District, 83
Vernon, 81, 82, 83
Versailles, 264
Versailles State Park, 24
Veteran's Memorial, 78, *79*
Vevay, 270
Victory Noll, Motherhouse of Our Lady of Victory Missionary Sisters, 188
Vienna, 17
Vigo, Col. Francis, 122, 320, 322
Vigo County, 18
Vigo County Historical Society, 125
*"Viking, The"*, 57
Vincennes, 11, 12, 15, 23, 66, 93, 151, 302, 319, 320, 321, 322, 323, 324, 325, 327, 328
Vincennes Roman Catholic Church, 18
Vincennes University, 299
Viquesney, E. M., 120
Von Arsdale, Thomas & Richard 74
Von Tilzer, Albert (Gumbinsky), 29
Von Tilzer, Harry, 29
von Steuden, Baron Friedrich, 170
Vonnegut, Kurt, Jr., 32
Voorhees, Daniel Wolsey, 125, 247, 250

Wabach Merry Bowmen (archery club), 258
Wabash & Erie Canal, 15, 68, 72, 122, 178, 185, 190, 192, 213, 235, 238l, 318
Wabash County Historical Museum, *191*
Wabash County, 188
Wabash High School, 191
Wabash Railroad, 72
Wabash River, 188
Wabash Valley Correctional Center, 134